7. Clark County, WI, Jan. 18, 2010: Shortly after leaving his picture here on a trail camera, the lion made his first serious jog northward, skirting almost certain death in Milwaukee or Chicago.

8. Cable, WI, Feb. 15 and 27, 2010: Tracked twice just two weeks and yards apart in the Northwoods of Cable, the second time within two miles of eight thousand cross-country skiers competing in the 37th American Birkebeiner ski race. More scat and DNA collected.

9. Lena, WI, May 20, 2010: Backyard trail camera catches the lion's last appearance in Wisconsin, heading east.

10. Wallace, Michigan, May 26, 2010: The lion trips another shutter in Menominee County, where no lions had been known to live since 1906.

11. Neebish Island, MI: Sometime early in the summer of 2010, the lion may have crossed into Canada via this archipelago braiding the St. Marys River.

12. Thousand Islands National Park, Ontario, late fall–early Dec., 2010: More suspected island-hopping by the lion, this time spanning the Saint Lawrence Seaway on his way back into the United States.

13. Lake George, New York, Dec. 16, 2010: Caught by a motion-sensing spotlight, walking through the backyard of Cindy Eggleston, as seen through her kitchen window as she was washing dishes. Conservation officers confirmed lion tracks the following day and gathered DNA from hairs plucked from the cat's snow bed.

14. Greenwich, Connecticut, June 5, 2011: Seen and photographed in the light of day by Brendan Gilsenan as the lion circled his house on a Sunday stroll. A scat of dubious quality failed to identify him, but the next sighting six days later smothered all scientific doubt.

15. Milford, CT, June 11, 2011: End of the road. The lion is hit and killed by a car on the Wilbur Cross Parkway in Milford, his body bearing no signs of former captivity, his DNA matching five other samples collected along the way.

HEART OF

A LION

HEART OF
A LION

A Lone Cat's Walk Across America

William Stolzenburg

B L O O M S B U R Y
NEW YORK · LONDON · OXFORD · NEW DELHI · SYDNEY

Bloomsbury USA
An imprint of Bloomsbury Publishing Plc

1385 Broadway	50 Bedford Square
New York	London
NY 10018	WC1B 3DP
USA	UK

www.bloomsbury.com

BLOOMSBURY and the Diana logo are trademarks of Bloomsbury Publishing Plc

First published 2016

© William Stolzenburg, 2016

Frontispiece image courtesy of Lue and Krystal Vang

ISBN: HB: 978-1-62040-552-9
        ePub: 978-1-62040-554-3

Library of Congress Cataloging-in-Publication Data has been applied for.

2 4 6 8 10 9 7 5 3 1

Typeset by RefineCatch Limited, Bungay, Suffolk, UK
Printed and bound in the U.S.A. by Berryville Graphics Inc., Berryville, Virginia

To find out more about our authors and books visit www.bloomsbury.com. Here you will find extracts, author interviews, details of forthcoming events and the option to sign up for our newsletters.

Bloomsbury books may be purchased for business or promotional use. For information on bulk purchases please contact Macmillan Corporate and Premium Sales Department at specialmarkets@macmillan.com.

To Kathy, of course, and the memory of Jean

CONTENTS

PROLOGUE

HALF PAST MIDNIGHT, June 11, 2011, on a highway seventy miles outside New York City, a mountain lion met his death on the fender of a northbound car. He was nearly eight feet long, tip to tail, and a solid 140 pounds. He was the first physical proof of a wild mountain lion in Connecticut in the last century. Soon thereafter he was to become the most famous mountain lion in North America, in any century.

The news of his demise triggered a flurry of national press and gossip. That such an unlikely beast from so deep in the past had so magically materialized in America's iconic megalopolitan corridor came with a certain irresistible irony, serving as fodder for wild speculations.

He was a drug kingpin's abandoned pet. He was an escapee from a roadside zoo. To an ardent sect of conspiracy theorists, the Connecticut cat was the smoking gun, proof at last that wildlife authorities had been clandestinely airlifting the big predators into the eastern woods to rein in a runaway population of deer. To the multitudes of citizens who swore they'd long been seeing such lions roaming their streets and backyards and local woods—the same such lions that just three months earlier had been officially declared extinct by the U.S. Fish and Wildlife Service—he was vindication in the face of all the authoritarian dismissals. He was undeniable evidence that eastern mountain lions—by the hundreds, maybe thousands!—were in fact still thriving beneath the experts' condescending noses.

He was in fact none of those things, but far more. Six weeks after scientists sliced and probed and sent bits of the lion's body to a genetics lab in

Montana, his tests came back and his incredible saga emerged from the molecules. He was a three-year-old mountain lion from the Black Hills of South Dakota. And he had wandered under his own power for the better part of two years and more than two thousand miles across the eastern two-thirds of North America. His journey had spanned at least six states and, most likely, Canada's largest province.

The lion had not simply walked a long distance, in the Guinness Book fashion easily imagined by any human pedestrian with a few months' spare time and a supply chain of cool beverages and warm lodging along the way. This lone cat had threaded a gauntlet that would have given an elite force of Navy SEALs the night sweats. He had slinked and scampered across five hundred glaring miles of naked prairie and industrial cropland, patrolled by a certain culture of guns and antipredator hatred that had already dropped dozens of his fellow pilgrims in their paths. He had slipped through metropolises of millions, abuzz with four-wheeled predators and guarded by skittish cops armed with orders to shoot. He had forded many of the mightiest rivers east of the Rockies (the Missouri, Mississippi, St. Lawrence, Hudson) and the busiest of eight-lane freeways, some of them rumbling to more than a hundred thousand vehicles a day. Through ferocious heat, cold, rain, and snow, feeding himself on the fly in a foreign land, he made his way as far east as a land-bound animal could go, to be stopped only by the Atlantic Ocean and two tons of speeding steel.

Only after the lion's headlining tragedy in Connecticut did America come to realize they'd already met this cat more than once along the way. He had made his first public appearance eighteen months earlier, on a December night outside Minneapolis, with a waltz through a suburban neighborhood captured on a police cruiser's video camera. The video went viral. The lion went east. After swimming the Mississippi and scampering around the north end of the Twin Cities, he stopped for a couple days in an urban nature preserve surrounded by freeways and car dealerships, to eat a deer and—more important, for history's sake—to leave behind his first fresh samples of urine and scat.

Before his pursuing biologists were through bagging that evidence, the lion was seen crossing a busy town ten miles east, on the icy banks of the

St. Croix River, bordering Wisconsin. Every stop of the way, reporters followed. The lion was adopted and named, written up like an outlaw on a cross-country getaway. He became at turns the Champlin cougar, the Twin Cities cougar, the St. Croix cougar. There were cheers, there were fears, there were threats of his demise by police fire should he be caught loitering in town. Citizens were publicly warned and instructed on defending themselves against attack. The lion fled for safer surroundings.

Through his first winter on the run he continued leaving his trail of crumbs eastward across Wisconsin: a line of pancake-size paw prints and a thatch of fur at the wooded edge of a dairy farm; at another farm, another sixteen miles east, more fur, more astonishingly intimate glimpses caught by a hidden video camera. In February 2010, in Wisconsin's wintry North Country, he treaded within two miles of eight thousand cross-country skiers at that moment gliding through the woods in the continent's largest ski race.

Late in May he made a couple more cameo appearances on trail cameras, the last one catching him as he passed into the wilds of Michigan's Upper Peninsula, eastward bound still. And then his trail went cold. Over the following months the lion went out of sight and out of the public mind.

So, when he next made his grandest entrance upon the public stage, more than a year later and another seven hundred sixty miles due east—amid the gated estates and manicured greens of Greenwich, Connecticut, thirty miles from Manhattan—it was just too much to imagine. Nobody could think to connect the dots. So far as anyone knew, here was a lion fifteen hundred miles and nearly two centuries removed from genuine lion country. He could be explained only by less fantastic scenarios, as in the odd pet gone loose or the government's secret weapon air-dropped from black helicopters.

The big cat's Greenwich splash played out on TV and YouTube, in the daily papers and social media. The Greenwich Mountain Lion's Facebook page, which sprang up during the commotion, would soon gather five thousand friends. A blurry photo of him scared a prestigious boys' school into closing its campus and the American Cancer Society into moving its annual charity walk to an indoor track in another town. Fanciful sightings streamed in from nearby communities caught up in mountain lion mania. It was lively theater while it lasted.

One week later and another forty eastward miles down the highway came the car and the end of his trail, with the DNA bombshell to follow. All those tokens of hair and bowel and bladder meticulously gathered in the wake of his Midwest crossing now revealed the genetic fingerprints linking the Connecticut cat with his South Dakota origins and the improbable chain of sightings between. This was history.

The lion's trans-American trek had reached more than twice as far as that of any such cat on record, conducted by a barely weaned teenager venturing solo across strange and perilous lands. For students of dispersal biology, the journey was a godsend of data and scientific discovery. Never before had such a secretive creature, untagged and uncollared and so free to wander, left such a revealing chronicle over so wide a terrain.

For conservationists championing the return of his kind, and for public officials fearing the same, he was either emissary or omen of wild things to come. He testified to all that a certain shrinking window into eastern America's ailing wilderness had not yet closed.

But among those following him from the sidelines, his passing carried the sadness of a lost friend. He was more than a statistic or symbol. He was a mindful creature with untold ambitions and emotions, so many of them hauntingly familiar. The lion at turns had displayed cockiness and fear, aloofness and laser-like focus, recklessness and rashness and tenacious resolve. He had survived on varying parts stealth and dumb luck, over half a continent hiding in plain sight like an Apache scout, then suddenly blundering before cars like a wino and parading across patios in the middle of the day. All, it turned out, was in blind pursuit of a mate. The lion had ultimately come so far looking for what some would call love.

His was, by any measure of natural history or emotional gravity, a heroic journey. It was a remarkable odyssey of one lone, impassioned cat that, in keeping to its endless turns of irony, would begin in the most idyllic and dangerous piece of lion habitat for two thousand miles.

ONE Black Hills

Once, in every corner of this continent, your passing could prickle the stillness and bring every living thing to the alert.

—WALLACE STEGNER

THE BLACK HILLS rise along the western border of South Dakota as a long dark island adrift in a prairie sea. They are a rogue eastern outlier of America's Rocky Mountains, one hundred miles from the nearest range to the west, the last major uprising before the land lies open, the trees fade away, and the Great Plains take hold for the next five hundred straw-hued miles across the midsection of America.

It is from the distances that the Hills were so shortsightedly named. Their amorphous blackness is a muted reflection of what on closer approach become bold granite mountains and green pine forests cut by sheer chasms, the whole of the kingdom ringed by floral valleys and a wall of red sandstone.

People gather here as desert trekkers to an oasis, in towns pressing against the foothills and wedged into the canyons. They come in tides of summer tourists to the monument of Mount Rushmore and the casinos of Deadwood, and in one rowdy torrent of more than half a million Harley riders rumbling to their yearly rally in Sturgis. The wildest residents of the Hills congregate most conspicuously as herds of bison, deer, pronghorn, and elk grazing the intermountain meadows, and as mountain goats and bighorn sheep tiptoeing about the cliffs.

Then there are the lions. By the summer of 2009, arguably more than two hundred mountain lions had come to live in the Black Hills. It was not an abnormal number, as lion populations go. But these lions seemed to have risen from the dead, and their resurrection had caused more than a little stir among the people whose ancestors had driven them from the Hills.

Obliterated as vermin a century before by westward settlers, the forgotten lions had recently returned from distant mountains. They had in just the previous thirty years evolved from the rumored existence of an occasional phantom drifting through, to a ubiquitous presence that had frantic citizens reporting missing house cats and unearthly screams in the night. The apparitions eventually began to assume living shape. Lions in the flesh occasionally took to lounging on roofs and back porches, sauntering through town, and leaving the odd deer dead on the streets of Rapid City. And soon enough, former lions in the flesh were appearing by the dozens each year, as carcasses.

In those thirty years, the mountain lion was officially reassigned, from a rare and guarded species of the state, to a targeted animal drawing hundreds of hunters to the Hills each winter. Police and game wardens took to shooting town lions as a rule. The courts came to grant all citizens year-round license to kill lions, so long as they claimed to have felt threatened.

Conservationists from across the country came in turn to the lion's defense, with lawsuits and letters to the editors, billboards and civic center seminars, all pleading for more tolerance toward the Black Hills' comeback cougars, all to be repeatedly overruled in favor of killing ever more of them.

It was one of the survivors, who on a late summer evening in 2009 came to stand on the edge of the Hills, looking out. He was little more than a year old and not long separated from his mother. He had survived his first year as hunters' quarry, public enemy, and roadkill candidate, dodging the armed sportsmen and police and the vehicular predators speeding through the heavily travelled Hills. He had dodged his own kind as well. Had any of the Hills' reigning males caught him trespassing, they might well have killed him. The young tom had reached a leap point in the life of male lions. He was a teenager toeing the line of adulthood, heeding a hard-wired imperative to find a mate and a place of his own. The hills of his birth promised him death if he stayed. Eastward before him lay the black abyss of alien prairie.

Of Lithe and Splendid Beasthood

For seventy million years the Black Hills had stood apart. They were at birth a turtle-shaped dome of molten granite arching through crusts of old seabeds and chasms of time during the last days of the dinosaurs. Over the eons the hills would become mountains rising four thousand feet above the plains, and the world of dinosaurs would give way to one of colossal mammals, magnificent beyond anything earth would ever again produce. They were giants by modern standards, and prolific in number and form. In North America there was a beaver as big as a modern bear, a ground sloth as big as an ox. There were elephantine mastodons, and a mammoth fourteen feet at the shoulder. There were deer, elk, moose, caribou, mountain sheep, and mountain goats little different from today, but also towering camels, wild horses reaching Clydesdale proportions, and a bison with horns spanning seven feet. All were chased by several varieties of wolves and a particularly frightful form of bear that stood as tall as a racehorse and apparently ran like one, too. There was a long-striding, pack-hunting hyena. And there emerged a guild of great cats as a carnivorous force unto itself.

Saber-toothed cats roamed the American wilderness, the most spectacular bearing six-inch canines for slicing through the thickest hides of mammoths. This same wilderness harbored the American lion, a blood relative of the African lion, but about a quarter again as large. An oversize jaguar—close kin to the spotted cat now typically associated with southern jungles—lived as far north as what would become the states of Nebraska and Washington. Across the open spaces sped the American cheetah, a sprinting cat with a whipcord spine and stilted legs, unleashing violent bursts of speed to overtake the second-fastest land animal on earth, the pronghorn. The line that led to the cheetah split off to yet another big cat, which, though neither the fastest nor the biggest nor the flashiest of the clan, was destined to inherit the Western Hemisphere.

The mountain lion—to be technically classified as *Puma concolor*, or "cat of a single color"—retained somewhat the trim runner's skull of the cheetah, while adding the muscled forearms and massive paws more befitting a true lion. Its hind legs compared to nothing else in the world of cats. They were heavily thighed and apparently too large by half, hinting at kangaroo. They were built for leaping. While its cheetah sister hurtled in high-speed pursuit over the open spaces, the mountain lion took to lunging and pouncing in explosive acts of ambush from behind the wooded edge, over the boulders and cliffs of canyon country.

Stretching seven to nine feet from nose to tail, females weighing about a hundred pounds and the biggest males more than twice that, the mountain lion yet amounted to an underling in the pecking order of the Pleistocene's land of giants. The quintessential saber-tooth, *Smilodon*, of the famously over-size fangs and muscle-bound physique, outweighed the mountain lion by six times. *Panthera atrox*, the original American lion, was bigger still. The mountain lion gave way to these alpha cats whenever paths crossed or a pile of fresh meat came under dispute. But the mountain lion bowed to none as the great cats' apex of athleticism. It could vault thirty-foot chasms, and scale trees like a squirrel. Its oven-mitt paws could pluck a rabbit on the fly or grapple a bull elk five times its mass. It had evolved a particular expertise for slinking invisibly to within striking distance, closing with a rush, and dispatching big prey with a surgical, spine-severing bite to the neck or a suffocating lock on the windpipe.

"Of all the beasts that roam America's woods, the Cougar is the big-game hunter without peer," wrote the naturalist Ernest Thompson Seton in his 1937 opus, *Lives of Game Animals*. "Built with the maximum power, speed and endurance that can be jammed into his 150 pounds of lithe and splendid beasthood, his daily routine is a march of stirring athletic events that not another creature—in America, at least—can hope to equal."

Thus forged in a crucible of intense competition, the mountain lion emerged as a carnivorous embodiment of adaptive versatility, every trick and talent of which would be tested in the forthcoming cataclysms. Late into the Pleistocene epoch, with the receding of the last glaciers, a tribe of people entered the North American continent from the west. They migrated over a temporary arc of exposed seafloor bridging Siberia to Alaska, Asia to North America. Entering the New World some fourteen thousand years ago, their tribe may not have been the first to arrive, but it was by far the most obvious. The people left their calling cards rather conspicuously strewn across the land, set in stone and bearing a bold universal message. They left spear points, massive beyond imagination, emerging from the dirt as sharp and deadly as the day they'd been flaked. The spear-wielding Clovis people—named for the little town on the dusty plains of eastern New Mexico where, in 1929, their weapons were first uncovered—would rapidly spread across the continent. A curious lot of their spear points were to be found embedded among the remains of mammoths, elephantine monsters who vanished from the American landscape within a millennium of the spear makers' arrival.

The camels and the ground sloths and the horses soon vanished, too. Those that had fed on them (the dire wolf, the giant short-faced bear, and the great cats) disappeared in turn. Suspiciously soon on the heels of the pioneering Clovis, three of every four of the Pleistocene's North American megafaunal forms were reduced to dust and bone. Scientists of the twentieth century would come to argue themselves hoarse over who or what did it, whether the continent's most mysterious mass extinction had stemmed from the environmental chaos of a glacial reversal, or from the business end of the Clovis spear. But with the megafauna's record of having survived a score of climatic upheavals over the previous one hundred thousand years, yet failing to survive their first meeting with the meat-seeking Clovis, the last-minute meltdown acquired an indelible odor of massacre.

Of the hemisphere's once-crowded suite of big cats, two survived, if barely. The jaguar retreated southward; the mountain lion appeared to have fled North America entirely. Of the two, only the mountain lion would ever fully recover—and then some. In time, after the smoke of the Pleistocene immolation had cleared, a few refugee mountain lions crept back. They entered their ancestral home, gutted as it was, to find the place not only habitable but positively inviting. The mammoth-hunting Clovis, with no more mammoths to hunt, had given way to cultures of smaller ambitions and shrinking spear points, turning to the hoofed herds of bison, elk, and deer that had survived to thrive in the newly peopled continent. The list of apex predators had been pared to a species or two of wolf, a grizzly bear more apt to dig for roots than to chase down meat, and a race of hunting and gathering humans who seemed to have struck a precarious semblance of balance with the land that fed them.

The homecoming lions found the landscape rearranged to their liking. By the time European explorers made landfall in the sixteenth century, the mountain lion had settled the New World from Atlantic to Pacific, Canada to Patagonia, rainforest basins to alpine peaks. And by the time the Europeans took to settling themselves, America's lion was soon again fleeing in full-bore retreat.

All Things Fierce and Savage

The first Europeans to glimpse the New World discovered a creature the likes of which they could only imagine as kin to the king of African beasts that adorned their medieval artwork back home. Amerigo Vespucci and Christopher Columbus, in separate reconnaissances of Central America, had both come back with reports of *leones*.

The English colonists who followed bestowed a welter of new names on America's singular cat (cougar, catamount, wildcat, tyger, puma, panther, painter, Indian devil, mountain screamer, and mountain lion, among many more) and an equally creative narrative of its anatomy and natural history. "It has a tail like a Lyon, its legs are like a Bears, its Claws like an Eagle, its Eyes like a Tyger, its countenance is a mixture of every Thing that is Fierce and Savage, he is exceedingly ravenous and devours all sorts of Creatures that he can come near."

The mountain lion was said to wail like a sobbing child lost in the woods, or perhaps like a woman being murdered. His hair-raising roars—later to be debunked as acoustically impossible, given his vocal equipment—could only be confused with those of the Devil himself.

Though the lion's chroniclers were hard-pressed to conjure solid evidence of human injury, any creature with such a hideous howl must surely be a devoted man-eater. The lion gained a reputation for chasing people, with the curious twist of hardly ever catching them. "Panthers have not seized any of our people, that I have heard," reported the pioneer botanist John Bartram in 1738, "but many have been sadly frightened with them. They have pursued several men, both on horseback and foot." The irony of such stories was not lost on Bartram, given that it was almost always the lion who got the worst of the encounters. "Many have shot them down, and others have escaped by running away. But I believe, as a panther doth not much fear a single man, so he hath no great desire to seize him; for if he had, running from him would be a poor means to escape such a nimble, strong creature, which will leap about twenty feet at one leap."

The lion was said to pounce upon its victims from the limbs of trees, where in fact it was the lion who was typically pounced upon. Those limbs were typically the last refuge of a lion on the run, where the savvy hunter following his hounds would casually approach to within spitting distance and shoot the treed cat at his leisure.

A few of the early chroniclers got it right, squaring the mountain lion's astonishing verve for tackling the fiercest four-legged beasts with its near-pathologic reluctance to prey on the most defenseless people. "As formidable as this Beast is to his Fellow Brutes, he never has the confidence to venture upon a Man, but retires from him with great respect, if there be a way open for his Escape," wrote the Virginian plantation master William Byrd II in 1728. "However, it must be confesst, his Voice is a little contemptible for a Monarch of the Forest, being not a great deal louder nor more awful than the Mewing of a Household Cat."

In their 1846 account of the cougar, the painter John James Audubon and his naturalist colleague John Bachman gamely attempted a balance between the tall tales of the frontier people and the few facts that could have been known of an animal so seldom seen. The stories they gathered told of silent footsteps treading the blackest of night, of the wilderness camper awakening to the snorting of terrified horses and the "glistening eyes of the dangerous beast glaring upon him like two burning coals." This was the cougar that ambushed people on their horses, in their houses, in their sleep, and ultimately, in their minds.

"We have given these relations of others to show that at long intervals, and under peculiar circumstance, when perhaps pinched with hunger, or in defence of its young, the Cougar sometimes attacks men," wrote Audubon and Bachman. "These instances, however, are very rare, and the relations of an affrighted traveller must be received with some caution, making a due allowance for a natural disposition in man to indulge in the marvellous."

The authors admitted that they themselves had only seen this animal—of which they so authoritatively wrote—all of three times in their lives. Each encounter featured a lion fleeing up a tree. The first was chased there by a schoolboy's little terrier. "We approached and raised a loud whoop, when he sprang to the earth and soon made his escape. He was, a few days afterwards, hunted by the neighbours and shot." The second cougar sprang, too, heading for far horizons and an unknown fate. The third never left the tree alive, to be finally dropped thudding to the ground by a dozen blasts from a shotgun.

Mercy rarely figured in the settlers' meetings with the forest's great cat. Colonists from the beginning were offered bounties to kill all such predatory vermin as wolves, bears, and lions. In the late 1500s, Jesuit priests in Southern California were offering a bull as reward for anyone killing a cougar. South Carolina enacted a law in 1695 requiring "all Native American braves to bring in the skin of a wolf, panther, bear, or two bobcats each year." If the brave brought in more, he would be rewarded; if he brought in fewer, he would be whipped. New Jersey, as of 1697, was offering twenty shillings per lion, regardless of the killer's race. The demonic panther burned in the witch hunters' fires of colonial New England. And rarely did a red-blooded settler of the new country pass up the chance to parade his dead lion through town, or to tack its hide to a shed as a badge of manliness.

Lions were rounded up in ring hunts and massacred. One such hunt was led by an ominously named character, Black Jack Schwartz, who one day in 1760, along with two hundred of his henchmen, all but surrounded an entire Pennsylvania county. With their bells clanging, fires burning, and guns popping, Black Jack and his men began driving all manner of wild creatures before them. Foxes, bears, bobcats, elk, deer, buffalo, otters, beavers, wolves, panthers, and myriad smaller creatures ran ahead, until meeting the opposing line of gunmen. Some of the animals in their panic broke through the lines and escaped; the rest were cornered and executed. The shooting went on for hours. When it ended, more than a thousand bodies were tallied, stacked, and burned, the stench of which was said to have driven settlers from their cabins three miles away. Among the dead were forty-one panthers. The hunters dressed themselves in the panther skins—an ill-advised boast that soon put a target on their backs when the local Indians came looking for those who had just plundered their livelihood.

There were many ways to kill the panther. Besides shooting, trapping, snaring, axing, knifing, or bludgeoning—all of which were commonly boasted of in the chronicles of panther slayers—there was a more round-about method that never required touching the animal. The cat could be starved off the land.

As the burgeoning American colony spread westward, clearing forests and wildlife as it went, so too went the forests and food of the mountain lion. By the mid-1800s, upward of 80 percent of the eastern forest had been cut for lumber and firewood, converted to pasture and cropland. The deer, bison, and elk that had lived there were rendered for meat and hides to feed and clothe the growing masses of the eastern cities, to the demise of the native peoples and predators who depended on them.

The bison and elk, presenting the biggest targets, were extinguished outright; the smaller deer, all but so. In 1830, market hunters were collecting a dollar a deer; venison was selling for pennies on the pound. Few forested enclaves remained safe. Railroads eventually punched through the last invio-lable tracts of the northern woods, and the market hunters loaded the trains to the last.

Deer evaporated across the countryside. The bottomless herds celebrated in the pioneers' journals inevitably gave way to rare sightings of skittish survivors. New Brunswick, New England, New York, New Jersey, Pennsylvania, the Virginias, Maryland, Kentucky, Tennessee—all watched their herds driven to desperate little enclaves in the last wooded pockets of refuge. In 1842 the state of Connecticut reported a single deer killed.

What the bounty hunter and the ring hunter and the local potshot couldn't quite finish in their quest for lion extermination, the logger and the deer hunter did. As much as a lion might survive the lean times on meat of beaver, turkey, rabbit, or even porcupine, such appetizers were ultimately lacking as long-term staples for a creature so purposefully built for hunting sizable prey. Nor was there any hint of last-minute reprieve from their gunners. For what the clear cutters and market hunters had done to the colonies' deer, the last mountain lions conveniently took the blame and the bullet.

So it went that the baby-snatching, horse-thieving, game-plundering, myth-shackled mountain lion fled before the settlers' advance. By the mid-1800s, signs of eastern lions had grown scarce. Delaware, Massachusetts, Connecticut, Maryland, New Jersey, the Carolinas, Maine, Vermont, Pennsylvania, Ohio, Missouri, and on down the line recorded their final bountied cougars and panthers. The sole survivors retreated to the last hidden peaks and hollows of the Appalachians, until the last hiding places were overrun. Deep in the mosquito-fogged Everglades and cypress swamps of southern Florida, a few refugee panthers held out for lack of enough people to finish exterminating them. But everywhere else swept the gunners.

Through the Midwest plains of Indiana, Iowa, Illinois, Wisconsin, Minnesota, Oklahoma, Kansas, Nebraska, and the Dakotas, the settlers cleared cougars like prairie flowers under the plow. The last prairie cougars gravitated toward the ribbons of riverside forests to shelter and rest and to hunt for deer, until the settlers did, too.

Not long into the 1900s, the cougar of the eastern forests and Midwest plains was gone, and those of the great mountains and badlands of the American West were already fast on the run. Rare was the gun-toting Westerner who didn't instinctively fire upon the hint of a mountain lion. For most, the killing of lions had become an unspoken civic duty; for others, a deed as mindless as crushing spiders underfoot. For a few, the killing of lions was to become a vocation bordering on obsession. And above and beyond all was Ben Lilly.

Lilly

Born in 1856 in southern Mississippi, with gun and knife soon thereafter in his hands, Benjamin Vernon Lilly would grow to become the country's most celebrated assassin of mountain lions. By the time he was finished eighty years later, Lilly had been variously credited with killing upward of a thousand lions and bears, from the swamps of the Deep South to the sky islands of the desert Southwest. They were many of the last.

Lilly as a boy took to the woods early and often. He ran away at twelve and roamed across Mississippi and halfway through Louisiana, sleeping in the woods and feeding himself on wild game along the way. He came back for a while with the idea of farming and starting a family. Yet farming and family life suffocated Lilly, who wandered away at every temptation into the bottomland thickets and swamps, where he gunned the deer and wild hogs by the score, and harpooned the biggest alligators. And here Lilly grew particularly fond of killing the swamps' remaining bears and panthers.

Somewhere early in the slaying of the great predatory beasts, something triggered in Lilly's soul. (He killed his first bear, goes the story, with a pocketknife.) Lilly came to take his readings from the Bible, his killing orders from God. He adopted hounds as his living weapons, training them to track and tree the panthers and hold the bears at bay. He would end the chase at close range with his rifle, or wade into the scuffle with his knife. Lilly was said to have yanked a panther from a tree by its tail. He killed another by bashing its skull in with a rock.

Lilly was a solid, compact man with an incongruent blend of bearish strength, pantherine agility, and cervine swiftness. He would sometimes entertain audiences by lifting his blacksmith's anvil with one hand, arm straight out, so the story goes. He would leap for the simple joy of it, leaving tape-measured legends of his broad-jumping ability. He could run ten miles on a whim. On the hunt, Lilly was a tireless predator, scouring the most ungodly unknowns for days or weeks on the run. He armed himself with a Winchester repeating rifle and a knife of his own design. The signature Lilly knife was a sinuous, eighteen-inch, double-edged dagger Lilly used to hack his way through the Louisiana jungles, to slice the vital organs and arteries of the monsters he met in close-quarter combat, and then to butcher them into hides and meat. Lilly tempered the steel of his blade with panther oil.

With Lilly's rising lust for lion blood, the outings grew longer, the farming business more sporadic. Legend has it he came home one day to a scolding wife, who suggested he at least make himself useful by shooting the resident chicken hawk. And as Lilly's biographer J. Frank Dobie recorded, "Ben took his gun. The hawk flew. Ben followed. More than a year passed before he re-entered the house."

Lilly's second marriage continued on a similar course of dissolution by absenteeism. He bought another house, fathered three kids, and visited once in a while between his self-appointed missions to rid humanity of its forest-dwelling demons. He became a wild denizen of the woods, developing an almost telepathic ability to navigate the deepest thickets and swampiest mazes. Lilly's predecessors had already driven Louisiana's apex predators from common occurrence to dwindling scarcity; before his arrival, a single hunting party had in one winter killed seventy-five bears. The last great beasts of Louisiana made for the thickest bug-infested hells remaining, only to meet there the most fearsome swamp monster of all, named Lilly. In his wake sprouted the Lilly legend, growing with every new telling of epic endurance and hand-to-hand slayings of supernatural beasts.

Those who met the great hunter were invariably surprised to find a soft-spoken man of pale blue eyes and a cherubic face draped by a beard cascading to the breastbone. He was honest to a fault, never drank or smoked. He carried a Bible, loathed the foul language of his fellow woodsmen, and honored the Sabbath as if his eternal life depended on it. If a hunt went unfinished through Saturday night, his quarry was granted a day's stay of execution; Ben Lilly would not lift a finger to work or hunt on Sunday.

But come Monday, woe to any creature that raised its head in Lilly's sights. Wild or tame, coming or going—it mattered little to Lilly. He was known to ax the horns off a belligerent cow. He was a pitiless wielder of the bullwhip, slashing through living hides with a crackling report like gunfire. He all but hated horses, shooting those who angered him and leaving one tied unfed for a week while he tended to other business. For a few of his most loyal hunting dogs, Lilly occasionally ventured a hint of sentiment, going so far as to inscribe an epitaph on the coffin of one hound named Crook, A BEAR AND LION DOG THAT HELPED KILL 210 BEAR AND 426 LION SINCE 1914. But woe again to those who fell short of his standards. He would gather the rest of the pack to witness, proclaiming for all to hear his formal judgement of execution, and then shoot the dog—or beat it to death.

Lilly grew into an accomplished marksman, practicing as he did on the universe of living targets. He practiced his aim on bees, bats, and songbirds. He blasted the bills off ducks. He hunted some of the last survivors of the ivory-billed woodpecker, en route to its extinction, and sold their skins to the Smithsonian Institution in Washington, D.C. Lilly didn't much care to hunt deer, but rarely passed up an opportunity to shoot however many he might happen upon. In one two-mile stroll to his neighbor's house, he shot eleven along the way. He plugged vultures circling on high and knocked squirrels out of trees, and for good measure peppered them all again as they fell. It was all in proper training for his ultimate quarry. "If a bear or lion ever jumps out of a tree and I am in sight, I will get three balls in it before it hits the ground," he wrote. "I never saw a lion that I did not kill or wound."

In 1901, Lilly left home and family for good. To his wife he signed over his land and all but five dollars, and went hunting. He normally traveled light, shouldering his gun and trailing his dogs, sometimes on a mule, but preferring his own feet to those of a horse. He subsisted on the corn he carried and the meat he shot along the way. He spent the next five years in the Tensas River bottomland of northern Louisiana, and began a long, slow meander into east Texas and beyond.

Lilly wandered west, leaving great voids of bears and lions in his wake. (It is arguable whether his westward leanings stemmed from wanderlust or the ratcheting scarcity of anything left to shoot.) He continued on across the Rio Grande into Mexico, killing lions as he went and shipping their skins and skulls to the Smithsonian Institution.

In 1911 he reentered U.S. territory, into the boot heel of southwestern New Mexico. At fifty-five years old, he was just embarking upon the golden years of his fabled killing career. He added the grizzly bear to his Most Wanted list. But with the rimrock and canyons and high pine forests of the Southwest, he was entering some of the last bastions of the mountain lion, and he developed an especial passion for hounding them in particular, and with recently added incentive.

The wild open ranges of the West had given rise to millionaire empires built on sprawling herds of cattle and sheep and bounties on any varmint that might eye a single one of them. The Indians had been all but driven away, and wild game was on the run, leaving the livestock predator as the last bogeyman standing in dominion's way. The new hoofed stock, bred for slowness of foot and mind, and a surfeit of fat, wandered loose on the open range, where their

cowboys and shepherds and other would-be caretakers were few. Certain
enterprising lions quite adroitly took to killing the deer's dumbed-down
replacements. Others came hunting in desperation. Such lions often came
wounded or maimed by a bullet or trap. Young lions orphaned by the hunters
wandered confused and starving into the flocks. And for the indiscretions of
a few such stock killers, all lions came branded with bull's-eyes.

By the time Lilly the lion hunter had reached his mecca in the Southern
Rockies, the war against the predator had advanced beyond the randomly
sniping cowhand shooting on sight and sowing strychnine like chicken
feed. It had become an organized offensive spearheaded by the U.S. government. In 1914, with an appropriation from Congress, the American citizenry
began subsidizing the extermination of America's native predators, sending
an army of mercenaries afield, with salaries and orders to kill. Walking into
this land, with the predators now officially branded as vermin and their
exterminators elevated to hero status, Lilly became a hired gun in highest
demand. His first year, he cleaned bears, wolves, and lions from the Diamond
A Ranch in the Animas Mountains. He took his pay and moved north to find
the next infested ranch in need of his services. Along the way, he killed ten
bears and lions in a single week and sold their scalps for ten dollars apiece.

Lilly blamed all dead livestock on predators, turning a blind eye to disease,
weather, accidents, and the sundry other greater dangers of open-range
ranching. He figured stockmen were losing five hundred dollars every year
for every bear or lion on their land. The ranchers revered Lilly's reputation
and bought his math. They gladly paid as much as fifty dollars each for as
many scalps as he could produce.

The deadliest mercenary in the war against lions preferred working freelance, selling his services and wiping landscapes as he went. Occasionally
Lilly took a salary as hired hitman for the U.S. Biological Survey, earning one
hundred dollars a month. He had become at once the mountain lion's
leading student and chief executioner. He was "the dean of lion hunters,"
and far and away the most eccentric. President Theodore Roosevelt wrote
famously of his first meeting with Lilly, whom he sent for in 1908 to join
him on a bear-hunting trip in Louisiana. Lilly had walked for a day and a
night without food or water through hard rain to reach Roosevelt's camp,

where he arrived near dawn to find the ground too wet to lie on. Roosevelt awoke to find the man "perched in a crooked tree in the beating rain, much as if he had been a wild turkey." For one who prided himself on his own machismo, Roosevelt had to bow to this strange and feral creature from the woods. "I never met any other man so indifferent to fatigue and hardship."

Lilly as a habit slept outdoors through the seasons, his bed amounting to a canvas drop cloth, adding a blanket or a warm hound for the coldest winter nights. He never wore a coat, making do with several shirts or a light sweater he could peel or add as the weather dictated. So attired, he once followed for three days on the path of a particular grizzly in the White Mountains of Arizona, through snows drifting twelve feet deep, with no food. To keep from freezing, he slept sitting by a fire.

"I felt weak," Lilly later wrote. "My dogs and I both needed water." As he was stumbling toward some ice to quench his thirst, he and his dogs crossed the fresh track of lion. "I felt like a new man and took out in a run. The lion was soon treed and killed. We got water and went back to the grizzly bear. After I skinned him, the dogs and I had a good meal. I wrapped up in the skin by the carcass and slept as warm as if I were in a stove."

Lilly bathed in streams and ponds. If the pond was frozen, he would break the ice to get in. If no pond was near, he would bathe in the snow. The soles of his shoes tended to evaporate from all the mountainous miles, so he took to resoling them with old tire rubber. For good measure, he tacked on a set of mule shoes. One pair of Lilly's fortified boots weighed in at nearly twelve pounds.

Lilly's backpack weighed upward of another 125 pounds, depending on how many lion skins and dog chains he was carrying. He was oblivious to the burden, particularly once he'd struck the trail of a lion. He would pursue as a man possessed, following and fasting for as long as the trail led him. He would then break his fast with equally epic displays of gluttony, one of which involved an invitation to a campsite dinner whose host watched in astonishment as Lilly downed a succession of steaks and loaves of bread, cantaloupes, and watermelons, one after the next.

As his legend grew, anybody seeking wisdom on the mysterious lion was automatically referred to Lilly. All manner of hunters and trappers, young and old, referred to him as Mr. Lilly. When tracking cats, Mr. Lilly could tell by the wear of the heel pad whether he was hunting a young fledgling or a battle-scarred lord of the mountain. He could tell female from male, and by the spread of the outside toe on her hind foot whether she was carrying unborn kittens. He could read in a swath of flattened grass the belly print of a crouching lion the moment before launching.

Yet for all his dedicated dirt time, for all the wild country he traversed, Lilly was no great naturalist. He didn't know a walnut from an oak. To him it didn't matter. His antennae were tuned to all things lion. He listened to the alarm call of the jay, not with the enraptured curiosity of a birdwatching Audubon, but with the cold calculus of an assassin seeking clues to the whereabouts of his quarry.

Lilly studied the cats he chased. He opened their stomachs to see what they'd eaten. He sometimes watched before killing. "One family I followed went eight miles with only one stop. The lioness lay down under some rocks; the kittens sucked and played all around her. When I killed her I saw that she was giving plenty of milk."

Hunters' lore would suggest that the greatest of their fraternity was he who became one with his quarry. Lilly came close. He lived the better part of his life on the lion's path, thinking like one. He anticipated its line of travel, and met it at the pass. And when he finally caught and killed one, he ate it, for the stealth and grace he believed its meat bestowed on him.

Lilly most closely resembled his prey by his wanderlust. Half a century before biologists armed with radio trackers and motorcraft began spying on the unseen meanderings of the lion, Ben Lilly was already long on their trail. Over hill and dale he followed, for as long as the scent stayed warm. And from his travels, he came to recognize what would later be reconfirmed as one of the pivotal tenets of lion life. "Some individuals seem kin to the gypsies," wrote the man who packed his world on his back.

Lilly tracked one lion for four years through the Blue River country of eastern Arizona. He had first identified her by an odd five-toed print she made with her left front paw. "She had, I judge, been caught in a trap that pulled one toe out of joint in such a way that it printed two points on the ground," he wrote. "She was being followed by two yearlings."

Over the following four years, and another hundred and more miles along the trail, Lilly twice again came upon the track of the five-toed female. He lost the first in a snowstorm; the second was fresh. "And after following it all afternoon, I killed the maker of it about sundown. That night a man and son in camp with me, asked me how far a lion travels. My answer was, 'As far as the ranges suit it.'"

For all he knew about lions, Lilly knew little of their place in the larger world of living things. He didn't anticipate what science would come to decipher of the lion's role as shepherd of the deer, as guardian against the overbrowsed forest. He believed there was no purpose for lions but to die for their sins. His God-given duty was to vanquish them as the "Cains of the animal world," cleansing the landscape of them wherever they might still roam.

He nearly succeeded. Lilly's diaries from his Southwest crusades speak of a hunter's feast followed by famine. In one week of 1914, he killed nine mountain lions and three bears. Yet for two months in the summer 1916, he "never struck a lion track." He typically averaged less than one dead lion or bear per week, hardly a chest-beating feat compared to the Boone-and-Crockett exploits of his frontiersmen predecessors.

Lilly had come late to the massacre. He was ferreting out those lions the invading army before him had overlooked, the survivors cowering in the crawl spaces. There were hunters who in their lifetime may have tallied more lion kills than Lilly, but none who scoured the land to the last with more tenacious resolve than he. The Lilly of legend appeared as a singular kind of animal, yet ultimately he was common kin to every other faceless hitman in the revolving league of lion exterminators. He was ultimately blind to his role as chief architect of his own demise, blazing through the vestiges of the wildness that sustained him.

Lilly spent his final years hunting the high plateaus and sky islands of the Southwest, slaying his dragons to the last. He ultimately came to rest in a poorhouse near Silver City, New Mexico, as a muttering, old, unshorn eccentric who on creaking knees and shuffling feet still occasionally wandered off into the mountains looking to kill. On his last hunt, near the age of eighty, Lilly, still true to form, took to the hills but took no food. Miles and more than a day afield, eventually remembering his hunger, he sniffed out some sustenance in the half-buried leg of a freshly slaughtered deer. Lilly's last supper of his last hunt had been bestowed by a lion.

By the time Lilly died in 1936, he and his fellow eradicators—many of them freelancing for ranchers and taking salaries with the newly minted U.S. Department of Predator and Rodent Control—had nearly accomplished their mission. The blitzkrieg of poisoning, shooting, and trapping had driven America's big predators to the edges. The wolf was gone from all but a tiny corner of northern Minnesota, the grizzly bear left clinging to a handful of inhospitable rock-and-ice holdouts of the Northern Rockies. The lion whose range had once spanned the country had been extinguished everywhere east of the Rockies, save for that one tenuous little lair in the cypress swamps of southern Florida. The majestic wilds of the West now harbored but a phantom's shadow of the great cat that once was.

As the exterminators drew near to shooting themselves out of business, they shrewdly created a new enemy. They declared war against the wolf's little cousin, the coyote. More adaptable in diet, more fecund and prolific and stubbornly resilient, the coyote endured the unprecedented new offensive, suffering hundreds of thousands of casualties by the year. As for the lion's demise, the eternal campaign against the coyote served to keep the bounty hunters afield and the lands ever more mined with traps and poisons, hounds and guns. As the wilderness disciple John Muir would so sadly observe from the sidelines, "None of our fellow mortals is safe who eats what we eat."

The last pockets of western lions imploded, as islands swallowed in a rising sea. All but the tallest and harshest and most humanly impenetrable fortresses eventually went under. Most vanished without comment or roadside marker. But one stood out, for its geophysical essence as a singular mountain sanctuary some one hundred miles distant from the last major range of the Rockies—and for its historical resonance as a seminal drama in the conquest of the American West.

Last Bastion

The Black Hills had weathered a procession of cultures coming and going, from the Pleistocene mammoth hunters, to archaic nomads chasing bison, to the final aboriginal tribes named Arikara, Cheyenne, Crow, Kiowa, Pawnee, and the mighty Lakota Sioux. Caucasians from the East first began tiptoeing into the Hills in the early 1800s, as little bands of mountain men and miners prospecting for furs and gold, but never lingering for fear of the reigning Lakota. The Lakota considered the Hills sacred, a vital source of lodge poles and wild game, to be trespassed under risk of death.

The white chiefs in Washington, D.C., upon surveying the western territories of their ongoing conquest, at first deemed the Hills strategically worthless. In 1868 they threw the Black Hills as a bone of appeasement to the Lakota, in a treaty that forever barred all white men from trespassing. Forever lasted a few years, until two Indians fresh from the Hills stopped into a trading post and poured some glittering dust on the counter.

The hint of gold in the Black Hills sent the fever racing through the white men's camps. Prospectors oblivious to treaty or threat of Lakota scrambled for the Hills. The seductive wafts of Black Hills gold and marketable timber eventually reached Washington. Ordained by manifest destiny and armed with its anti-Indian workhorse weapon of deceit, Washington moved to void the Lakota's treaty.

"I am inclined to think that the occupation of this region of the country is not necessary to the happiness and prosperity of the Indians," wrote the U.S. secretary of the interior, Columbus Delano. "And as it is supposed to be rich in minerals and lumber it is deemed important to have it freed as early as possible from Indian occupancy."

In July of 1874, a wagon train came rolling southwestward from a fort outside Bismarck in the Dakota Territory. It trailed more than a hundred wagons pulled by seven hundred mules, along with three hundred head of cattle for meat along the way. It was attended by a thousand soldiers, sixty Indian scouts, several geologists and naturalists, four reporters, a photographer, and most essentially, two miners. Leading all was a flamboyant, golden-haired Indian fighter and rising lieutenant colonel named George Armstrong Custer.

Custer's party rolled as an enormous mobile picnic, the soldiers picking prairie flowers from horseback, the cavalry band striking up Custer's favorite battle tunes over breakfast, the day's merriment capped with bottles of fine wine. Two weeks and nearly three hundred miles upon the prairie, they came within sight of the Black Hills oasis rising out of the plains. They ogled the verdant forests and crystal streams, the flowing grasses and painted flowers and soothing summer air. Custer wrote to his wife, "We have discovered a rich and beautiful country."

They marched into the forbidden land of the Lakota, searching for their excuse to steal it. On July 27, while panning the waters of French Creek, the expedition's miners found it. Custer immediately trumpeted their discovery of gold—conveniently omitting the Lakota's rights to the land—with his enticement to all interested invaders: "And it is the belief of those who are giving their attention to this subject that it will be found in paying quantities." The word carried as fast as the whipped pony could cover the hundred miles to the nearest telegraph, and by August 2, the New York Times was retrumpeting the news to the country.

Between feeding his reporters their daily diet of golden propaganda, Custer and his entourage continued their merry tour of the Black Hills, hiking peaks and shooting animals along the way. On August 7, Custer bagged a grizzly bear, and kneeled upon its carcass for a photograph. His chief zoologist, George Bird Grinnell—who would later go on to organize the first Audubon Society and the New York Zoological Society—had also reported seeing a "panther," which he believed "are quite numerous in this locality, as on several occasions I saw indications of their recent presence, and once found the partially devoured remains of a deer that had just been left by one of these animals."

The Black Hills had wolves, too. Together with its grizzlies and lions, the Hills harbored the triumvirate of the country's last apex carnivores. Together, their mere presence suggested a pinnacle of ecological integrity all but expunged from the evaporating American frontier. Upon Custer's arrival, the Black Hills had embodied the rarest form of unbroken wildness. Soon upon his departure was to come its unravelling.

Midway into August, with grounds for the Lakota's eviction in hand, Custer's band finished its tour and headed back for Bismarck. By the time it returned two weeks later, the rush was on. What had been a trickle of snooping scouts became the stampede of fever-struck prospectors and speculators clawing for their fortunes in the Hills. "A wall of fire, not to mention a wall of Indians, could not stop the encroachment of that terrible white race before which all other races of white kind have gone down," reported war correspondent John A. Finerty.

> At the news of gold the grizzled 49'ers shook the dust of California from their feet and started for the far distant "Hills." The Australian miner left his pack and started by saddle and ship for the same goal; the diamond hunter of the Cape, the veteran prospector of Colorado and Montana, the reduced gentleman of Europe, the worried and worn clerks of London, Liverpool, New York, or Chicago, the sturdy Scotchman and the light-hearted Irishman, who drinks the spirit of adventure with his mother's milk, the miners of Wales and Cornwall and the gamblers of Monte Carlo came trooping in masses to the new Eldorado.

The mining town of Deadwood sprouted, in all its glorious Wild West stereotype, thick with saloons, brothels, and gunfighters. Wyatt Earp, the variously occupied gambler, bouncer, pimp, prospector, and lawman—and later, in Tombstone, Arizona, a starring gunman in the shootout at the O.K. Corral—spent a winter in Deadwood during the rush, seeking his fortune. The ferocious competition had him boarding an outbound stagecoach by spring. Wild Bill Hickok, whom Earp regarded "as the deadliest pistol-shot alive," was shot through the back of the head playing poker in a Deadwood saloon, supposedly holding aces and eights at the time. The trail that Custer's wagons had blazed became a road of gold diggers. The Lakota named it the Thieves' Road. With the Lakotas' paper rights to their land tattered and tossed to the winds, some ten thousand foreigners stormed the Hills and settled in as the new owners.

The Lakota of course got mad, and two years later got even. Great throngs of them, led by the immortal warrior Crazy Horse, surrounded and slaughtered Custer and 268 others under his command in the Battle of Little Bighorn. But it was to be the Lakota's last great stand. New U.S. armies came to avenge the embarrassment of Custer's beating; new people came storming the Hills. Survivors from the Indian nations were systematically massacred, starved, and marched off to prisons. Their genocide was preview to the oncoming plunder of the Black Hills' wildlife.

The Hills' invading hordes took no prisoners. Deadwood's miners demanded meat, which came from the Hills' deer and elk, slaughtered by market hunters and delivered to town by the wagonload. Within five years of the U.S. invasion, the deer of the Black Hills went from fabulously abundant to frightfully scarce. By 1883 the governor of the Dakota Territory stepped in to outlaw their hunting for eight months of the year.

The surrounding plains were withering in step. As the prospectors picked apart the Black Hills, not far north the last appreciable gathering of American bison was soon to be destroyed. Bison had once roamed the American steppe from Canada to Texas in horizon-spanning herds of millions. But with the eventual rise of the English eastern city and its market-driving fashions came an insatiable demand for buffalo robes. The demand was eagerly supplied by an entrepreneurial guild of professional buffalo shooters and skinners, armed with the Sharps buffalo rifle firing a bullet to match the caliber of modern antiaircraft artillery. In 1868, with the pounding of the last Union Pacific Railroad spike and the arrival of the iron horse to haul hides by the ton, all the lethal pieces had come together, triggering the final and most explosive spree of plunder. It became known as the Great Slaughter, a stupendous decade of death leaving millions of skinned bison rotting on the plains. One could walk miles upon their dead bodies. The last skittish little bands of bison became targets of trophy hunters and museum collectors. "Few, indeed, are the men who now have, or evermore shall have, the chance of seeing the mightiest of American beasts, in all his wild vigor, surrounded by the tremendous desolation of his far-off mountain home," wrote Theodore Roosevelt, who was among those who came gunning for their trophies before the opportunity was forever lost.

For the lions of the Black Hills, the new round of exterminations portended theirs in turn. Into the voids of the vanquished swept the empires of cattlemen and sheepmen and their antipredator mercenaries. It was a particularly bad time to be a wild predator in the Black Hills—or, for that matter, anywhere in the New West. Livestock associations lobbied their governors for bounties. Professional wolfers and lion hunters of the Ben Lilly breed stormed the last sanctuaries. In 1889, South Dakota in its first year of statehood put a bounty on its mountain lions. Within seventeen years, South Dakota recorded its last bounty.

For sixty years thereafter, the Hills remained empty of resident lions. (Although, South Dakota continued to offer a reward for any lion scalp brought in, just in case.) Across the West, fugitive lions melted back into the last and least-ventured hideaways. They hunted in the dark; they lay low by day in the streamside thickets and rocky ledges. But the Black Hills, increasingly slashed with logging roads, evermore crawling with people, and too far removed from reinforcements, became too leaky a lifeboat to weather the storm.

Over the years, cadres of scientists came forward to challenge the government's scorched-earth policy toward predators as an ill-conceived waste of lives and money. They questioned the economics of spending nearly thirty dollars killing predators to avenge every dollar's worth of sheep supposedly lost to them. They asked why, when the occasional stock-raiding lion called for a surgical strike against the offender, the weapon invariably deployed was a sledgehammer to the entire race. Yet for decades, the predators' defenders were ignored, their damning reports buried in the government stacks.

With the 1960s came a tipping of the American conscience, a swelling of societal concerns for the oppressed and persecuted, and with it a rising call for saving such wild things as mountain lions. Even among the lion's hunters came a notion that perhaps more profit was to be made in keeping a few of them alive, as sport. State after state—with the exception of Texas—stopped referring to lions so simply as predators or vermin, and began referring to them as game. They abandoned their lion bounties and replaced them with hunting seasons. During the seasonal lulls in the gunning, lions hiding in the West's last unflushed corners began poking their heads out, filling lion-less voids, reclaiming lost ground.

Or so went the more popular telling of the tale. Though the end of the bounty era would coincide with an upswing in lion sightings, it would turn out their apparent resurgence was not for any lack of incessant hounding. Through the 1970s, '80s, and '90s, the tallies of dead lions continued on a steepening climb, far beyond those recorded during the early century's era of eradication. But so, too, had climbed the censuses of living deer and elk, the lion's primary prey. It was something more than mercy that had staged the lion's comeback. It was a resurgence of food.

By whichever means, bold young lions had indeed begun wandering to the edges of their little worlds, and then beyond. Eventually they reached the eastern foothills of the Rockies, where there was nowhere to go but down upon the plains. So, from the Laramie or the Bighorn mountains of Wyoming came a lion walking eastward, across the grasslands of the Powder River Basin, and finally into the last beckoning highlands of the Black Hills.

Eventually came another, and another. The first lions found the Black Hills rich again with deer. And in time, the pioneers, male and female, found each other. By the late 1970s, woodsmen and game wardens of the Hills had begun running across the occasional lion track or stashed leftover of deer; the word from the gun shops and bars held that the sightings added up to more than the passing visitor. The Black Hills lions were growing from within.

In 1978, just twelve years after abandoning its bounty on mountain lions, the South Dakota legislature certified their return, declaring them an endangered animal of the state, to be protected under law. The homecoming celebrations would be brief. Soon after its protection, the first lion to unwittingly test the waters met a deer hunter, who shot him dead. The judge who dismissed the case said he would have done the same thing.

But the lions kept coming. The rare news of a winter track turned into three or four reports per year. The sightings and signs were clustered at first in the southern half of the Hills, and in time spread throughout. Lions started leaving their calling cards in towns. Two deer were found dead near the streets of Rapid City, home of some sixty thousand people, the Hills' closest approximation of a metropolis.

Authorities stopped wondering if, and started guessing how many. By the late 1990s they estimated that the Black Hills was harboring a breeding population of maybe twenty-five mountain lions, with perhaps as many more living in the surrounding plains. The Black Hills once again, after ninety vacant years, had come to harbor a self-sustaining community of mountain lions. There would be a new order to the ecology of the Hills. The legions of archers and riflemen would find themselves joined by a hunter of awesome innate skills, a creature capable of bringing down the biggest and fleetest animals with no weapons but its own body and brains. The stockmen would take note, too. And along with the lions returned the latent hostilities of a bygone era.

Among the more vocal townsfolk there was talk of plunder and looming danger. If mountain lions were so brazenly taking deer on the edge of town, went the thinking, it was but a matter of time before all the deer were gone, all the sheep were slaughtered, before children were being plucked off the streets. This was a brewing emergency demanding a preemptive strike. Hence, in yet another rapid reversal of fortune, the comeback lions of the Black Hills were to be rebranded, from natural phenomenon to criminal at large.

Wizards of Oz

In 1998 a graduate student of South Dakota State University named Dorothy Fecske began the first scientific study of the Black Hills recolonizing lions. Her study, funded in part by the South Dakota Department of Game, Fish and Parks, was ostensibly aimed at discovering how many cougars the Black Hills might be harboring. Ultimately, it would serve to justify how many were to be shot.

With the winter snows of 1998, Fecske began venturing into the Hills to capture her subjects. Mornings after a fresh snowfall, she and a crew of lion chasers, including a veterinarian and a houndsman, headed out in trucks through the back roads of the Hills. Upon finding a line of tracks crossing a road, they would unleash the hounds and follow their baying through the hills, until the baying came to settle on a spot. They would come running to find the dogs barking up a tree, and a lion glaring down from above. They would estimate the cat's weight, load a prescribed dose of tranquilizer into a dart gun, and fire into the big muscles of the cat's shoulder or haunch. The drugged lion would grow groggy. Up the tree went the appointed climber, to loop a line around a leg and lower the cat.

The ground crew worked quickly. They measured the cat's length and weight, and drew a sample of blood, checking its vital signs as they went. They estimated its age, inspecting its fangs for signs of wear, its coat for any vestigial spots of kittenhood. Finally, they wrapped a plastic collar around the lion's neck and injected the reversing drug, to wait and watch as the lion's muscles awakened. And with a gathering of strength and a drunken gait, the big cat would be off, wobbling away into the Hills with a radio beacon now betraying its whereabouts.

In time, Fecske's crew thus processed and released fourteen lions, to begin adding fact to the rumor-laden résumé of lions in the Black Hills. With receiver in hand, Fecske would fly passenger in a Cessna two-seater, casing the Hills, charting the cats as they roamed. The signals began to amass into clusters and polygons, sorting into what amounted to lion territories. The lions ranged widely. The males in their yearly wanderings covered some three hundred square miles; the females less than a quarter as far. It was the female's habit to limit and focus her travels, to learn every cliff and copse of woods and potential ambush of prey, to feed not only herself but as many as three or four lion cubs every other year.

The male lion followed a different course. His strategy was to possess female lions. He would patrol a territory as far as his time and energies allowed, to gather as many mates and sire as many offspring as possible in one lion's lifetime, and to challenge all competing males along the way. His was a fiercely defended territory. It was an established fact of mountain lion society for males meeting on contested ground to fight, sometimes to the death. Fecske's lions held true to the rule. In the spring of 2000 the transmitter of a young lion named M-7 began emitting a new beat, of an animal that had stopped moving. The signal had become known as the mortality sequence. Fecske's crew traced the signal to find M-7 lying in a bloodied heap. In his youthful wanderings, M-7 had inadvisably crossed paths with M-2, a larger, older tom with an established territory and zero tolerance for intruders.

It was this concept of territory and competition on which mountain lions sorted the Black Hills among themselves. Contrary to the doomsday pontifications of armchair outdoorsmen, imagining lions multiplying like rabbits and sweeping countrysides like the Plague, Fecske found true lion society operating as an orderly self-policed population. It was on this system that she began to extrapolate.

Given the average territory size of her sample subjects, Fecske figured there was room for only so many males over the whole of the Hills. Adding an average of three female territories for that of every male, plus a reasonable ratio of kittens and teen lions, Fecske estimated as many as 149 cougars living in the Black Hills. It was an admittedly rough estimate, as Fecske would dutifully warn in her ensuing dissertation: "Caution should be taken when interpreting simulations until additional information . . . is obtained on the population."

Cautions notwithstanding, those deciding the lions' fate had already begun the paperwork toward knocking back those numbers. In 1999 the governor of South Dakota granted the state's wildlife commission the authority to remove the lion's legal protections as a threatened species.

For one among Fecske's crew, the commission's move smelled a bit too suspiciously of the cart before the horse, decisions before the data. Sharon Seneczko, a young veterinarian who ran a small animal clinic in Custer, had volunteered to help track the lions of Fecske's study, to see to their safety under the stress of capture and anesthesia. As time went on, catching and collaring cats, hearing the talk about town, listening to her clients at the clinic, it dawned on Seneczko that the hounds and the dart guns were the least of the new lions' concerns. There were grumblings among the deer hunters and stockmen of too many lions in the Black Hills. The state wildlife commission, beholden to South Dakota's omnipotent agricultural and sport hunting lobbies, had shown its hand. Seneczko heard the growing drumbeat of a predetermined march toward legal slaughter of the lions, using Fecske's data as cover. "They were gaining information to open a season on them," said Seneczko. "There was going to be a big clash between mountain lions and people."

In January 2003 the South Dakota Department of Game, Fish and Parks, and the eight-man commission that oversaw it, declared that they wanted to kill off some of the Black Hills cats—or perhaps a lot of them. They had introduced a bill to the state senate Agriculture and Natural Resources Committee that would complete the dismantling of the lion's protections as a threatened species. They would reclassify the lion as big game, to be legally chased and shot—the forebodings of Seneczko coming to pass.

The game agency came armed with Fecske's fresh estimate of lion numbers, spiked with its own message of impending danger. There were upward of 149 lions living in South Dakota, most of them in the Black Hills, and that apparently meant that trouble was just around the corner.

"No one in the state was attacked by a mountain lion last year," said game secretary John Cooper to the committee, "but two hunters reported they were stalked by lions. Neither one of the people was attacked, but I'm certain there was a laundry bill there."

So went the logic: too many lions in the Hills, its citizens therefore in danger, a sport hunt therefore to remedy both ills. Sailing through committee, the hunting bill soon came up for a vote in the full senate, its fear-based rationale repeated.

"Currently management plan research indicates we should be aggressively managing this species," said Cooper. Chimed a lobbyist for the South Dakota stock growers, "I don't think we need to wait until we have a human death before we manage the lions."

But next there came a warning of a different sort, from the veterinarian who had tended to some of the same lions now under the gun. "There is no scientific evidence that the public would be safer if mountain lions were allowed to be hunted," testified Seneczko. Killing the big cats at random would only invite more trouble.

Seneczko was no standard bleeding-heart lion hugger. Her boyfriend, Donny Morgan, was a hunter and a houndsman, the same houndsman who had helped tree the first subjects of Fecske's study. Morgan had a lion head mounted on his wall. Seneczko, too, accepted the killing of lions for sustenance and self-preservation, perhaps even for the occasional trophy. But what the game agents and livestock lobbyists were pitching amounted to something else.

Seneczko echoed the concerns of leading scientists drawing on decades of study in lion country. She feared the ensuing chaos of a lion society suddenly devoid of its leaders. She loathed the cruelties and dreaded the consequences of orphaned kittens and reckless teens left to roam—the ones most likely to come starving into the farmer's goat corral, to snatch the family pet from the backyard. "The killing of lions should only occur as a last resort and on a case-by-case basis."

The lawmakers were having none of it. Unanimously, they passed the bill, and with that the mountain lions of South Dakota became big game animals. The only details to be resolved were how many to shoot and how soon to begin.

The news spread, and cadres of lion champions from across the country huddled. The Cougar Fund of Wyoming, the Mountain Lion Foundation of California, the Eastern Cougar Foundation of the Atlantic states, the Prairie Hills Audubon Society of South Dakota, and Seneczko's new local force—the Black Hills Mountain Lion Foundation—together they prepared for the storm Seneczko had long seen coming. Some among them worried simply for the future of the Black Hills cats, whose history already included one extermination at the hands of humans. Others worried more broadly, for the future of lions where none now lived.

In the decade leading up to the battle over the Black Hills lion, citizens from distant points east had begun startling to the incongruous sight of big cats suddenly appearing in their neck of the plains. What had begun as a sporadic trickle of freak prairie sightings appeared to be gathering pace. Over just the previous two years, scientists had tallied some two dozen confirmations of lone lions far upon the open spaces of the Midwest. The cats had recently roamed into the eastern plains of the Dakotas and Nebraska; a few had passed beyond, into Minnesota, Iowa, Missouri, and Arkansas. The local stories coalesced into national headlines. From its resurgence in the western ranges and badlands, to its promising forays toward the eastern forests, the lion had become that rare form of conservation news known as a success—or, as famously declared by the ranking dean of mountain lion scientists, Maurice Hornocker, "the most amazing big-carnivore comeback story in the history of the world."

For those wishing the cats well, the breaking news on eastward lions appeared on first take a heartening picture. On closer inspection, the lions' victory parade began to resemble more a death march. The remains of the pioneering lions were coming back plugged with bullets or pulverized by motor vehicles—and not surprisingly so. The pioneers were venturing into a land of people a century removed from life among lions. Now, suddenly, flashing through the beams of their headlights, napping between their rows of corn, strolling through their suburban backyards, came a mythical creature from a dimly remembered past, obviously bent on human carnage. The fatal flaw of the comeback story, the applause-hushing fact conveniently missing from the headlines and pull quotes, was that no survivors were to be found.

Of the bodies examined, nearly all turned out to be young males from points west, likely prospecting for love. A rare few were female. Not one confirmation amounted to a wild-born kitten. For a lack of mates and an excess of dangerous people en route, not one young lion's odyssey for immortality had been consummated. So far as anybody knew, the lions' eastward pilgrimage had become a tragic venture tantamount to suicide.

An intriguing number of their paths were funneling back to one particular source. It appeared the Black Hills had become a critical port of departure for the mountain lion's opening attempts to reclaim the continent. And now that port was coming under direct attack.

The South Dakota game department's concern was not to escort the lions eastward, but to accommodate a certain sect who wanted them dead before they left the Hills. By the spring of 2005, the department had published its plan, and had begun pitching it in a series of town meetings across the state. The plan was to open the Hills to hunters the following October, to kill twenty lions, or five females, whichever came first. According to the plan, "The most important season objective will be to determine if a prescribed mountain lion season can reduce the amount of human-lion conflicts while still maintaining a healthy, viable mountain lion population in the Black Hills."

Over the next two months, the department held twenty public meetings across the state, pitching its plan for the hunt. The meetings tended to be anything but cordial. With a suggestion of twenty lions to be randomly sacrificed, the hunt was too lenient for some, too draconian for others. Lion haters took the mike and warned that there would be rampant killing of livestock and devoured children if more drastic measures weren't soon deployed. There were calls to wipe the lions out. Lion defenders spoke their piece, of the missing logic and ethics behind this new unprovoked war on the Hills' returning native. Voices rose, fingers were pointed, threats were issued.

Standing square in the crossfire was the department's lion point person, a young biologist named John Kanta. He had been chosen to deliver his agency's party line, reviewing the lion's Black Hills history with humans, from exterminated pest to protected species to public menace—thus the need to begin killing it again. With no formal training in cougar biology, Kanta compensated with an even-tempered talent for entering the proverbial lion's den and emerging with all limbs intact.

Kanta was yelled at, cursed at. His home phone rang in the middle of the night. "I'd have people say, 'John, you're a dumb son of a bitch. You must have shit for brains.'" Kanta would come to be known as Teflon John. Ranchers in particular made their feelings clear. If the department didn't do something about the lions, they would do so themselves.

While Kanta skillfully soothed the flaring tempers and steered the hearings off the shoals, his senior colleague John Wrede sat watching and shaking his head. Wrede, a wizened thirty-year veteran of the agency, a conservation officer and big-game manager who over the years had witnessed firsthand the return of the banished lion to the Black Hills, was thinking things that no agency man was free to say. Wrede silently sympathized with the lion's defenders. He, too, saw fundamental flaws in the unwavering prescription for curing South Dakota's supposed plague of lions with more bullets. He saw a disturbing imbalance in the debate, biased as it was by hatred. "It was encouraging to hear cougar conservation proponents use research and documentation to support their pleas for moderation and approaching any hunting season with a great deal of caution," he later confided. "It was very discouraging and downright angering to listen to some of the ag producers and suburbanites first berate the advocates as environmental wackos and bunny huggers before launching into their fear-driven diatribes in support for sending the cougar back to the endangered species list."

The lion's defenders returned fire with a flurry of protest. They went head-to-head with the lion haters at the town meetings. They held seminars at the Rapid City civic center, ran a full-page ad in the city paper, imploring all to consider a more peaceful mode of coexistence with the Black Hills' native cat. They peppered the game department with letters, challenging its science, questioning its motives. Wrote cougar biologist Rick Hopkins from California—the one western state prohibiting the hunting of its lions— "Upon reading this proposal, we are reminded of the Wizard of Oz when he implores Dorothy and Company to ignore the man behind the curtain."

For their part, the wildlife commissioners who would ultimately decide the lions' fate saw the game department's recommended kill quota of twenty cats, and raised it by five, while expanding the hunt from the Black Hills to the entire state. Certain powerful ranchers outside the Hills wanted every lion dead. Conspicuous among them was a representative in the South Dakota legislature named Betty Olson, who owned a cattle ranch eighty miles north of the Black Hills. "We should make it easier to kill lions," she argued.

With every turn of the political gears, the lions' champions saw their time running out. Little more than a month before opening day, they filed a petition to repeal the hunt. The commission denied it. Three days before the hunt, they filed suit. The judge struck it down. Thirty-six hours later, the lion hunters took to the Hills.

Escape

What the game department had loosely labelled an experimental hunt, what the pro-lion people saw as persecution, was nonetheless destined to become a fact of life for the lions of the Black Hills. Experiment or slaughter, the sanctioned killing would continue every year thereafter, casualties and controversy rising in step.

By the summer of 2009, the mountain lions of the Black Hills were either threatening to overrun the country or threatened with annihilation, depending on the observer. It had been yet another busy year of lion sightings and shootings. Some sixty cats had been recorded dead, all but four of them at human hands. For the fourth season running, the lions' defenders had protested the heavy gunning, and for the fourth season running, the state's wildlife commission had in turn raised the hunting quota. For all the commotion, the Black Hills' leading newspaper would come to rank the return of the lion (along with political scandals, antiabortion crusades, epic droughts, and forest fires) among South Dakota's topmost stories of the decade. Rhetoric aside, the body count in the war of lions versus people—recording hardly a single human harmed, but hundreds of big cats and kittens shot dead—darkly painted the Black Hills of the twenty-first century as once again an especially treacherous place to be a mountain lion.

The killing would ultimately show both sides wrong about certain things they thought they knew of lions. Yet it was not the collective dead, but rather one young survivor, who would so thoroughly dismantle every inbred prejudice and statistical probability meant to peg the most contentious creature of the Black Hills. Four years after the shooting officially resumed, on that late summer evening of 2009, the young lion came walking out of the woods, looking eastward.

TWO Into the Void

One doesn't discover new lands without consenting to lose sight of the shore for a very long time.

—ANDRÉ GIDE

BY THE DARK of night the young lion walked out of the forest and into the valley, through fields cordoned by barbed wire and veined by the meandering creek. As many times as he had ventured this way before, down into the streamside groves and foothill savannas of the prairie's edge, he had eventually back-pedaled to the more familiar mountain trails of home. But here he was again, drawn to the edge, alone and itching to leave. The evolutionary biologist would say that he was maximizing his chances of finding prospective mates and infusing new lands with his genetic stock; that he was minimizing his chances of inbreeding with his mother and sisters, or having his skull crushed by an older rival. The romanticist would say he was longing for love and adventure.

A chorus of crickets mingled with the occasional hum of tires on the interstate running through the valley. After weeks of pacing about the periphery of the Hills, something had triggered in the maturing lion's chemistry. And like a restless young bird finally lifting north with the first glimmer of spring, this night he was heading for the far side of the highway and would not be coming back.

Lion Science

In the years following Dorothy Fecske's inaugural study came a succession of academic collaborations between South Dakota State University and the

South Dakota Department of Game, Fish and Parks, shining new light on the Black Hills' nascent society of lions. The capture techniques were honed, the directory of collared cats grew long. By 2009 nearly three hundred lions had been caught and released wearing ear tags or radios broadcasting their whereabouts to young researchers canvassing the Hills in small planes and trucks. Their findings would corroborate much of what scientists elsewhere had come to learn of the wild ways of mountain lions. There had been a world of new understandings gained over the past forty years, all ultimately stemming from the first systematic examination of lion society by a young biologist named Maurice Hornocker.

Hornocker had started his training as a lion student in the 1960s, offering local houndsmen fifty dollars for every cat they could tree for him. What to do with them thereafter was for Hornocker to figure out. He was a novice tree climber and cat handler, who had dealt with all of one small female lion before meeting his second subject on a cold December morning in the Bitterroot Range of Montana. With climbing spurs and a rope, Hornocker went up to retrieve the lion, a massive tom lying woozy from a tranquilizing dart in his thigh, seventy feet aloft in the crook of a swaying pine. As Hornocker tells it, "I reached for one of his hind legs to slip the noose over his foot . . . Letting loose a deafening growl, he swung his huge head around the tree trunk not three feet from my face. Eyes blazing and fangs bared, he lurched his body, attempting to move from the fork. As he did so, his tail whipped across my chest. Instinctively, I grabbed that thick tail and with all my might pulled the big, now unbalanced, cat from the tree, literally launching him past my face and into space. I watched the big lion sail through the air as if in slow motion and fall into the deep, cushioning snow, where he skidded harmlessly down the steep slope."

In time, Hornocker's cougar-processing skills grew more graceful, and with the recruitment of a veteran woodsman and lion hunter named Wilbur Wiles, he began formally applying them in a vast and roadless tract of mountain forests of central Idaho known then as the Idaho Primitive Area, in what was to become the modern template of cougar field research. (Hornocker had abandoned Montana after hunters shot nearly all his subjects.) Hornocker and Wiles fitted the cats with numbered collars and ear tags, then trailed and treed them again and again, bushwhacking upward of twelve hundred miles each winter through the snow-buried mountains to estimate their numbers and trace their wanderings. They also took stock of the lions' food. They surveyed deer and elk to gauge how predator and prey were getting along.

Five years into the study, they were joined by student John Seidensticker, and the team began illuminating the big cat's clandestine life as never before, by way of the radio collar. It turned out Hornocker had served his wildlife apprenticeship under the legendary Craighead brothers, Frank and John, the pioneering wildlife researchers who, with ham radio technology, garage bench ingenuity, and a few close escapes from grumpy half-drugged bears, had cobbled together the first rudimentary protocol for tracking the grizzlies of Yellowstone National Park. The radio collar gave the Craigheads and the world a vivid new look at the social life and spacious wanderings of grizzlies as no mountain man or binocular-clad biologist before them ever had. Adopting the Craigheads' telemetric approach, Hornocker would soon do the same for mountain lions.

Where once the images of lion life typically amounted to short and violent snapshots begun by chasing hounds and concluding with a hunter's rifle, now the chases slowed to the lion's unharried pace. Instead of hours, the cats were tracked for days and years. Young cats were some-times tagged within weeks of birth and followed until their deaths. As the tracks and radio fixes were plotted and pinpointed, a veil began to lift, and the big cat gradually emerged from the historical fog of myth and hearsay.

The lions' weekly wanderings gathered as patterns and polygons inscribing what Hornocker would interpret as territories. The largest of these territories were policed by big mature males, lording over entire river valleys and mountain peaks, posting their territories with scent and scrap-ings, spraying trails with their urine, laying their feces as cornerstones. The territory of a single male might circumscribe those of three females. Among Hornocker's lion colony, the ruling toms rather politely respected each other's boundaries. (Although, lion researchers elsewhere would later docu-ment a more savage counterpart to Hornocker's peaceable kingdom.) By whichever means, the lion's territorial nature made for a stable community with built-in safeguards against overcrowding.

Such inherent laws and limits of cougar society described a creature other than the serial slasher of hunters' yarns and ranchers' nightmares. The unhunted lions of the Idaho Primitive Area did not multiply unchecked, eat themselves out of house and home, and then resort to stalking human settlements. Deer numbers did not inevitably collapse under the weight of lion predation.

As for the lion's purported thirst for human blood, Hornocker and a generation of disciples to follow would intimately test and reject the hypothesis hundreds upon hundreds of times, using themselves as bait. They climbed within arm's reach of snarling cougars cornered in trees. They walked unarmed into lion dens writhing with kittens, at times while mother cats looked on. Tracking signals would locate lions catnapping next to popular hiking trails while scores of pedestrians unwittingly passed. The mountain lion, for all its people-killing potential, habitually chose retreat, if not indifference.

The tenets of cougar society as revealed in the Idaho Primitive Area were eventually to be seconded by cougar scientists across the breadth of the species' hemispheric range—across the Great Basin Desert of Nevada and the Chihuahuan Desert of New Mexico, the canyon country of southern Utah, the western slope of the Colorado Rockies, the North Rim of the Grand Canyon, the potato fields of southern Idaho, in the Santa Ana Mountains of Southern California, in the Yellowstone of northern Wyoming, in the Canadian Rockies of Alberta, the open steppes of Chilean Patagonia, the cypress swamps of southern Florida, and eventually in the rock-and-pine island of the Black Hills. Chief among the repeating themes: Lions were programmed in and practiced at controlling their own numbers; lions, as winnowers of the weak and drivers of the herds, were a positive force for deer and an antidote to overeaten forests; and lions, contrary to their accompanying warning labels, suffered a vastly greater history of people overkilling them than the converse.

None of this knowledge squared well with the lion's dramatized role as decimator of deer and lurking scourge of human societies. Nor did the science cast a particularly flattering light on what had become the de facto mode of mountain lion management as recently adopted in South Dakota—which was to randomly shoot them. Game agencies across the West were holding yearly public hunts for their mountain lions—with the exception of California, whose citizens had repeatedly voted against hunting their cougars since 1972; and its alter ego, Texas, where the cat was still considered vermin to be shot year-round without limit. All agencies had staff or contractors killing additional scores of lions they deemed dangerous. But on what scientific grounds, few could honestly answer.

In 2002, thirteen of the lion's leading authorities had come together to suggest a science-based overhaul of the prevailing seat-of-the-pants approach to managing mountain lions. The result, published in 2005, was a slim volume called *Cougar Management Guidelines*. The *Guidelines* updated the science of cougars and their prey, cougars and their habitat, cougars and livestock, with a particularly revealing chapter devoted to cougars and the practice of hunting them. The *Guidelines* offered a dozen detailed recommendations and cautions for those public servants purporting to manage their lions so simply with bullets. Though written in measured academic tones, the *Guidelines* bluntly indicted those pitching cougar hunts as a means to more deer and safer streets. Two of the recommendations in particular, headed in boldface, hit squarely between the eyes:

Sport hunting to benefit wild ungulate populations is not supported by the scientific literature

Sport hunting has not been shown to reduce risk of attack on humans

In the years following the return of the Black Hills lion, none of the prophesied Armageddons had come to pass. Those sounding alarms of the Mongol hordes descending were to be left groping for evidence of their carnage. A few goats, llamas, miniature horses, barnyard fowl, and untended house cats had apparently been taken, most of them, as lion biologists had already predicted, by wandering teenage males and orphaned young. But of the thousands of cattle, sheep, and horses pastured among the Hills and surrounding prairie, whose owners were among the loudest voices for the lion's annihilation, all of three such animals were officially recorded as lion prey. As for the gather-your-children-and-bolt-your-doors doomsayers, their grim reaper had apparently fallen asleep on the job. Hardly a lion in the Hills was to be found whose home range did not encompass a human residence. Such endless opportunities for mayhem led to a single, if murky, account of an attack: In 2008 a fisherman claimed he'd been clawed. Tracking hounds deployed within two hours of the incident could detect no scent of lion, though investigators did find several spent cans of beer.

Nor had the lions' numbers crashed as forewarned by their allies. Eighty cats would be killed in the first four years of the South Dakota hunt, the number rising more steeply by the year, the number in 2009 more than twice as many as the first hunt. Another sixty lions had been killed during that time by police and private citizens, on suspicion of danger and claims of self-defense (a disproportionate number of the dead again represented by young footloose males). Yet even as the Black Hills came to approximate the death camp for lions, their living numbers somehow appeared to keep pace. As much as the rising body count incited lion conservationists to louder protest, the inevitable collapse they warned of kept failing to happen.

The mountain lions of the Black Hills, for all their tightening surveillance under gun sights and radio beacons, had upheld their species' age-old aura of mystique, a certain element of surprise that continued to confound the population modelers and outdistance the electronic gadgetry of science. True to form, the lions had socially partitioned the Hills among mature territorial males and females and offspring more or less tied to their mothers. But beyond these bell curve exemplars of lion society there crept a more elusive creature who would scatter such tidy concepts of home and family to unimagined horizons.

Hornocker had been the first of many to formally meet and ponder these outliers of lion society. Just as he would come to assume that he had treed and pegged every resident lion on the mountain, along would come a young stranger from points unknown. The flow went both ways. Among the young lions born in Hornocker's study area, some would suddenly leave their mothers and siblings and wander off the map. Most would never be heard from again. But a few would reappear, their collars turned in by hunters more than one hundred miles away. Hornocker labelled this roving class of lion as transients.

Such transients Hornocker came to see as critical to the integrity of lion populations. These were the daring young scouts who went in search of new lands and mates. They were the immigrants who filled missing ranks and brought new blood to established colonies. In their risky, gallivanting way, the transients served as the ironic balancing rods of cougar society.

With the proliferation of wired cougars, the appreciation for the terrain-gobbling capacities of the transient expanded exponentially. It was not uncommon to find young males venturing upward of two hundred miles from their birthplace. In 1984 a young male was tracked from the Bighorn Mountains of northern Wyoming to where he was killed west of Denver, Colorado, three hundred miles away. Young females, though more apt to settle down near their birthplace, sometimes set out on impressive jaunts of their own. One such cat spent a year trekking more than two hundred miles eastward from her mountain home overlooking the million-person metropolis of the Salt Lake Valley of Utah, to the rural White River Plateau of Colorado, where she was shot by a hunter. When her trackers connected the dots of her daily wanderings, they found she had walked 833 miles, crossing the biggest river and busiest interstate in Utah, in addition to fourteen major highways and five ecoregions spanning three states, from the jagged peaks of Utah's Wasatch Range to the Red Desert of Wyoming to the western slope of the Colorado Rockies.

The idea of modern lions living as isolated colonies in their mountain fortresses, stranded by impassably hostile moats of river and plain and highway, soon gave way to a new image of lions as a single scattered nation of related tribes, clandestinely trading by the dark of night in living bodies and new blood, ultimately delivered—come hell or human obstacle—by the roving transients. For the Black Hills, this secretive stream of immigrants from the West began to answer the riddle of the seemingly bottomless source of slain lions being carted out every year. As for those leaving the Hills, their unique launching point on the eastern precipice of the lion's inhabited world begged the bigger question of where on earth they might be heading.

In 2003, the second phase of the Black Hills biological investigations began with Dorothy Fecske's successor, a graduate student named Daniel Thompson. Whereas Fecske had dealt with the most basic questions of how many and where, Thompson would peer more intimately into the lives of individual lions. Chief among his plans was to scour the Hills for birthing dens, to tag lion cubs and follow them through their forays, to that most daring leap in the mountain lion's life, when the young animal left its mother and set forth on its own. Thompson, a newcomer to the fraternity of lion researchers, and his upstart subjects of the Black Hills were about to redefine just what lengths a determined young lion on the edge of the abyss would go to in search of his destiny.

Thompson's early observations would more or less mirror those of his fellow cougar students across the land. He found mother lions giving birth to as many as four kittens, little camouflaged puffs of spotted fur weighing barely more than a pound, hidden in the most inhospitable rock slides and densest tangles of underbrush. Within two weeks the eyes would open baby blue, and the kittens would begin stumbling about the den.

These first fuzzy days of awareness were a particularly trying time for the mother lion. Her forays for food were necessarily short, but urgent. Her task was to replenish herself without venturing too far from her unguarded brood. So she was tethered to these increasingly active cubs with their growing demands to keep the milk flowing. The kittens were metabolic balls of fire, forever hungry, and growing fast. Within three weeks, they had doubled their weight.

As their senses sharpened, their world of curiosity expanded to match. They would wobble to the edges of the den, and beyond, into the ever-beckoning boulders and brush on the outskirts of their brightening little world. Upon mother's return, they would occasionally find themselves dangling gently from her jaws and being carried to new dens. This was as much a shell game against would-be predators as it was early training for the hunter's life. They were to become intimate with every nook, every over-look and hiding place and deer trail, over the miles of terrain, on the expanding scale they would one day consider home.

Within a month, the young lions' gums had sprouted the first hints of fangs that would one day sever arteries and spines, to be followed by emerging molars for shearing muscle and sinew. With the emergence of teeth came the first offerings of meat, and as the cubs gained their feet, their mother began leading them to her kills, and leaving them while she hunted for more. Left to themselves, the rambunctious cubs rumbled, strewing bone and hide and miscellaneous body parts like toys in a toddler's play-room. Thompson would come upon these mobile den sites as to the scene of an explosion—or, as one veteran lion researcher described it, "that of a minor tornado." The kittens' play grew rough; they stalked and pounced, wrestled and bit, launching mock attacks in training for real battles to come. Their mother began leaving for days at a time. The needs grew larger, the mother's forays longer.

Though Thompson and his crew aimed their den visits to coincide with these forays, there would come times when researchers and mother lion would inadvertently meet. If the mother refused to leave, Thompson respect-fully retreated. He rarely had to. More often it was the lion who gave way, to wait anxiously nearby while these fearsome strangers handled her kittens. The worst Thompson ever received for trespassing the lion's most sacred space was a concealed growl of warning.

The same could not be said for those lions who fought for the rights to these females. Nearly every adult male that Thompson captured came battered from fighting other lions. The warriors came with faces raked, fangs broken, noses torn, necks punctured, and ears severed. Some were dead when Thompson found them. Some would have been better off that way. Thompson came upon one cat wandering dazed in circles, his skull crushed by another lion's jaws. Thompson, out of mercy, killed the cat.

These were the battle-scarred warlords of the Black Hills. Their territories were their kingdoms and their livelihoods, providing them the essentials of life and legacy, in the form of food, shelter, and the mates through which to immortalize their genes. For these rewards they would fight tooth and claw until driven out or killed. And for these same rewards, some also tended to kill kittens.

Of the eighteen kittens that Thompson tagged, four would die from what appeared to be the bite of a big male. Thompson found the kittens lying dead and uneaten. (He wondered how many more he might have missed.) Infanticide was a major danger facing mountain lion kittens. Roving males' seemingly counterproductive penchant for killing kittens came with an evolutionary explanation. For a courting male to dispatch a litter of kittens was, in theory, an effective strategy for resetting their mother's hormonal status from that of maternal caretaker to that of receptive breeder. The death of a mother's cubs would hasten her coming into heat, to more quickly bear young sired by their killer. It was a doubly diabolical means of clearing the way for her new suitor's genes while, with the same lethal swipe, expunging her former suitor's genes from the pool

Those young lions surviving their own kind would eventually face a barrage of human threats standing between kittenhood and old age (which, in the Black Hills, had come to describe a ten-year-old cat). Thompson, who concluded his investigations before licensed lion hunters first took to the Hills in 2005, found the lions getting run over on the roads, shot by poachers and game cops, strangled in trappers' snares, and otherwise dying by miscellaneous and mysterious causes. How many others were dying unnoted was anybody's guess. How many were leaving the Hills of their own accord, and to what end, became Thompson's seminal question.

By the time the cubs approached their first birthday, they had grown from spotted stubs to tawny, gracile felines slightly smaller than their mother. They had become capable, if clumsily, of killing on their own. They had practiced the lion's signature death bite, a severing of cervical vertebrae by two-inch canines driven with precision and power. They had practiced stalking and surprising live animals—with the Hills' assortment of turkeys, coyotes, porcupines, and deer as candidates—most of which escaped, but a critically increasing proportion of which became food. Their training was nearing the end.

Their mother began leaving them farther behind and longer alone. She would soon be coming again into heat, bringing the inevitable courting toms and their inherent hazards to unwelcome cubs. Eventually would come the family's last meal together, and the mother would leave and not return.

For a while, Thompson might find the abandoned siblings wandering and hunting and feeding as one. In time they, too, began to splinter. In the coming months, the young females drifted and settled into their own home sites in the nearest uncontested patches of marginal habitat on the periphery of the Hills. One left the Hills altogether, trekking sixty miles into Montana. But it would be two unrelated young males who soon widened Thompson's eyes to the horizon-gobbling capacity of a mountain lion on a mission.

M-16

In February 2003, Thompson's team treed and collared a yearling lion wandering alone in the southern reaches of the Black Hills. They weighed him at eighty pounds, labelled him M-16 (Male Number 16), and sent him off wearing a new radio collar.

Through the following spring, M-16 held close to his capture site. In June, he began to move. He went west to the edge of the Black Hills, and then followed the high country across the Wyoming border to the Hills' northwest corner. From there he commanded a clear view of the Bear Lodge Mountains, a small satellite range of the Black Hills separated by a valley of prairie and cattle pasture, with the long black line of Interstate 90 splitting the gap.

Thompson knew what was coming next. It was there that many of the outbound cats of the Black Hills would make their first tentative little leaps out of the motherland, to the most convenient stepping stone of the Bear Lodge before heading west into the quintessential cougar country of the Rockies. M-16 was getting ready to bolt. Thompson ramped up his flight schedule with the hope of getting a bearing on the cat as he headed out.

On September 3, Thompson located the cat still pacing the western edge of the Hills. A week later, he flew again. The radio signal for M-16 had vanished.

Thompson assumed that M-16 was heading west, away from the prairie, toward the more fitting mountain lion country of Wyoming. But that left a dauntingly big world yet to search. Thompson's radio receiver ordinarily covered a radius of roughly thirty miles. He asked his pilot for more.

Pilot Leo Becht climbed to twelve thousand feet, levelled off, and without warning banked into a tight spiral. Becht spun the plane on its side through the 360 degrees of the compass, wingtip antennae scanning all horizons for the beep that would reveal the lion's direction. (Borrowing from Tom Clancy's novel The Hunt for Red October, Becht called his maneuver a Crazy Ivan, after the Russian submarine captain—Ivan, of course—notorious for veering his ship suddenly sternward to look for spy boats following in the blind spot of his radar.) Thompson, for his part, focused on retaining his breakfast while otherwise listening for the faintest pulse in his headphones. North . . . west . . . south . . . east. Thompson listened through full circles of silence. The cat was gone.

Through the autumn and winter and into the spring of 2004, Thompson went back to tracking his other subjects in the Hills, though forever thereafter with an ear cocked for the wayward signal of M-16. "You're always curious," he said. "You're always wondering. You never stop looking."

In early June, nine months after his last signal from M-16, Thompson received a call from the manufacturer of his telemetry collars, informing him that one of the units he'd registered with them had been turned in. The serial number was that of M-16. The collar had been attached to a mountain lion found dead beside railroad tracks eighty miles west of Tulsa, in the prairie plains of Oklahoma. The straight-line distance, between the northwest corner of the Black Hills to where M-16's body was found, measured 667 miles.

Thompson struggled to accept what seemed at first glance a simply incredible journey. M-16 had apparently dispersed more than twice as far as any mountain lion ever recorded. He was hundreds of miles east of the nearest population of mountain lions; he had all but crossed the Great Plains, the long way, to a place where his kind hadn't roamed for a century. Thompson, a budding student of the budding colony of Black Hills lions, had just scored a major coup in mountain lion science. He had recorded by far the longest point-to-point journey ever known of a mountain lion. The immediate impressions were astounding, to the point of suspicion.

Plaguing nearly every state wildlife department east of the Rockies was a well-worn chorus of lion rumors, chief among them the accusation that government officials were covertly controlling runaway deer herds by secretly releasing the big cats. Thompson, as a close collaborator with South Dakota's game division, had grown weary of the tired old tale. One common version involved black helicopters airlifting the animals into secret enclaves. Another had the cats being hauled in by boxcar and unloaded in the middle of the night—which, given M-16's railroad connection, only promised to rekindle the conspiracy flames. However ridiculous the cloak-and-dagger explanations on the one hand—could the cat somehow have been carted to the middle of Oklahoma and dumped?—there remained the biological improbabilities of the other: Could it be the cat had actually walked all that way from the Black Hills? Thompson sent a forensics expert to clear the air surrounding the dead Oklahoma lion.

The carcass of M-16 was taken to a lab at Oklahoma State University and examined. He weighed 114 pounds, a reasonable weight for a wild lion his age. His stomach contained the remains of deer; he had been eating wild game. There were no broken ribs, but the animal's spleen and guts had been blown from the body. The official cause of death was "blunt trauma to the right lateral thorax," as one might expect of such an animal being struck crosswise by a locomotive.

How M-16 had made his way, Thompson could say little for sure. His facts amounted to one dead cat and two geographic coordinates, separated by nine months and at least 667 blank miles. Between origin and destination, M-16 had necessarily crossed interstate 80 of Wyoming and 70 of Colorado, and maybe, too, the north–south thruway of I-25, linking the congealing metropolises of the Colorado Front Range. He'd crossed the major prairie rivers of the Niobrara, Platte, and Arkansas, flowing east across his path.

As for narrowing M-16's route, Thompson envisioned him maybe heading south along the eastern edge of the Rockies, down through the Laramie Mountains of Wyoming and along the Colorado Front Range, before veering east into the prairie. He imagined him finding his shelter and sustenance on the plains by following a corridor of riverside forest. The single most obvious conduit was the Arkansas River, its snow-fed headwaters falling from the mountains west of Colorado Springs, spilling out onto the plains in a long, meandering crawl across Kansas, and then south into Oklahoma, to where a westward-jutting oxbow passed within ten miles of the journey's end. It seemed most logical to assume any prairie-bound cat automatically clinging to whatever ribbons of forest it could find along the way. Then again, who was to say such a lion wouldn't strike out straight across the open expanses? Which was precisely what another of Thompson's cats was even then preparing to do.

M-31

Two weeks before M-16's demise, Thompson had tagged another young male lion, in the hills west of Rapid City. According to protocol, he named him M-31. Following the now-familiar preflight pattern, M-31 hovered close to his capture site in the Hills for a couple of months, and then abruptly decamped. In late July, his radio signal reappeared just beyond the northern edge of the Hills, along a verdant little drainage called Whitewood Creek. More to the point, he was on the far side of Interstate 90. He had crossed the unofficial boundary separating the Black Hills from the prairie.

Thompson kept close tabs on the cat, waiting for his next move, while the cat in turn teased and bided his time. There among the shady oaks and ashes and whitetail deer of Whitewood Creek, M-31 stayed for a month, staging his exit. Thompson checked again on the second day of September— almost a year to the day after M-16 had bolted for Oklahoma—to find M-31 had made a portentous eight-mile jump northward along the creek. His flight was under way. The next time Thompson returned, M-31 was long gone.

But which way? The northward view through the cockpit framed a blank canvas of prairie. Beyond the muffled drone of the propellers there was silence. Once again, pilot Becht summoned Crazy Ivan. He tipped into his dizzying spiral, wingtip to the sky. The antennae began tracing the horizon. Thompson pricked his ears to a faint but sure pulse from his headphone. It was coming from the north.

The two flew sixty miles over the plains, to find M-31's signal coming from a pine-crested outcrop of chalky white bluffs and spires named Slim Buttes. It was a tragically fitting site for a fugitive to hole up. Slim Buttes once sheltered a village of Lakota people, until another September dawn, in 1876, when two thousand U.S. Army soldiers—out to avenge Custer's humiliating defeat at Little Bighorn eleven weeks earlier—ambushed the people and ransacked their village. Slim Buttes now stood as a lonely white cathedral of rock rising out of the prairie, with westerly breezes echoing across the amphitheaters of ancient limestone. And one mountain lion with wanderlust hidden among its ravines, leaving his airborne trackers wondering about his next move.

Between the Black Hills and Slim Buttes, there was little to suggest M-31's logic. He had abandoned the shade and cover of Whitewood Creek, now far behind, and headed north across the prairie; he had inevitably run against the Belle Fourche River, with its brushy banks and inviting eastward flow, and ignored its invitation, too. He had forded the Belle Fourche and headed north across more unpromising prairie. Perhaps by then he had spotted the distant outline of Slim Buttes and followed by simple line of sight, on the prospect of finding shelter or a female lion there. By whatever reasoning, M-31 had belied the most obvious academic hypotheses of how a mountain lion should have woven his way through such a seemingly alien habitat. It seemed he had simply drawn a bead on the buttes, and more or less shot the gap.

Finding the refuge too small for permanent residence and lacking in female lions, M-31 was not long for Slim Buttes. Thompson and Becht were back looking within a week, though this time no amount of elevation or stomach-flipping aerobatics would raise a trace of him.

"Where would I go if I was a big cat out there?" Thompson asked himself. "What would a cougar do?"

The two canvassed a few likely drainages leading eastward, guessing that M-31 might be heading for the Missouri River. The Missouri—longest river in North America, guiding path of Lewis and Clark on their search for the Pacific, and staging point for every major pioneering trail thereafter serving the European swarming of the American West—seemed a most likely corridor for a lion looking to slip unnoticed through the glare of the Great Plains. Born in the Centennial Range of Montana to the west, it ran southeast through the prairie centers of the Dakotas, draining downstream toward the Ozark Plateau of Missouri. Its banks rose in rugged breaks and bluffs, its floodplains forested here and there by towering hardwoods. Notwithstanding the occasional minefield through the metropolitan fortresses of Bismarck, Omaha, Kansas City, and St. Louis, it seemed a perfectly logical prairie route for a through-hiking mountain lion. But again, M-31 was guided by a more mysterious compass.

On December 6, three months after his last signal from Slim Buttes, Thompson received a call that a cougar wearing a collar had been spotted twenty miles west of Grand Forks, as confirmed by the North Dakota Game and Fish Department. The straight-line distance between Slim Buttes and Grand Forks measured more than three hundred miles, never mind how many times that distance he'd meandered in getting there. Sometime after leaving Slim Buttes, M-31 had veered northeast and crossed both the Missouri River and nearly the breadth of North Dakota, all the way to the Minnesota border. How, wondered Thompson, had M-31 crossed the mighty Missouri, or slipped unseen through the one-hundred-mile wasteland of harvested corn- and soy fields lying west of Grand Forks? M-31, meanwhile, was not hanging around for questions.

A month later and another ninety miles northeast, biologists picked up M-31's signal at the Roseau River Wildlife Management Area in northern Minnesota. He was two miles from the Canadian border.

Through January and February, M-31 lingered about the Roseau, where the marshland willows were thick and the deer plentiful. The ping of his radio signal became commonplace among the Roseau's managers, though never would they get so much as a glimpse of him. He crossed into Canada for a week or two, and then circled back to his now-familiar haunts and hunting grounds in the Roseau. Inevitably he was drawn onward, and with the spring thaw his signal disappeared into Manitoba, never to be reported again.

Dan Thompson would later author his dissertation and two scientific papers on the phenomenon of mountain lion dispersal, as observed from

the busy eastern port of the Black Hills, and starring the exploits of M-16
and M-31. Beyond the two headlining heroes, the Black Hills cats had largely
upheld the expected norms for their species. Young females were tending to
settle near their mother's home, occasionally venturing to other colonies to
the west. Young males were without exception leaving for distant ranges
beyond the Hills. (Three of Thompson's subjects established their own
territories in lion country of Montana and Wyoming, and held them for at
least a year, until killed by hunters.)

But it was the odd eastward-venturing cats that cast the most unexpected
light on the protocols of lion colonization. Their means of getting from
points A to B typically contradicted the predictions of science. Rather than a
methodical march through the most inviting corridors of cougar habitat, as
imagined through the biased human eye, the pioneering lion proceeded in
fits and starts, detours and backtracks, with periods of rest and refueling
broken by suicidal scrambles through the most ungodly stretches of anti-
lion country imaginable.

"They'll follow these riparian corridors out of the hills, into the prairie,"
said Thompson. "They'll use mountain lion habitat for a while, get some
food in them, then boom! Off to another pocket. They're very visual. When
they move, they go fast. They seem to do it in jumps."

Both M-16 and M-31 in their brow-raising jaunts had laid to rest any
notions that they were driven to such lengths by hunger or lack of habitat
along the way. The would-be pioneers had found prey aplenty (and probably
a bit rusty at the getaway, too, given that the prairie deer hadn't been chased
by a lion for dozens of generations). The eastward adventurers had also
pierced the doubters' theories that the endless horizons of naked prairie and
agricultural desert, booby-trapped with hostile cities and menaced by
barrelling eighteen-wheelers and railroad trains, posed insurmountable
barriers for the supposed lion of the mountains. It was a more elusive target,
reasoned Thompson, that drove the incredible journeys.

"They're looking for a mate," said Thompson. "If you keep going in any
direction you're going to find suitable habitat and food, but not necessarily
a viable breeding population. If you decide to go west, you'll find other
lions. If you go east, you gotta keep going a l-o-n-g ways."

Open Season

There would be no collar or radio signal sounding the departure of the particular young lion who left the Black Hills in the waning summer of 2009. He was among the nameless and tagless who had evaded the researchers' hounds and traps. Nobody reported seeing him as he dropped down out of the Hills under cover of darkness, slunk across the sleeping freeway, and struck off into the prairie. He was, for lack of labelling, the nameless lion. Although, soon enough, that would change.

Among the Black Hills' cohort of young males, nine out of ten would head northwest, lured at first by the Hills' little-sister range, the Bear Lodge, before detecting the No Vacancy signs of older toms and moving on to try their luck farther west, in the heart of the Wyoming Rockies. But the nameless lion was among the contrarian few who would instead come to fix on more mysterious bearings leading them east.

Over the previous decade, the Midwest plains had been visited by a quickening trickle of supposed sightings and signs far removed from any classical definitions of cougar habitat. A group calling themselves the Eastern Cougar Network had begun charting the phenomenon, gathering reports of sightings, tracks, pictures, video, body parts, and carcasses, and dotting the U.S. map with them. The Network's map appeared as if a shotgun had sprayed the Midwest with colored BBs. The eastbound lions were showing up in incongruous islands of humanity far upon the open spaces: Omaha, Sioux City, Bloomington, Kansas City, Wichita, Cedar Rapids, Chicago. There were Thompson's cats, M-16, meeting a train in Oklahoma, and M-31, last heard by radio heading into Manitoba. Thompson's successor, Brian Jansen, would collar a Black Hills cat that ventured fatally into the city of Saskatoon, Saskatchewan.

For every confirmed cat, hundreds more were reported. Upon official investigation, most became house cats and golden retrievers, deer and raccoons and sundry other mistaken identities, mischievously salted with amateur hoaxes and bald-faced lies. Typical was the photograph of a particularly huge cougar shot and killed in the Cascades of Washington State, the dead body hoisted in a bear hug by his killer. The photo went on a national Internet tour, with captions variously pinpointing its demise to Missouri,

Pennsylvania, Iowa, Wisconsin, Kansas, and Alabama, in addition to several states where cougars actually exist.

But dead bodies told no such lies. Since the year 2000, at least forty-five cougars in the flesh had been recovered—two captured, the rest killed— beyond the western breeding populations. All but eight were identified as males, and not one was estimated beyond four years of age. There was indeed a movement afoot, led by intrepid young males ultimately dying to meet a mate.

Therein lay the rose-shaded illusion of the brightly dotted map. To the lay public and the sundry journalists who served them, the galaxy of sightings gave the snapshot impression of a glorious mass migration, of a cougar comeback in the making. The map was, in fact, a memorial of the dead, of cats run over, shot, or suspiciously vanished. Not one was known to have survived the Midwest gauntlet.

The appearance of Midwest lions tended to incite the sort of mob violence more historically reserved for fairy-tale ogres and Frankenstein's monster. Officers of the law came with orders to kill. Typical had become the reception of one young lion who ventured across South Dakota to arrive, by early June 2004, in the southeast corner of the state, in Yankton.

Yankton, a little city of fourteen thousand people on the northern bank of the Missouri River, harbored a deep U.S. history, some of it pleasant. Lewis and Clark and the Corps of Discovery, on their way up the Missouri, had camped there in late August 1804, where they feasted on dog and exchanged gifts with the resident Yankton Sioux. A few decades behind Lewis and Clark came the inevitable waves of settlers, land grabs, and evaporating cordialities with the Sioux. Soon after gold was discovered in the Black Hills, Yankton became a busy steamboat port supplying the rush, and in 1861 it was named the capital of the Dakota Territory. What was once Sioux land filled with foreign people. Their homeland overrun, their game gone, their treaties broken, and their reservation rations running short, bands of renegade Sioux began attacking settlements farther east along the Minnesota River. Settlers from miles around fled for the safety of the Yankton Stockade, though it never was attacked. Come the year 2004, Yankton had been homogenized to a conventional little American oasis of green lawns and shade tree suburbs and shopping plazas, bounded by horizons of industrial crop fields and the sprawling Missouri River. Soon after 6:00 A.M. on June 4, Yankton got a bit less quiet when the phones began ringing at police dispatch, with reports of a lion in town.

One of Yankton's citizens had been taking out the trash when the big cat ran from under his deck. A neighbor looked through her kitchen window to find a mountain lion looking back. "He just stared at me for twenty-five or thirty seconds, then sauntered off." By the time the local conservation officer, Andy Alban, arrived on the scene, the Yankton police had evacuated several houses and set up a perimeter. Across the lawns, they followed the lion's footprints left in the morning dew. Alban turned a corner, and there stood the lion.

The cat ran; Alban and his men chased. They flushed the lion from some shrubs and cornered him under a camper parked in a driveway. Alban then proceeded with department protocol. The protocol of the South Dakota game department called for destroying lions found in human communities.

Alban drew his gun and fired the first shot. His fellow officers fired in turn. The wounded lion fled, found no better cover, and then returned, seeking refuge again under the camper. Alban fired the last shot.

"It was deemed a potential risk," Alban later explained. "It was deemed appropriate to make sure the animal was dispatched."

The animal was later cut open and examined. He was a young lion, about two years of age and 115 pounds. His stomach held the remains of deer, mink, and badger, a mix of riverine and prairie prey. Alban had recently fielded several reports of lion sightings upriver; he speculated that the lion had found his way to Yankton via the rugged banks and coulees of the Missouri, and then, for some reason, had detoured up Marne Creek and wound his way through town, where he got lost and confused.

The citizenry of Yankton wasn't unanimously happy with the lion's ending. People questioned the barrage of bullets where tranquilizers or traps might have served. (The owner of the camper under which the lion was repeatedly shot came home to find sixteen hundred dollars' worth of bullet damage.) Hoping to impart a cheerier spin on the slaying, the city had the lion stuffed and displayed at the Yankton Community Library, where they planned a name-the-cat coloring contest for elementary school students. The novelty wore off, and the stuffed lion was eventually shipped across town, to hide in an obscure corner of the Dakota Territorial Museum.

For all its small-town excitement, the Yankton lion's dead-end saga was more notable for its increasing familiarity. The year before, a fellow transient had made his way to the outskirts of Sioux City, Iowa, only to be discovered by farmers, who shot him. Same fate for the Saskatchewan cougar of 2008, who got lost within the city limits of Saskatoon, got found by a policeman, and got shot.

None of which boded well for the young lion now working his way across the plains. No matter which of the 179 degrees of eastward bearings the cat might follow, each had him wading into firing squads and withering odds. On the northern route through North Dakota awaited more hunters and zero-tolerance policies against lions who wandered within sight of people. Heading southeast along the Missouri River corridor tempted the fate of the Yankton cougar.

Nor were the wildlife officials of South Dakota interested in making his escape across their borders any easier. During the Yankton dustup, a regional supervisor for the game department told a reporter that the state "might consider having a mountain lion hunting season if the problem of migration continues." Within a year, the state opened its first lion-hunting season in the Black Hills. And by 2008 the wildlife commissioners had granted all landowners beyond the Black Hills license to kill lions the year round, further arming South Dakota's eastern plains with a ready force of citizen snipers. The sanctioned ambush would soon prove doubly effective. In November 2009 a female transient—the rarest, most precious component of the mountain lion's colonization equation—made her way down the Missouri to within just ninety miles of Yankton, where a local hunter legally bagged her.

The Great Plains had become the mountain lion's Great Wall. Yet the possibility of escape lived on, so long as there remained yet another pioneer impervious to the odds. And as of December 2009, there was still at least one, making his way east.

With the early days of winter, the Great Plains' dwarf forests of corn had been rendered to stubble, and the land lay cold, windy, and barren. Somehow the lion was still moving unnoticed, finding cover by day in the odd windbreak or gully, scrambling overland by night. He had remained invisible in plain sight as only a cat could, through a bleak terrain where the mere glimpse of him would have brought men running with guns. He had managed to feed himself on the go, through a land stocked with creekside deer, grassland jackrabbit, rock pile porcupine, and the ubiquitous feral house cat. By December the lion had put the Black Hills and nearly six hundred miles of prairie and cropland behind him when he came walking into a new land of thickening woods and gathering people. He was on the verge of breaching the wall. And after the months and many miles of phantom's stealth across the lonesome plain, the lion came inexplicably sauntering into the spotlight on the national stage, as if he owned it.

THREE The Search

A delusion is something that people believe in despite a total lack of evidence.

—RICHARD DAWKINS

TWO HOURS BEFORE DAWN on December 5, 2009, Sgt. Bob Penney and Ofc. Jeff Martin of the Champlin, Minnesota, police department were finishing another long night on the dog watch shift. The two were returning to their cars after handling a call of domestic violence at an apartment complex one block west of the Mississippi River when something drew Martin's attention to the highway. A large animal was trotting across the road, heading his way. Martin's immediate impression was that of a big yellow Labrador retriever.

At that instant an onrushing car came squealing to a stop within feet of the animal. The animal trotted on. Martin processed the image that had just passed through the headlights, of a big brassy creature with a swooping tail as long as its body and a kamikaze's disregard for speeding automobiles. *That's no dog*, thought Martin. He nudged Penney.

"Did you see that?"

"See what?"

"I just saw a mountain lion walk across the road. It almost got hit by a car."

"Martin, you've been working too many night shifts."

"I'm not kidding. It should be coming out on the other side of those houses."

Martin and Penney returned to their squad cars and headed toward the river to intercept the big cat. They came to a frontage road lined with houses.

Martin started the video camera mounted on his dash and swung his spot-light to the side of the road. There, immediately illuminated in the beam, was the unmistakable image of a massive, muscled feline with a fire hose tail, sauntering between trees across somebody's front yard.

The cat quickened his stride and headed for the river.

"Right there," Martin radioed Penney. "He crossed the road . . . Right in the middle of the road! . . . A mountain lion!"

The lion slipped between houses and down the bank toward the Mississippi. Penney and Martin pursued on foot. A few steps into the dark of the riverside forest, with handguns at the ready and flashlights scanning the shadows, the pursuers stopped. They looked at each other and then looked up, simultaneously arriving at the same unspoken question: *Don't such animals as this like to climb?*

The chase had rather suddenly lost its appeal. Penney and Martin backed out of the woods into more comfortable surroundings and gathered their thoughts. In their collective thirty-five years with the force, neither had ever imagined seeing a wild mountain lion, never mind chasing one through a northern suburb of Minneapolis. And if not for the camera's unblinking testament, they may never have admitted they just had.

"I'd probably have said, 'Yeah, we saw a dog,'" said Martin.

"They would have thought we were crazy," said Penney. "There's no way anybody would have believed us."

Come Monday, everybody believed them. Officials from the state's Department of Natural Resources had confirmed the video's subject as none other than a mountain lion, exuberantly overestimating its weight at a whopping two hundred pounds. Viewers of the evening news in St. Paul and Minneapolis were tuning in to Martin and Penney's video. People across the country were replaying the clip on the Internet. The unknown lion was now the talk of the Twin Cities.

It had been more than a century since the last resident mountain lion was vanquished from Minnesota, though with modern times, the state had begun receiving the occasional if fleeting visitor. In 1991 a lion was discovered bedding down in a barn outside Worthington, a plains commu-nity of ten thousand people in the southwest corner of the state. (Apparently the barn also housed a herd of goats and several house cats, who went unharmed.) The lion fled, only to be treed and tranquilized a few weeks later and sent to a game farm in Colorado.

The Worthington cougar was succeeded over the next fifteen years by another seven confirmed sightings within Minnesota borders. And with them the inevitable rumors began to spread among certain deer hunters and conspiracy theorists, of a clandestine stocking program and government cover-up meant to conceal a burgeoning population of Minnesota lions. Yet none of the cats would prove to be anything but lone western transients passing through, or unwanted pets gone loose. Some came with claws removed by their former owners, some with an unusual affinity for human company. In 2001 an escaped female was found resting on the porch of a house west of Duluth. So she was shot. Her two hungry cubs came looking for her. They ended up behind bars at the Minnesota Zoo. Another lioness was discovered lying beside a walking path near Bloomington. So she was shot.

Rude receptions notwithstanding, it seemed the visits were on the uptick. The Champlin lion was the fourth confirmed in Minnesota over the past three years. Less than three months earlier, a cougar had been struck and killed on a bridge near Bemidji, in the northern tier of the state, a cat whose DNA was later traced to the Badlands of North Dakota.

The Champlin cat now raised the same questions. Dan Stark, the Department of Natural Resources' predator expert, went to inspect the scene of Martin and Penney's viral video, looking for clues to the cat's origins. His first and safest guess was captivity, a former prisoner on the lam, one of maybe ten thousand such animals being held in city zoos and roadside attractions and hidden backyard pens across the nation. Stark found the ground frozen, the snow spotty, and the tracking all but hopeless. The only visible sign of large carnivore activity amounted to the scat of a dog.

Or perhaps the cat had wandered from afar. For the biologist Stark, the idea of a wild lion on the move offered the more intriguing possibilities. It had been less than five years since lion M-31 of the Black Hills famously toured the northern reaches of Minnesota en route to Manitoba. M-31 had proven that Minnesota was not too far for a South Dakota cat with ambitions. As for the Champlin lion, his entrance by way of the Mississippi River made sense for a wild cat visiting from points west. Upriver from Champlin, the city gave way and the land opened into the cultivated circles and rectangles of crop fields and dairy pastures of Minnesota farm country. If the cougar was intent on staying hidden, the Mississippi's patchy corridor of deer-laden forest offered what seemed a logical passage.

But if the Mississippi's banks had been the lion's lifeline, they would soon be his noose. From Champlin downstream, the square-mile sections of fields and fencerows were giving way to city blocks and busy streets. The Mississippi was leading him straight into the urban heart of Minneapolis and St. Paul, where some three million people awaited.

Following the Champlin video, police stepped up patrols and warned residents to be on the lookout. On the following Tuesday, the Pioneer Press of St. Paul joined in, devoting prime column space playing up the cat's least likely intention.

"Stay calm. Don't turn your back, crouch, play dead or run. These actions can prompt a predatory instinct in the cougar to attack."

"Back away slowly and keep your eyes on the cougar. Avoid sudden movement."

"If you are attacked by a cougar, fight back."

Twelve hundred miles east, from a village in the Wallkill Valley of southern New York State, Chris Spatz was reading the warnings and shaking his head. Spatz was the newly appointed president of the Eastern Cougar Foundation, a small, feisty team of scientists and scholars dedicated to seeing the cougar reclaim its rightful place in America's eastern forests. Spatz had been watching the Midwest developments with more than casual curiosity. He knew all too well the probable end point of the lion's Twin Cities saga. He believed that the cat's potential place in history deserved deeper consideration than any fifteen minutes of media hype preceding its likely execution.

Vision Quest

Spatz grew up in northwestern New Jersey, in the shadow of the Kittatinny Ridge, where he heard his first tale of the panther. "There was this idea that the cat was out there," said Spatz. "There was an article in the Easton *Express*, mid-seventies, talked about a cat that was sighted every night for a month. He was moving down the ridge. People saw this thing over a month. I remember hearing the hunters talking about it. My dad was talking about it."

Spatz's father was a history teacher, amateur naturalist, and spontaneous adventurer who every weekend would load his two boys into the family car to explore the woods and canoe the waters along the Kittatinny. One day the elder Spatz decided to take up rock climbing. He bought some strange gear, headed up a cliff; the boys followed. "When I look back on it, he didn't really know what he was doing," said Spatz. "But he soloed a lot of stuff before people started soloing. The guy had nine lives."

Spatz's father began leading the boys farther afield, to the Kittatinny's northern arm, into the Catskills and Shawangunks of southern New York. The Shawangunks, a tilted slab of ancient seabed, had become legend among rock climbers of the world, mentioned in the same breath as Yosemite and the Alps. The Shawangunks reputation rested not in the least bit on the sheer drop of their cliffs, the biggest barely reaching 250 feet. Rather, the Shawangunks had risen to prominence for their unforgiving angles and impossible overhangs, providing prime breeding habitat for odd strains of superhuman flies and spidermen, defying gravity by the tips of their fingers and toes. Climbers called their vertical haven the Gunks. With the 1960s, a new culture of rock 'n' roll came to attach itself to the radical old rock of the Gunks. A psychedelic crew of climbers distinguished themselves by their dusk-to-dawn parties and fragrance of smoked cannabis wafting from the base camps, all legitimized by day with unparalleled feats of nerve and sinew and first ascents of unclimbable cliffs, some of them scaled without the aid of rope or chock, a certain few of them ritually performed without clothes. They proudly referred to themselves by the same epithet derisively snorted by their genteel rivals. They were the Vulgarians.

When the Spatz trio first visited the Gunks in the 1970s, in the waning days of the Vulgarians' reign, the elder Spatz found the scene still too raucous for his loner's tastes. But Chris left harboring a seed of longing for the "dropout, dirtbag subculture." In 1981, while enrolled at Trenton State College, Spatz joined an outing club, and the Gunks became his weekend home and family. The joke was that Spatz returned to Trenton only to pick up his mail.

Spatz charged through his young man's wild phase a little wilder than most, slam-dancing to punk rock at the fabled City Gardens of Trenton, climbing naked upon the cliffs of the Shawangunks. He was for a time an English major, if an ambivalent one. Between the requisite classics of Joyce and D. H. Lawrence, he was absorbing the civil disobedience of Thoreau and the angry wilderness elegies of Ed Abbey and his disciples. He gravitated to the radical edge of the environmental movement, to the group Earth First! (Motto: "No Compromise in Defense of Mother Earth!" Logo: a clenched fist.) He sent away for a copy of Ecodefense, Dave Foreman's monkey-wrenching manifesto, featuring detailed instructions on sabotaging bulldozers, spiking trees, and sundry other do-it-yourself slingshots and trip wires aimed at the Goliath pavers and plunderers of American wilderness.

He answered at first to nothing more than a chronic itch for climbing, but with time he became aware of a seductive creature from his past, prowling about the edges of his consciousness. The panther that had once stirred the imagination of his youth had started coming to him in ever-more-familiar apparitions, beginning one summer day in 1985, as he was scaling an overhang in a hidden palisade of rock called Lost City.

"I started belaying my partner, and did what climbers do, spend a lot of time ogling the landscape. The cliffs stretched off into the distance on either side above the valley mantle of trees . . . I felt suddenly the great age of the place. Even though it was the height of eastern terrarium summer, the scene reminded me somehow of the desert cougar diorama at the American Museum of Natural History. I don't remember if I had heard of a recent sighting, but it kind of dawned on me how perfect cougar habitat the ridge is. That's when the Gunks began speaking to me about cougars, of phantom cougars haunting, animating the crags."

Over the next two decades, Spatz drifted in and out of the cougar-haunted Gunks, his obsession interrupted by a few traumatic detours—the near death and yearlong recovery of his father in a cycling accident, grad schools in Boston and New York, an eight-year apprenticeship studying Jungian psychoanalysis and counseling schizophrenic crack addicts at a halfway house outside Princeton. He was still searching. When he was eleven years old, he'd read everything he could find on the immortal Lakota leader Crazy Horse. As a boy, Crazy Horse had followed a red-tailed hawk to a peak in the Black Hills, where he received the vision that forever after set him on his warrior's path. Spatz came to question his own religion, one that had never prepared him for such a vision. When he was twenty-six, he went west to study with descendants of Crazy Horse, on the poverty-stricken Pine Ridge Indian Reservation in South Dakota. He was going to live there and become a medicine man, and find his path. A month later, a deflated Spatz was fleeing back east for New Jersey with the realization that he was a white boy on a vision quest in the wrong land.

He would invariably return to the Gunks, to root his feet again in the vertical rock, to seek his visions while soaring over the valley on his finger-tips. And he began recalling more than ever that moment of revelation upon the cliffs of Lost City, when the land folding beneath him had come alive with phantom panthers.

Between knocking off new routes on his climber's tick list, Spatz started talking to people here and there, collecting reports, and reading any scrap he could find on the eastern cougar. He was earning his rent and gas money tending bar, where his patrons regaled him with more tales. Everyone he talked to had a mountain lion story. By 2006, he had gathered fifty reports of lions, if not one shred of proof. All amounted to nothing better than blurry photos and fleeting glimpses backed by unshakeable belief. The lion was supposedly every-where. Spatz was getting nowhere. Then in April came the fall.

Spatz and a climbing partner were exploring some intriguing crags in a secret enclave called Witch's Hole. Spatz scouted what seemed a promising line on the cliff, and scrambled up an adjacent block for a better look. The rock of the Gunks was revered for its hardness. Rarely did it ever break.

The block beneath Spatz's feet broke, sending him airborne, headfirst. He had time to think about it on the way down: *This is going to hurt.* He hit the top of a tree, ricocheted to the horizontal, and pancaked onto the hard ground.

He lay for a minute, wondering. Then he tried moving. *I'm all right.*

But for a banged-up ankle, Spatz had just lived the climber's worst night-mare and awakened with all body parts properly attached. He took it as a sign, his Crazy Horse vision by whatever crazy means. An old calling had crumbled with the fall, and a new one began taking form. He was forty-four years old. He was not going to conquer the last unclimbed rock of the Gunks. He was going to find the cougar.

Spatz therewith shelved his climbing shoes and within a month was hopelessly headlong into his cougar search. He had met a police officer and his wife in Vernon, New Jersey, on the edge of the Wallkill Wildlife Refuge, with the most amazing news yet. They had not only glimpsed the eastern cougar, but had shone a floodlight on a mother and half-grown cub for fifteen minutes in their backyard. The cougars had discovered a litter of feral house cats hiding near the shed, and were tearing the litter apart. So went the story. Spatz ran out and bought his first remote wildlife camera, with a motion-triggered shutter. He hurried the hour's drive down to Vernon and placed the camera at the scene of the sighting. Two to three times a week he made the trip to Vernon to retrieve his pictures. Two to three times a week he returned with pictures of everything but cougars.

Something had certainly led the Vernon couple to believe beyond doubt that they'd been visited by cougars, creatures that should never have been mistaken at that distance—creatures that somehow Spatz was not privileged enough to see. He wondered how such a sure thing could so simply vanish into the ironic wilderness of New Jersey. He didn't know whether to doubt the sighting as some form of hallucination, or to fear its authenticity. There was talk of killing the cougars if they came back.

The thought of documenting New Jersey's first living cougars in nearly two centuries only to have them shot under his watch sent Spatz scrambling for help. He went in search of other seekers. He soon realized that he was not nearly alone in his obsession to find his panther. He dug up an article from a 2004 issue of *Harper's Magazine* by a writer, Jay Kirk, who had preceded Spatz down the rabbit hole of eastern cougar lore—into a world of true believers, UFOs and black helicopters in the night, spontaneous human combustion, and campaigns of denial and high-level government conspiracy—and who had emerged to declare it "quite possibly the most metaphysical mystery in American natural history."

Nearly every eastern state was sprouting citizens' organizations soliciting and dispensing reports, collectively authoring a new natural history of the cat that science was somehow incapable of cataloging. The Eastern Puma Research Network, led by a Baltimore radio reporter named John Lutz, who while otherwise operating under the theory that the cats were being covertly imported by a massive government conspiracy, was logging sightings by the thousands across the Mid-Atlantic. The Friends of the Eastern Panther, founded by a retired businessman from New Hampshire, Ted Reed, were seeking panther signs in the far Northeast. Jay Tischendorf, a young wildlife veterinarian and former mountain lion research assistant to Maurice Hornocker, began sending out a quarterly roundup of the movement, via his own newsletter called the *Eastern Panther Update*.

Among the citizen searchers, Tischendorf was of the rare breed who possessed both a wildlife degree and hands that had actually held a wild, breathing cougar. There were in fact few big carnivores of the country that Tischendorf had not handled. Before vet school, he'd spent a decade as a journeyman wildlife technician, traipsing with his dog across the country, living out of his car, tent, trailer, and tipi, while serving as apprentice to some of the preeminent figures of big carnivore biology: Dave Mech and gray wolves, Lynn Rogers and black bears, Maurice Hornocker and his lions. Tischendorf learned along the way the crafts of houndsmanship and field anesthesia, with a minor specialty in flushing ghost cats from the graveyard of natural history. In 1986 he was hired as part of Hornocker's team to search Yellowstone National Park for mountain lions rumored to have returned after their eradication during the national predator-cleansing campaigns of the early 1900s. Within just two weeks of systematic searching, the team had replaced the rumors with proof, and eventually had lions in the flesh wearing radio collars and contributing to an estimate of eighteen resident cats previously hiding inside one of the nation's showcase parks.

Tischendorf had come to believe there were lions waiting to be discovered in the East, too, history be damned. The lion's harrying had been mercilessly thorough, from the colonial witch hunts and ring-hunt massacres, to the pioneers' clear-cuts and relentless bounties, all sputtering with tragic monotony to an inglorious end by the late 1800s, in the slaying of the final lonely cat of every last ridge and valley of the East. Or maybe not.

Long past the time when the dead cats quit appearing in the town squares and bounty ledgers, a creature matching their description began startling Easterners all over again. Half a century after the eastern cougar's extirpation, talk of big cats began ramping up, the stories surfacing with the 1950s and accelerating through the '60s and '70s. Every autumn, deer hunters from New York to North Carolina were coming home with new tales of cougars slinking through the woods. Country motorists were glimpsing great long-tailed cats flashing across their headlights. Farmers found them skulking about their corrals. Journalists trumpeted their return: THE PANTHER PROWLS THE EAST AGAIN!

The new spate of sightings and night screams coincided suspiciously with a growing popularity of cougars in the pet trade. But it also came with a certain systemic belief that the woods were being haunted not by some sporadic half-breed escapees, but by a secretive clan of wild survivors who had never actually left. These were renegade cats of supernatural stealth and cunning, who had magically dodged the hounds and the lynch mobs and otherwise slipped invisibly through the firing lines. And fast on their tracks came a certain new breed of seekers compelled to prove their existence.

In the late 1930s, a wildlife manager from New Brunswick named Bruce Wright had started gathering anecdotes of cougars, and canvassing the woods for tracks. Through the decades and scores of stories, the evidence mounted in Wright's mind. He came to believe the eastern cougar lived, if in tiny numbers, scattered about the deepest pockets of what remained of the eastern wilderness. His college professor and mentor, Aldo Leopold, the most prominent wildlife biologist in the country, believed so, too—but with a worry that the cougar's resurrection would be short-lived should Wright ever blow its cover. Leopold warned Wright, "We must not tell anybody."

Wright told everybody. He began writing of the cougar accounts, at first in scientific journals and later in magazines and books aimed at the masses. He reasoned that full disclosure was the eastern cougar's only chance. He pointed to the infamous ring hunt of 1760, when Black Jack Schwartz and his bloodthirsty mob slaughtered forty-one Pennsylvania panthers and a thousand other forest creatures in a day—a scorched-earth mentality that was apparently still quite alive in Pennsylvania: "Recently an estimated 700 hunters turned out to comb one mountain for a panther there, and a cash prize of $300 was offered for its dead body," Wright wrote. "Volunteer patrol planes, mobile Red Cross units, and various other agencies took part in the hunt, but the panther got away."

Wright knew that word of any wild panthers at large would eventually get out, with or without him. "A bounty has already been placed on their heads by certain newspapers who have offered a reward for 'the first panther shot in the state.' The fact that the reward has not been claimed does not alter the fact that the public is being led to believe that this is an animal that should be shot on sight, instead of an extremely rare beast that deserves complete protection in the eastern part of the continent." Wright's mission was to control the message.

In 1959, Wright published his first book, *The Ghost of North America: The Story of the Eastern Panther*, after which the sightings came faster. More magazines and another book followed. By 1972, Wright had come to believe that eastern North America, from New Brunswick down the Appalachian chain, harbored upward of one hundred cougars. Many citizens believed there were that many and maybe thousands more.

Whether Wright was authenticating the cougar's presence or innocently engendering a new myth of it, one had to wonder. Though otherwise meticulous in analyzing his evidence—the terrain and distance between cougar and observer, the time of day and season of sighting—Wright faithfully accepted many of the stories on word alone, and was later found to have mistaken many dog tracks for cougars'. A good number of his readers, including certain wildlife experts who should have known better, overlooked Wright's suspect sources and misidentifications and forwarded his hypotheses of the eastern cougar's existence as fact.

In 1973 the eastern cougar was among the first American animals listed under the country's new Endangered Species Act, never mind that nobody could lay a finger on a single living specimen. Cougars or not, the listing by law demanded action. In 1977 several citizen groups in North Carolina threatened to file suit if the U.S. Forest Service continued clear-cutting the Nantahala National Forest, where the now-protected cougar was rumored to roam. Within a year, U.S. Fish and Wildlife Service biologist Bob Downing was sent out to settle the issue: Find the cougar or declare it gone.

Downing could do neither. He sent out questionnaires and requests to local newspapers and national magazines for evidence of cougars. He sent letters to every resource agency employee throughout the Southern Appalachians, and enlisted help from wildlife experts all the way to Massachusetts. He followed up on fresh sightings to look for signs himself. The reports flooded in. There was apparently a world of eastern cougars out there, though strangely none that Downing could find.

If nothing else, Downing learned that a wild cougar in the hand was worth hundreds in the bush. Beyond a handful of skeletons and stuffed hides that he managed to track down as physical proof of bygone cats, he was left to hack his way through viney jungles of tall tales and swear-on-the-Bible fabrications.

> I am intrigued by the tendency of witnesses who get only a fleeting glimpse of an animal to make a split-second interpretation that it was the rarest animal in the East (a cougar), rather than a common one (dog or deer) . . . People have sent me tape recordings of screams, and they all sounded exactly like grey foxes barking. People often hear a sound that is unfamiliar to them and, instead of associating it with a common animal, they report it as the rarest of all, the cougar. In more than 60 instances where I saw a suspected cougar track (or a photo or cast of one), all but four turned out to be of dog, bobcat, or bear, or were too indistinct to make a determination.

And as cougar scholars would later note, even a couple of those promising four that Downing credited might too have been dogs.

The barrage of trackless sightings and cryptic photos offered up as indisputable evidence left Downing weary of the chase, if not morbidly amused. State after state offered up its own head-shaking history of laughable blunders and cougar tomfoolery. Downing investigated a dead cougar found in Arkansas, and found there a dead dog in its place. A black panther killed in

South Carolina turned out to be a house cat. North Carolina in particular kept Downing busy chasing bogus leads and missing bodies. A skull claimed to be a cougar's turned out to be a bobcat's. Another cougar skull reported by telephone somehow disappeared before an expert could lay an examining finger on it. One man declared he'd killed a cougar that was molesting his hogs. The bones found where he'd left the cougar's carcass were those of a dog. Twice, in separate cases, carcasses claimed to be cougars turned out to be African lions.

Even those few cases backed by flesh-and-blood cougars came bearing red flags. In Pennsylvania, a mountain lion shot by a John D. Gallant in 1967 was indeed a cougar, albeit a tiny young female with deformities suggesting a previous malnourished life of captivity. Nine years later, in West Virginia, a mountain lion was killed and another one captured close by, both of them bearing certain parasites and lackadaisical behavior more descriptive of caged cats turned loose.

Downing's final tally for his exhaustive searching would amount to a few dead and dusty cats from the deep past, a couple of fresh tracks worth pondering, one suspicious scat, and otherwise not one kitten's hair of confirmation that the eastern cougar—as a wild, breeding, viable biological species—still lived. "All that I have been able to prove in six years of effort," he concluded, "is that proof of their existence is difficult to obtain."

Downing's cold splash of fact did little to dampen the raging fever of belief. The legions grew, the stories multiplied, hardening with time and repetition into legend. The legions soon came to include Tischendorf.

He'd begun wondering while in high school, since first reading the sensational writings of the eastern cougar's supposed comeback; of the garden club of elderly ladies who had threatened to sue the U.S. Forest Service to keep the loggers out of the Great Smokies of Tennessee; and of the federal biologist Bob Downing who was thus dispatched to untangle the truth. Tischendorf would later drive to South Carolina to meet Downing, who invited his young protégé over for dinner and a conversation on cougars. Tischendorf left with the fever. He started gathering everything ever written of the eastern cougar. He read through the life's work of the eastern cougar's leading evangelist, Bruce Wright. He tracked down a rare old copy of Wright's 1959 classic, *The Ghost of North America*, and bought it for one hundred dollars. He tracked down another and bought that one, too. Wright had been a champion swimmer, a World War II frogman commando for the Canadian Navy, a student of Leopold, a waterfowl biologist, professor, ecologist, cryptozoologist, historian, and writer—the sum of which, to Tischendorf's mind, made Wright's faith in eastern panthers all the more unquestionable. "It is difficult for me to believe," Tischendorf would later write in a posthumous tribute to his hero, "he could have been totally mistaken in his interpretations of the evidence."

Tischendorf eventually grew impatient. It had been a decade since Bob Downing completed the official eastern cougar recovery plan, calling for a far more extensive search than he alone had been able to muster. It had been forty years since Bruce Wright flagged the hotspots of cougar activity in the North Country. The feds had since sat on Downing's recommendations, and few biologists had considered Wright's flaggings worth a second look. Tischendorf the scientist began to sympathize with his fellow cougar champions on the amateur side of the divide, with the Ted Reeds and the John Lutzes and the disgruntled multitudes of believers forever lambasting the bureaucrats for their campaigns of denial in the face of the citizenry's overwhelming evidence. From the parapets of his newsletter, Tischendorf took to firing his own literary slings and arrows against the naysaying establishment.

"Why all the secrecy and/or denial? . . . After all these years of unequivocally denying the cats' existence, are they afraid of having to taste a little crow?"

"That this evidence is based on a combination of mistaken identity, escaped zoo animals, or released pets is an idea so far-fetched, and so non-scientific, that it defies comprehension. Yet this is exactly what many professional biologists and wildlife managers have been claiming for years."

"Today the truth stares us in the face—or bites us on the buttocks. The cougar is here, and we're not a bunch of half-baked hopefuls clinging to some impossible belief in tawny ghosts from a primeval past."

In 1992, Tischendorf went in search of Wright's ghost cats himself. Collaborating with Reed and flanked by Harley Shaw and Susan Morse, two of North America's preeminent cougar trackers, Tischendorf and a team of six spent two weeks searching thirty-six hundred square miles of forest above New Brunswick's Bay of Fundy, where Wright had once pinned his highest hopes of the cougar's persistence. After sixteen days in the field and more than two thousand miles logged by truck, snowmobile, snowshoe, and hiking boot, the team returned with neither hide nor hair. (In 1996 the journal *Cryptozoology* would publish Tischendorf and Morse's scholastic recap on the expedition, "The Puma in New Brunswick, Canada: A Preliminary Search," sandwiched between field reports titled "Observation of a Yeti in the Himalayas of Tibet" and "Sasquatch Investigations in the Pacific Northwest, 1993.")

Tischendorf was unfazed. "Though the three-week adventure netted no proof that the cats existed," he wrote, "we could neither prove that they didn't." In 1994 he led the first eastern cougar conference, a two-day event at Gannon College in Erie, Pennsylvania, attracting 150 eastern cougar enthusiasts from twenty-two states and three countries. His hope was to bring believers and skeptics together, citizens and civil servants alike, to unify the factions into one panther-seeking force that would finally put to rest the rumors and put the big cat on the conservation agenda of every resource agency east of the Mississippi. His result was a widening of the rift. One after the next, the believers ascended the podium, professing their undying faith in the untouchable cat and their bald indictments of its deniers. (John Lutz: "The Puma is similar to a UFO with four feet. Although thousands of reliable people have reported sighting him, government wildlife officials still deny he survives.") The wildlife officials and skeptics, but for a lonely soul or two, declined their invitations and stayed home.

Tischendorf was now a little less unfazed. Straddling the widening chasm between faith and science, he felt his faith begin to falter. Among the most damning contradictions to his own pro-cougar belief were ones he was unwittingly arguing himself. His New Brunswick search, from which he and six others had returned empty-handed, had covered an area the size of Yellowstone National Park, where a few years earlier, with one colleague and two weeks' time, he had found cougars enough to count. Tischendorf had demonstrated in Yellowstone that which was common knowledge to any cat biologist or houndsman operating in established cougar country, that sooner or later one of the cats would wind up in hand, alive or otherwise. Of the thirty to fifty wild panthers still roaming the swamplands of South Florida, one or two were getting crushed on the highway every year, their carcasses collected for all to show and tell. Yet for the next fifteen hundred miles northward beyond the panther's known range—where some such as Lutz believed more than a thousand lived and bred—no such roadkill. It was one thing to believe in the citizen's ghost cat, to believe that so many thousands of sworn sightings couldn't all be wrong; it was another to produce the occasional warm body that Tischendorf's own profession rightly required as proof.

And it was still another to produce that most mysterious variant of the eastern cougar, the black panther. Wherever people were reporting big eastern cats of any sort, a significant lot of them were reporting them as black. Lutz's list of eastern cougar sightings had by 1994 grown beyond two thousand, more than a quarter of which were ascribed to black panthers. Lutz explained them as escaped leopards, the big spotted cat of Asia and Africa, occasionally appearing in a dark-coated form; or as black cougars, a creature unknown to science. For a while, Tischendorf gallantly defended these, too.

"Hard as it is for many to swallow, it's not impossible that there are, right here in North America, black pumas. Just because no authority has ever officially recorded one doesn't mean it can't exist."

He tried explaining the black panther by way of misidentification: "Are they glimpsing released/escaped leopards, jaguars, and jaguarundis?" He tried by way of semantics: "Are some of the reported 'black panthers' actually just dark brown or tawny color?" And genetics: "Isn't is possible a gene for black fur surfaced and has been passed along and even increased in frequency and expression?"

Still struggling against his own logic, he went on to cite thirdhand a story of a black puma born in 1992 to a cat breeder in Michigan. The cub, according to the storyteller, was apparently sickly and had been eaten by its mother or siblings. No photos were taken, no witnesses were gathered, no tangible evidence offered. No problem, argued Tischendorf.

"This sounds, I know, like the typical tall tale. Yet what would anyone gain from fabricating such a story, especially when it makes themselves out to be a bumbling fool for not carefully documenting *with photos and witnesses* the incredibly rare birth of a black puma?"

He backed that tale with another, from a ranger in southwestern Colorado, who one night saw a black puma crossing the road. The man, an acquaintance of Tischendorf's, was "a Green Beret medic, is very observant, and as a federal law officer he's very cautious and precise in what he reports," wrote Tischendorf. "Knowing Ev, I tend to believe him."

Tischendorf wanted to believe, in a way that his hero Bruce Wright had wanted to believe. Seven percent of Wright's most reliable sightings had described the big cats as black. Wright first tried excusing the observers for having mistaken wet panthers and backlit panthers for black panthers. After testing those hypotheses and finding them wanting, he threw up his hands and sided against his better judgment. "I have now no alternative but to accept the word of the eyewitness that there are black specimens of *Felis concolor* in northeastern North America and that they are not particularly rare."

Tischendorf eventually tired of his own tail-chasing gymnastics. He started inching away from the radical edge of the cougar cult, looking for allies seeking more tangible forms of the missing cat. They, in turn, were looking for him. In 1998 he received a note from Todd Lester, another disgruntled disciple of Lutz's, who was forming a new search team.

Lester, a charismatic young coal miner from the Appalachians of West Virginia, had fallen under the cougar's spell one rainy morning in 1983, while out searching the woods for a lost coonhound. Instead of his missing dog, he came upon a huge long-tailed cat striding silently down the hill. He and the crouching lion traded long hard looks before the creature turned and vanished. "It took part of me with it," Lester would later write, "and I just haven't been the same since."

Lester spent the next thirteen years pursuing the cat that had stolen away with a piece of his soul. Each morning, he would emerge from his night's work five miles underground to begin his new calling, searching the woods with his hounds, posting flyers, hosting an Internet forum, gathering tracks and sightings and hearsay that might finally lead him to proof of the creature he'd met that day in his West Virginia wilderness. During a four-year stint in the air force, based out of Homestead, Florida, he spent all spare moments tracking real panthers through the Everglades. For a while he was drawn into the fold of John Lutz, with his thousands of sightings and conspiracy theories and unwavering contempt for nonbelievers. And like Tischendorf, he, too, was soon parting company with Lutz, in search of physical facts and common ground with those ultimately wielding the power to save the cat. "I knew individuals would never be able to influence the agencies to protect cougars in the East," said Lester. "We needed an organization."

Through his Internet grapevine, he met kindred champions of the cat. First came Chris Bolgiano, a writer from the mountains of southern Virginia, who was working on a book about mountain lions. Drawing on a long list of sources from her research, Bolgiano helped Lester gather the nucleus for his fledgling cougar campaign. The two aimed high, and scored. They were soon joined by the retired Bob Downing, conductor of the East's most extensive cougar search in modern times; Dave Maehr, carnivore biologist and leading authority on the Florida panther; professional forester and wildlife tracker Susan Morse; mammalogist Donald Linzey, who'd been gathering sightings since the 1970s, and his son, the attorney Thomas Linzey; Helen McGinnis, former Penn State coyote researcher turned independent cougar chronicler; and Melanie Culver, a Ph.D. geneticist who would verify the source of all those telltale bits of cougar bone and hair and scat the searchers were sure to discover. And now they had Tischendorf.

With their meager funds, the new Eastern Cougar Foundation bought twenty motion-detecting cameras and hid them in the forest in the hope of capturing the phantom on film. They captured images by the hundreds—images of deer, bear, coyote, bobcat, raccoon, opossum, grouse, wild turkey, and rabbit. They collected reports of eastern lions, so many of them demonstrably wrong. Unmistakable footprints of cougar paws, under more objective eyes, became those obviously belonging to dogs and bears; photos and videos of great cats became images of bobcats; black panthers became black house cats. Some observers claimed to have decisive photos and physical evidence in hand, but refused to let any "experts" have a look. There was the usual assortment of cougar screams in the night, which, when filtered through trained ears, sounded suspiciously like owls or foxes or any number of resident denizens of the eastern woods. It was Bob Downing's dilemma all over again. In a forest abounding with every creature but cougar, it was the cougar who was most faithfully credited with every smudged track, blurry photo, and disembodied utterance.

The hallucinogenic cougar had cast its spell far beyond the dark eastern woods. It lived as well in the glaring light of true cougar country. From their studies of cougar society in the Santa Ana Mountains of Southern California, biologist Paul Beier and his colleagues came back with an astounding catalog of misidentifications and wild goose chases better suited to bar conversation, a few of which they couldn't resist sharing in their official report.

At 12:45 P.M. on February 5 1990, Orange County Animal Control called to report that an adult cougar and a spotted cub were in a clump of pampas grass at 24252 Cataluna Circle in the City of Mission Viejo. An animal control officer had been called to the scene by a local resident, saw the cats himself, watched the cats enter the pampas grass at noon, and had watched the clump of grass continuously since that time, calling for assistance with his hand-held radio. The officer was certain that he was watching so closely that the cats could not have escaped. When we arrived we crawled into the pampas grass to flush the animals into the open where the assembled Animal Control Officers and CDFG wardens could attempt to shoot the cougars with tranquilizer darts. We flushed a 10-pound yellow house cat.

Beier's team responded to another sighting in a neighborhood immersed in cougar territory, where a resident said he'd been watching just such a creature for two days lounging near his woodpile. Beier's team paid a visit, to where "the informant and several other observers said they had just seen the cougar bed down behind the trailer. The informant stood by his spotting scope while we went to investigate. As we approached the trailer, a house cat ran out from under the trailer and the observers shouted: 'There goes the lion.'"

Beier, working in prime cougar country, where an accurate sighting was entirely plausible, concluded that upward of 95 percent of the sightings he fielded were in fact bogus, his follow-ups largely a waste of time. All of which boded poorly for the new Eastern Cougar Foundation team as it started sifting through the sightings. Over the years, the backlog of back-room yarns and sworn-to encounters piled high, while the accompanying physical evidence miraculously failed to materialize. Not all the submissions were born of ignorance or innocence. The cougar profusion also came fueled by a raft of amateur con artists and third-rate liars. One die-hard deception (distributed by a certain fearmongering faction) presented the demonic visage of a mountain lion, fiery eyes aglow, menacingly poised by a photo editor's sleight of hand behind the grinning image of a deer hunter. Another common ruse of the aspiring hoaxster was to photograph stuffed cougars posed in sylvan eastern settings, a laughable stunt readily debunked by noting the classic placid pose of the museum specimen, if not the dead man's stare on the manikin's shriveled face. The Internet empowered the pranksters and propagandists to giddy new heights of lowbrow mischief. Among the more notorious farces featured the image of a huge road-killed cougar from Arizona, who unfortunately ended up getting killed all over again in a dozen other states and provinces:

Look at what James Snipe hit with his car on a county road southeast of Liberty, Miss.

Look at what James Snipe hit with his car on county road 32 north-east of Foley AL.

Look at what James Snipe hit with his car on state route 161 east of Iuka [IL] road.

Look at what Wally Tiernan hit with his car on Highway 178 approximately 16 Miles East of Greenwood, South Carolina.

They say there are no lions in Wisconsin, well take a look at this cat that was hit by a car just north of Apperson Drive on Hwy 47, only two miles from our house.

See what's been roaming the neighborhood, north of Kempt, Nova Scotia.

This lion was hit between Grantsville and Walker WV by a car. Game and Fish had to come and put him down. He charged at the Fish and Game guy in the process. Look at his PAWS!

This lion was hit between Cherry Reservoir Road and High Knob area (near Wise, VA) by a car. Game and Fish had to come and put him down. He charged at the Fish and Game guy in the process. Look at his PAWS!

This lion was hit on Highway 30 near Jefferson, IA, by a car. Fish and Game had to come and put him down. He charged at the Fish and Game guy in the process. Look at his PAWS!

One hoaxster submitted a plaster cast of a cougar pawprint he claimed came from West Virginia, a pawprint later tracked to a cougar foot he had purchased online.

Wading through such piles of trash, year after year, checking the empty cameras, fielding the third-party reports and dead-end leads and half-baked hoaxes, the ECF team of believers grew jaded. One by one, the remaining romantics, Tischendorf finally among them, swallowed reality's hard pill. The phantom cat of the East had given up the ghost. There was no conspiracy, no cover-up. There was no cat.

But from the lost cause sprang a certain new reason for hope. And Tischendorf now realized he'd been half ignoring it all along. The East offered neither photos nor bodies—but the Midwest certainly did. Tischendorf had obliquely hit upon it as early as 1993, when he mused to his newsletter subscribers, "It's like a puzzle, and every piece is important . . . Maybe the Minnesota cougar originated in South Dakota? Maybe Minnesota occasionally gets others moving down from Manitoba or up from Wisconsin?"

He now remembered the 1991 cougar captured in Worthington, Minnesota; the Missouri cougar shot by coon hunters in 1996. In 2002 a cougar was shot in western Iowa. Trail cameras of Midwestern deer hunters were occasionally but surely capturing unmistakable close-ups of real cougars.

There was one vital detail connecting this otherwise random crop of lone cougars sprouting across the Midwest. Nearly all the Midwest's cougars were young males. "Cat after cat," noted Tischendorf, "male, male, male. What the heck." Finally it clicked. "These, by gosh, are dispersers. These are young males heading east."

And it was not hard to guess where they might be coming from. The once-rumored colony of cats in the Black Hills of South Dakota had by the late 1990s become fact—fact enough that by 2005 the state's wildlife commission had set about killing them off. Two of them, wearing Dan Thompson's radio collars and the names M-16 and M-31, had famously escaped over the state line and ventured to the unthinkable eastward outposts of Oklahoma and Manitoba.

After seeing what true heroics a determined cat from South Dakota could perform upon the hostile open spaces of Middle America, Tischendorf no longer bothered to defend the traceless sightings and threadbare theories of supernatural eastern cats and government conspiracies. He could now begin to imagine the rare eastern phantom as a live and vibrant young male of the flesh, all the way from the edge of the Rockies, trekking east "until his proverbial hat floated."

It was soon after Tischendorf's baptismal return to the hard ground of facts that he fielded an anxious note from an amateur cougar seeker in New Jersey. Chris Spatz was worried for the cougar family that had taken up residence in the backyards of Vernon.

By now Spatz had expanded his one-man cougar quest beyond Vernon. Lacking official funding and professional credentials, he had nonetheless impressed New Jersey's Division of Fish and Wildlife into permitting his three cameras in the nearby High Point State Park, where supposedly a cougar had denned, where supposedly a cougar had bounded across

Route 23, where reportedly a bow hunter had spied a long-tailed cat spotted like a cougar kitten. Likewise Spatz would soon begin searching his home turf in the Shawangunks, securing his permits and scraping together some money for a camera to spy in the woods of the Minnewaska State Park Preserve.

Still no cougar. Spatz had sought guidance from the leading shaman of the search, John Lutz, but soon tiptoed away, spooked by one too many of Lutz's rabid conspiracy sermons, with their pervasive vibe of paranoia. He came calling to the Eastern Cougar Foundation, and Tischendorf immediately took him under his wing.

Tischendorf was impressed with Spatz's dedication, and empathetic with his naïveté. He recognized the fever. He knew firsthand the dead end to which Spatz was hurtling. Spatz was openly frustrated. Everybody but he was seeing lions. "Why aren't I getting any evidence?" he asked Tischendorf. "Why no tracks, no scat, no deerkills?"

Tischendorf put a big brother's arm around Spatz and answered, "Do you really want to know?"

"Yeah."

"Do you *really* want to know?"

"Yeah-yeah, dammit! Tell me!"

"Chris. They're not here."

Spatz sat blinking. Tischendorf recounted his own painful coming of age, his eternal fruitless chasing of ether-based rumors from the East, when all anyone had to do was go a few hundred miles west to find dozens of real bodies and clear pictures. Spatz sat blinking. Tischendorf welcomed him onto the team.

Spatz thus joined the Eastern Cougar Foundation and their new cause. They were abandoning the search, embracing the rescue. No longer burdened with chasing the vaporous beast of myth and dreams, Spatz could now channel his passions on bringing the real thing back. He rapidly absorbed the ECF library, started writing columns for their newsletter and presenting cougar slide shows—RETURN OF THE LEGEND!—at public gatherings. Little more than a year later, the foundation appointed the hard-charging Spatz as its new president.

Charting its new course, the ECF spoke of pressuring the U.S. Fish and

Wildlife Service into physically carting the animals home from the West. Beyond that political long shot, the best the little band could immediately offer was to smooth a path for the lion's return, and root for the one-in-a-million pioneer from the West to do the heavy lifting. Fourteen months later came the Champlin lion.

For Spatz and team, the Champlin lion had entered their radar as a rare emissary of the cause. And now so suddenly it seemed the Twin Cities were about to crush him in his tracks. Here at last was a ray of hope heading their way, with what to Spatz read like an all-points bulletin in his name and a bull's-eye on his head.

MINNESOTA COUGAR FACES A DEADLY FATE IF IT STAYS IN TOWN, read the St. Paul headline, followed predictably by assumptions of the cat's murderous intent. Spatz's ire ratcheted up another notch, reading that the Minnesota Department of Natural Resources (DNR) "had no plans to try to capture, anesthetize or relocate the cat spotted recently in Champlin. If the cougar climbs a tree or doesn't flee if found in a public or residential area, it likely will be killed . . ."

Spatz hurried off a heated letter to the editors, with a copy to the DNR.

"Contrary to the purported threat of a cougar wandering Twin City suburbs, the statistical chances of the cat attacking a person are about as rare as being struck by a chunk of meteor," Spatz wrote. "Deer collisions injure and kill far more people every year than all other wildlife combined. Has the Pioneer Press called for euthanizing every deer in your suburbs?"

But the lion wasn't waiting around for any cease-fires. By the time Spatz's letter reached the editors, the Champlin lion had already put Champlin behind him. Soon after leaving officers Penney and Martin in the dark, he crossed the half-frozen Mississippi. Whether by luck or design, he then abandoned the river as it turned south for the Twin Cities. He instead struck off due east, skirting the cities' northern edge, through a landscape of strip-mall suburbia, with clots of development interrupted by old fields and farmsteads. On Monday night, even as most eyes were still replaying the surreal Champlin video, police were receiving another call of a cougar running through somebody's yard, this one coming from a residential neighborhood in Vadnais Heights, twenty-three miles east.

The Vadnais Heights authorities sent out a text alert to the neighborhood, with the oddest of warnings: KEEP AN EYE OUT FOR A COUGAR. The cougar then disappeared for three days, while he did the watching.

On the afternoon of Thursday, December 10, the naturalist Dana Larsen-Ramsay crossed his path. She did not see the lion; she felt him. She was leading a new manager on a tour of her company's preserve. Her company was the H.B. Fuller Company, a leading manufacturer of adhesives. The H.B. Fuller Company cared about more than glue, and around its spacious Vadnais Heights headquarters, it had set aside the Willow Lake Nature Preserve, a 295-acre oasis of oak woods and sedge meadows surrounding the namesake lake, the whole of it surrounded in turn by Twin Cities suburbia, industrial lots, car dealers, and six-lane highways.

Larsen-Ramsay, the preserve's director, was showing her new company manager around the grounds. The trail she took was normally busy with birds and deer; on this afternoon it was eerily silent. The two didn't see anything. "Not a squirrel," said Larsen-Ramsay. "It was really strange. It seemed so quiet and devoid of wildlife."

That night, Larsen-Ramsay took a call from neighbors who lived on the northern border of the preserve. They said they'd seen a cougar in their yard. Larsen-Ramsay winced. As the local naturalist, she'd grown used to receiving well-intentioned gifts of resident wildlife—the crow in a box that magically emerged as a starling, the pigeon mistaken for a pheasant, the woodchuck for a badger. The next morning Larsen-Ramsay paid a polite visit to the neighbors, took one look at the tracks in the snow, and called the Minnesota Division of Natural Resources.

The paw prints were nearly four inches wide. Her husband, Jon, who stood six feet four inches tall, compared a track against his outstretched hand. Between the cat's snowshoe prints trailed the sinuous, telltale divot of a long tail dragging. The tracks came to a chain-link fence, gathered them-selves together, and continued on the other side, six feet away. By late that afternoon, the DNR's carnivore biologist Dan Stark was with Larsen-Ramsay at H.B. Fuller searching for the lion.

They meandered up a hillside, past a grove of sumac where the snow had been trampled and pocked by the resident flock of turkeys and herd of bedding deer, to the yard where the cat had leapt the fence. The tracks led to the porch, passing within inches of the sliding glass door. The cat had then wandered across the next several yards before sailing over the fence again and back into the preserve.

Stark and Larsen-Ramsay followed through a stand of oak and aspen and down toward the lake, where in the darkening woods they came to an inlet stream with a footbridge passing over it. Stark pointed his flashlight to a yellow oval of urine in the snow and then refocused on the tracks. There were two sets of tracks entering beneath the bridge on one side and one set of tracks exiting the other. At that moment, the searchers had a Penney-Martin moment. They looked down under the bridge, then up into the trees, reading each other's minds. The snow was less than twenty-four hours old; the cat's tracks of course, fresher still. With darkness closing fast, Stark collected a sample of the urine, and the two retreated to resume their search by daylight.

Next morning, Larsen-Ramsay and her husband met Stark with his infant daughter in tow. Larsen-Ramsay teased Stark for bringing cougar bait. The search team returned to the footbridge where the cat had performed his disappearing act, and picked up his trail tracing the western end of Willow Lake. The prints passed by a gazebo, where beneath a nearby cherry tree Stark collected a dropping. It was large and blocky, beyond anything possible for a coyote, the preserve's biggest resident carnivore.

The cat led his trackers into a lakeside thicket treacherous with buckthorn. He emerged upon a hiking trail, and onto a boardwalk bridging the southern arm of the lake. He strolled the boardwalk for a ways, then hopped off to walk the ice before gaining the opposite woods, where he soon passed through a deer yard. His tracks mingled with those of the deer. He walked past cedar trees shaped like lollipops, trimmed as high as the deer could reach. (To save their trees, the Fuller company had taken to having the deer culled every year, but the deer were obviously winning the contest.) The lion walked right through, and kept going, for reasons Larsen-Ramsay would later uncover. He emerged from the forest, ascended a meadow at the eastern boundary of the preserve, and came to a six-foot chain-link fence bordering the six divided lanes of Highway 61 and a strip of car dealerships. The lion did not pace this way or that, or hesitate by any interpretation of the tracks. He floated over the fence in a bound and continued on across the highway. The lion left the deer-laden haven behind him, pointing into the hard geometric landscape ahead. He was heading east.

Larsen-Ramsay said good-bye to Stark and returned to the footbridge in the forest where the night before they'd pondered the spooky convergence of tracks. This time she backtracked the second set of tracks. They led uphill, past the H.B. Fuller offices, past the picture windows of the lunchroom behind which hundreds of employees gathered every workday. Larsen-Ramsay followed to a tall grove of red pines. And there the tracks stopped at what little remained of a deer. It was the same grove through which Larsen-Ramsay had guided her manager two nights before, when the air had gone so still. Larsen-Ramsay remembered the chill she'd felt, her hindsight now vividly colored by the image of a hidden lion watching as they passed. Now, too, she had at least one explanation for the lion's unwavering eastward exit soon thereafter: The tank was full.

Stark, on his drive home that afternoon, checked for tracks on the far side of the highway where the lion had exited the preserve. There was nothing. None of the lion's signs had survived the plows and the heavy traffic of what would turn out to be roughly thirty-six hours since his departure. No matter. Stark already had a better clue as to where his quarry might be found. The night before, even as he was shining his flashlight beneath the footbridge, there had been a report of a lion prowling a neighborhood in Stillwater, Minnesota, ten miles east. Next day, DNR conservation officer Alex Gutierrez confirmed it, following the meandering tracks a mile through backyards, along fences, past a church, around a neighborhood pond. From there the lion had been seen crossing a busy thoroughfare, heading east, toward an enormous commercial complex of big-box stores, strip malls, and fast-food eateries. The lion was two miles from the St. Croix River and the Wisconsin border.

The morning after, Spatz's letter to the editors appeared in the *St. Paul Pioneer Press*. Having fired his barbs over the lion's impending execution, Spatz offered constructive alternatives to the lethal fallback policy.

"In states such as California, where wildlife officials routinely handle cougars marooned in the suburbs, their first response is to secure the area, back everyone off several blocks and let the cat escape on its own. California officials know from decades of experience that such an animal poses little risk to the public."

Spatz prophetically went on to suggest that the Twin Cities' visitor was perhaps a lost wanderer from the Dakotas, looking only for a free path to slip through. And if by chance the Minnesota authorities soon found themselves facing a cornered cougar in town, the Eastern Cougar Foundation had a team of experts, with decades of field time and hundreds of big cats trapped and tranquilized, standing by, ready to help.

Spatz had little hope of anyone taking him up on his offer. His immediate aim was to plant a seed of hesitation in any gunman's mind, to buy enough time for the lion to get away. If his hunch was right, this was a wild pioneer from the Black Hills who'd already survived nearly half the impossible journey home. Spatz's colleagues had been corresponding with authorities in Wisconsin, where it seemed the climate might be a bit more welcoming for such a visitor. Spatz thought, *If we can just get our cat over the line.*

FOUR Crossroads

From a certain point onward, there is no longer any turning back. That is the point that must be reached.

—FRANZ KAFKA

ON THE MORNING OF December 16, a few miles outside the village of Spring Valley, Wisconsin, Barry Anderson was on his tractor chugging through a foot of snow covering his hay field. In the middle of his path appeared a line of fresh footprints too huge to ignore. He hopped down for a look. Anderson was a veteran deer hunter familiar with the signs of his local fauna, none of which squared with the likes of these. The shape of the tracks roughly matched those of Anderson's house cat; the size of a single track was large enough for his cat to have stood inside with all four paws. Anderson followed the tracks for a few hundred yards into his woodlot. They were coming from the west.

Spring Valley lay sixty miles east of the Twin Cities and the nearest TV stations, where Anderson and his wife, Mary, got their nightly news. They were among the many who'd been following the lion's whistle-stop tour of Minnesota's chief metropolis. Anderson's farm was, moreover, just thirty-two air miles from Stillwater, where the lion had last surfaced five nights before. There had been some question as to whether the cat would brave the powerful St. Croix River into Wisconsin. Anderson now suspected he had the answer at his feet. In the forty-five years he'd been farming this land, he had never seen sign of a mountain lion, but he was pretty sure he was now following one.

The tracks struck Anderson as fresh, the silence eerie. He looked around.

Maybe it's moved on, he thought. *Maybe it's watching me.* Anderson measured a track at five and a half inches across, took some pictures, and rode home.

A soft-spoken man normally shying from attention, he hesitated before finally sending the pictures to the Wisconsin Division of Natural Resources. Anderson was soon after fielding a phone call from a reporter at the St. Paul *Pioneer Press*, and the Wisconsin DNR was sending some men his way.

Adrian Wydeven, the Wisconsin DNR's leading authority on its once and future mountain lion—the last of Wisconsin's native lions had disappeared in 1908—in his eighteen years of searching had fielded hundreds of reports of lions in Wisconsin, nearly all amounting to fertile imaginations and every form of animal but lion. He'd seen mountain lions magically conjured from house cats and raccoons. He'd answered to calls of cougars screaming bloody murder in the night, and come away penciling in the probable work of porcupine or owl. No easy sell, Wydeven took one look at Anderson's pictures of the footprints on his farm and immediately forwarded an e-mail to thirty of his lion-minded colleagues from Montana to New York, under the unambiguous subject line COUGAR IN ST. CROIX CO., WI.

Wydeven, too, had been tracking the cat's chronicle since its opening act in Champlin. He'd been trading notes with Minnesota's cougar man, Dan Stark, the two of them growing more convinced with each new eastward emergence that this was something other than somebody's abandoned pet. Neither doubted the animal's inclination or ability to cross the St. Croix River, mostly frozen as it was. That the cat had then veered southeast toward Spring Valley, fording Interstate 94 along the way, made lion's sense, too. He was gravitating toward terrain ever more folded by steep river valleys and forested edges, into a big cat's Candyland overstocked with deer and ready points of ambush. Wydeven notified his cougar network to stand by, that the local DNR wildlife biologist Harvey Halvorsen was heading for Spring Valley to investigate.

Halvorsen arrived on Friday morning, December 18, with colleagues Mike Soergel and Brett Olson, and immediately picked up the footprints trailing through Anderson's field where the farmer had promised. Halvorsen, in his twenty-year Wisconsin career, had followed the tracks of bears and fishers, bobcats, coyotes, and wolves, enough to know at first glance that these were the tracks of nothing of the sort—the asymmetrical slant of the toes, the absence of claw divots, the enormity. The tracks had the signature meander of a cat on the hunt. They wound their way around some hay bales and then slanted close by the wood's edge, tending toward cover and optimal prospects for surprising prey.

And in the typically unpredictable fashion of the universal cat, the tracks then veered into the open, across a field and toward a farmhouse. It was a fortuitous detour for the trackers. The wind upon the open expanse had cleared a patch of snow to reveal odd marbles of ice. The ice balls reminded Halvorsen of those his dog chewed from between his toes after an outing in the snow. He squinted to find the ice balls spiked with hairs. He wrapped a sample in a paper towel and sealed them in an envelope.

The tracks then veered away from the house and eastward again, into the woods. The lion led the men through a tangle of downed aspen and into a wall of antipersonnel shrubbery. *Zanthoxylum americanum* was colloquially known in Wisconsin as prickly ash or, more colorfully yet, as a string of epithets issued from those who had ever met its medieval arrangement of flesh-piercing barbs. A hellish habitat for humans, the prickly ash thicket was in turn a living fortress fondly sought by deer, grouse, turkey, and rabbit. And now it had become the hunting ground through which the lion, on coiled limbs, had stealthily crept; through which Halvorsen and his men, on hands and knees, now suffered to follow.

Apparently even the lion had lost a round or two with the demon plant. The searchers' pains were rewarded with a thatch of hair impaled on a prickle. Halvorsen added the hair to another envelope and emerged to continue tracking the lion as the lion was now tracking a deer.

The lion followed the deer into the woods, down through a gorge, and onto the open ice of the Eau Galle Reservoir. Halvorsen stood on the edge of a cliff overlooking the lake. Through binoculars, he could see the tracks of deer and lion leading as one across the ice. The deer eventually trailed off, but the lion, it oddly seemed, had continued on his way. Halvorsen, holding fast to a strand of barbed wire, began inching his way along the rim of the cliff. He looked to his feet and blurted, "Holy bucket!" There were the tracks of the lion. He had doubled back to the base of the cliff and then scaled it.

How, Halvorsen could not fathom. But he could now more easily begin to imagine this lion as the same adventurous creature who had so deftly evaded the masses through the northern metro of Minneapolis before crossing the St. Croix.

The lion's Twin Cities fans were already imagining it themselves. There in the morning edition of the *Pioneer Press*, even as Halvorsen was out inspecting the Spring Valley tracks, was one of Barry Anderson's photos, along with an editor's map figuratively connecting the dots: Champlin to Vadnais Heights to Stillwater to, now, Spring Valley. Over the next few days, Barry and Mary Anderson became the reluctant celebrities of Spring Valley. Along their walks about town, the Cougar People were ribbed by friends who thought they'd been seeing things and regaled by believers with cougar stories of their own. A few failed to find any humor in all the hoopla. Said Anderson, "There were some people who wouldn't walk outside."

Wydeven, for his part, wished the lion well. The lion was the embodiment of the wilderness that had first drawn him to his life's work. As a kid growing up in the 1960s, he'd taken to camping in wild places and daydreaming of a life tracking wildlife through the Wisconsin North Country of legend. By then, Wisconsin's mountain lion had been missing for more than half a century, and the state's last lone wolves had just recently been driven from their final holdouts along the Minnesota border. But the young Wydeven had clung to his romantic vision of a hardened survivor or two still out there, eluding the trappers, still haunting the Northwoods. Soon after the passage of the U.S. Endangered Species Act, his vision came true. In 1974 a wolf pack was discovered operating along Wisconsin's northern border, and within a year, wolves—albeit dead ones—had officially begun marking the species' return. The survivors spread. By 1982, when Wydeven joined the Wisconsin DNR as a wildlife technician, there were upward of twenty-seven wolves censused as residents of the state. By 2008, with Wydeven then nearing two decades as leader of the state's wolf survey, there were close to six hundred. The wolf had outpaced both the biologists' most optimistic population models and Wydeven's wildest dreams. The mountain lion, though, remained the biggest meat-eating beast still conspicuously missing from Wisconsin's wilder past.

The mountain lion had once been a fixture of the Wisconsin megafauna. It was routinely celebrated in effigy by Wisconsin's ancient Indians, who had taken to heaping up great mounds of earth, the mounds sometimes shaped as animals—as buffalo, elk, and deer; bear, wolf, eagle, and panther. White fur traders in the late 1600s began mentioning the panther, among giant catfish and other "monsters."

The records continued through the 1800s, with added violence: A cougar was discovered and subsequently shot on an island in the Mississippi River in 1839; a cougar was shot along the Black River in 1863; another was killed that same year near Dodge, with a tomahawk. In the winter of 1867, not far from where the St. Croix cat of 2009 made his last Minnesota appearance before crossing, an "enormous catamount" prowling near Stillwater was pursued and shot by a local posse. And on it went through nineteenth-century Wisconsin, with panthers, cougars, and catamounts, treed, trapped, and otherwise hunted down, until the first decade of the 1900s, when, for complete lack of lions, the sightings and the killings stopped.

Of all the dead bodies, only one was ever spared for posterity, if barely. A lion shot in eastern Wisconsin in 1857 was stuffed and displayed in the biology halls of Lawrence College, to be unceremoniously trashed during a spring cleaning. It was rescued from the heap by a janitor, who then passed it on to a barkeeper to suffer yet another sorry life as mascot of a beer tavern, before finally being rescued by the prominent biologist A. W. Schorger, who ransomed the faded manikin for fifty dollars and had its ratty hide properly retired to a museum cabinet at the University of Wisconsin.

Thus by the first decade of the twentieth century, the lion's ten-thousand-year history in Wisconsin came sputtering to its ignoble end. Thereafter followed nearly a century of silence, to be broken in the 1980s by a tentative little spree of sightings that started the rumors swirling. They swirled to a point that Wydeven could no longer ignore. In 1991 he officially opened the search for evidence of mountain lions in Wisconsin.

A string of false leads soon left him wondering whether every cougar reported was either a mistaken identity or somebody's pet gone loose. And through the next seventeen years and hundreds of sightings, little of that changed. There had been nothing to give him firm hope—no lions that Wydeven could lay a finger on, or find a decent photo of, or gather a hair's worth of evidence to say with any assuredness that once again there was a wild-born cougar walking Wisconsin—until January 2008. Then a young male similar to the one now crossing the state surfaced in southeast Wisconsin, outside Milton. The Milton cougar, the first Wisconsin cat confirmed in a century, would lead Wydeven and his colleagues on an eighty-six-mile inter-state adventure before crossing the border and meeting some unsympathetic cops and a bad end in Illinois.

In the spring of 2009 came another lion to Wisconsin, this one treed by hounds a hundred miles northeast of Minneapolis, in the farm country of Spooner. Wydeven arrived to find the Spooner cougar lazily posing for photographs in an oak. After a career spent chasing ghosts, Wydeven had to pinch himself at the spectacle peering down at him. *Am I dreaming this?* He was close enough to have poked the lion with a broomstick.

It was as close as Wydeven would get. After two days and as many botched attempts at tranquilizing the cat to collar it, the Spooner cougar disappeared without further trace. But dead or gone, the Spooner cougar, and the Milton cougar before him, had opened doors to the possibilities of a recolonization. If history repeated itself in Wisconsin, as it had with the first big cats to appear in the Black Hills of South Dakota, there would soon be another on the way.

The Twin Cities cat was that cat. His emergence in Spring Valley during the final weeks of 2009 marked the century's third verified cougar sighting in Wisconsin, all coming within the space of two years. How or where the first two had vanished, by good intentions or bad, one could only guess. Wydeven was anxious to get a collar attached before this cat, too, disappeared for good.

Wisconsin was, on first glance, a wondrous place for a hunter of deer. America's Dairyland, of the trademark cow pastures and postcard silos, was also forested over nearly half the state's sixty-six thousand square miles, the mixture of woods and fields and edges, the concurrence of food and shelter, amounting to one of the richest deer herds in North America.

And with the deer came their hunters. Every autumn, Wisconsin's woods were to be swarmed by some six hundred thousand registered gunmen and archers. There were more deer hunters in Wisconsin than citizens in all of Wyoming.

Lately their swarms had been joined by families of unregistered deer hunters invading from the north, called wolves. Having barely survived the antipredator blitzkriegs of the early 1900s, Wisconsin's wolves had started rebounding in the 1970s, to cautiously open receptions and improving attitudes in Wisconsin. But with the new millennium and the multiplying wolves, there would come a turning point, when the animals began spilling out of the deepest woods and wilderness redoubts and into Wisconsin's vaunted dairy pastures and deer yards. Complaints of missing livestock and pets started piling up, from a handful in the 1990s to four dozen in 2008. Deer hunters who came home minus their trophies started blaming too many wolves. Attitudes went south, and the wolves' tenuous welcome went with it. In 2010 the feds answered the grumblings, and the Great Lakes wolf was removed from protection under the Endangered Species Act. Given the green light, the Wisconsin DNR's curious solution to saving the wolves from the lynch mobs was to offer them up legally as game. Wisconsinites would soon be shooting up to half the state's population of wolves in a single season.

Little of which boded well for the Spring Valley lion now entering from his tour of the Twin Cities. Now was not the best of times for another top-order predator to test the public mood, particularly one bearing the mountain lion's deer-slaying, pet-snatching baggage. And if Wydeven hoped Wisconsin's visiting lion would tread discreetly for his own good, the lion apparently had other ideas.

Downsville

One day after Halvorsen's Spring Valley investigation and another sixteen miles east, on the edge of a cornfield outside Downsville, Wisconsin, a young dairy farmer named Jason Weber and his hunting buddy Aaron Worden from Green Bay were scoping deer from a tree overlooking Weber's fields. They were wondering what in hell was going on. The two were well hidden, high in their tree stands, downwind beyond sight or smell. Yet the deer were on high alert, heads raised, ears scoping, tails flicking from a severe case of the jitters—so odd for animals more typically seen grazing the fields like Weber's dairy cows. "They were running scared," said Weber. "You know something's going on when they're acting like that." Weber figured maybe there was somebody out hunting. But there shouldn't have been anybody out hunting; it was Weber's land. As it got dark, Weber and Worden climbed down and headed toward the farmhouse for dinner, shaking their heads and echoing each other's sentiments: "Holy crap the deer are spooky tonight." At the edge of the field where they'd been hunting, they stepped around one of Weber's automated trail cameras. Approximately twenty minutes later, at 5:32 P.M., the camera's shutter triggered.

The next morning, while Weber was out finishing chores, Worden retrieved the memory card from the camera. He went inside, and began clicking through to review the past night's parade of visitors, expecting the usual collection of deer, raccoons, and coyotes. Weber soon heard Worden beckoning from the house, "You have to come see this."

The image was slightly blurred by the animal's motion, but its identity was abundantly clear. There striding through the frame, its eyes ablaze from the flash, was a mountain lion.

Next day, wildlife biologist Jess Carstens of the Wisconsin DNR was hurrying out to Weber's farm, looking to confirm the sighting before the trail went cold. Photos being an especially popular medium of the prankster, Carstens was on alert for a scam. He had his investigation planned: Check the scenery, the landmarks, the trees. Make sure the image hadn't been Photoshopped. Verify its log times. He met Weber and asked to see the camera. Weber escorted him through the snow on his tractor. Carstens knew before they arrived that there would be little need to verify anything.

The snow was busy with lion prints. The two men started tracking on foot. At the edge of the field, they came to a strange mound of piled cornstalks. From out of the pile peeked a face. The face belonged to a young buck deer, his eyes glazed in a frozen stare, his remains partially eaten and half-buried in the classical fashion of a lion's cache. The deer was still soft to

Carstens's touch. It had been killed the night before, at the earliest, or maybe as recently as that morning.

For Carstens and Weber, now peering down the lion's trail where it led into the woods, there came the same waft of hair-raising unease so familiar to those who had just recently walked the lion's path before them. Penney and Martin, Stark and Larsen-Ramsay, Anderson, Halvorsen, and now Carstens and Weber—all had felt the unnerving presence of something lurking on the edge of their senses. "It was a weird feeling," said Weber. "Being out there. That trail going up into the woods." Standing unarmed, Weber recalled watching his barn cats on the hunt. How stealthily they stalked. What damage they could do to little birds. Weber the hunter now knew the nervous twitch of the hunted.

Carstens the biologist looked toward the woods and rock outcrops. More than plenty of cover for a lion, he noted. *Maybe he's up there*, he thought. *Maybe he's sitting somewhere watching us.*

Now minding their surroundings with awakened eyes, the two moved Weber's trail cam to the deer carcass. They took one last glance around and left in the hope of the lion's return. Given the lion's recent minglings with the Twin Cities populace, neither man imagined him now particularly afraid of them or their scent, and rightly so.

That evening, shortly after 6:00 P.M., the lion returned to his kill, and all but mugged for the camera. He stood broadside, filling the frame with his muscular profile, lording over his cache.

This time there was video, too. The snapshot lion came to life in astonishingly intimate clips of motion. There came a pulse-skipping moment of high alert, the cat's ears flicking forward, neck craning, eyes locking onto something off in the black.

That something was likely Weber starting up his tractor. News of an approaching storm had the farmer forgetting all about the lion and hurrying out that night to finish harvesting a patch of corn by headlight. One might have imagined the next clip featuring the tail end of a lion fleeing the commotion for the next county. What appeared instead was the lion now reposed and settled in with his leftover deer, his head dipping, his jaws casually tearing and chewing, all the while the inky backdrop surreally animated by Weber's headlights creeping like tiny twin specters through the cornstalks.

The forecast was dictating the DNR's next move as well. Carstens was on the phone with Wydeven, with talk of capturing and collaring and accompanying the lion by radio on the rest of his journey. But with a big snow coming, they would opt to let the lion do as he chose, to see where he showed up next. Or maybe they would entice him to a rendezvous with another hidden camera. They thought about dragging a deer carcass and its luring trail of scent behind a truck to a promising patch of wildlife habitat ten miles east of Weber's farm. Imagining the public feedback to a state vehicle seen dragging a dead deer down the highway, they thought again. They discreetly trucked a fresh carcass to the site, bugged it with a camera, and waited.

By now the Twin Cities were catching up on their celebrity cat, with the Minneapolis *Star Tribune* posting Weber's photo of him striding alongside his pygmy forest of corn. The news recounted the lion's whistle-stop tour of the northern metropolitan area, his reemergence over the Wisconsin line, and now his dramatic landing in Downsville. The hysterical rhetoric had calmed, to a tone hinting ever so subtly of familial longing: "It appears Minnesota has lost its cougar to Wisconsin."

Chicago

All tallied, the lion had covered seventy-six linear miles since surfacing in Champlin, all the while determinedly heading east by southeast. On Christmas Eve, a Chicago newspaper picked up his story, with a hook: "If the mountain lion continues its 5–7 miles a day pace eastward this means it will make Chicago in about 50 days."

This was no journalist's idle speculation, scraping for drama on a sleepy news day. It was déjà vu. The lion was now heading down a path pioneered less than two years earlier by the first mountain lion in Wisconsin's modern era, by the cat first dubbed the Milton cougar. What had ultimately become of the Milton cougar foreshadowed a bad end for the lion now following in his footsteps.

The Milton cougar had entered the public eye on the evening of January 4, 2008, near the cat's namesake village in southeastern Wisconsin, running through the headlights of the car that nearly hit him. Regional wildlife supervisor Doug Fendry took the call, preparing himself for yet another false alarm and the probable hoofprints of a horse or deer. "But there was something in the tone of the guy's voice," said Fendry, "a certain confidence in the way he described it." Fendry went out and photographed the tracks, melted and marred as they were from the previous night's thaw, and sent them to Wydeven. Wydeven, then seventeen years into his own wearisome cataloging of tabby cat cougars and golden retriever lions, dismissed them as dog.

Two weeks later and just a mile or so down the road, Fendry got another call, this one from DNR dispatch. The local conservation warden Boyd Richter was at that moment on the trail of an honest-to-goodness cougar. Richter not only had a clear line of tracks in the snow, but also what looked like urine and blood and the prospect of a firm DNA profile. Fendry and Richter's supervisor, Jeremy Plautz, convened, and hurried to the scene.

Richter had responded to the report of a raccoon trapper named Kevin Edwardson, whose story began with a neighbor's tip of some large, suspicious tracks in his driveway. Edwardson picked up the tracks leading into an old abandoned barn. No tracks led out. Edwardson crept inside.

A dusting of snow had blown in through the dilapidated barn, conveying a perfect set of enormous tracks as they ascended into the hayloft. Edwardson followed. There was silence, and enough hay to hide a small army of ninja assassins. Edwardson tossed a stone against the back wall.

From behind a pile of hay, a mountain lion stepped out. He walked a few steps forward, veered at the sight of Edwardson's frozen figure, and sailed through a side window. The lion floated ten feet to the ground outside and hit the snow running, bounding twelve feet at a stride, across the field and into the far woods. But not before cutting a foot in his scramble.

Wildlife officer Richter arrived to find the scene as Edwardson had described. When he saw the lengths of the strides through the snow, he called for backup. He was soon joined by a pair of local videographers and by Plautz and Fendry, all following the tracks for two miles through subzero wind chill, gathering photographs of footprints and a bag of frozen urine. The lion's trail led his trackers on a long loop, eventually crossing a set of human footprints. The footprints were their own; the trackers were being tracked. They came to a frozen drop of blood. Fendry pried a plug of it from the snow with his pocketknife, and Richter cradled the precious nugget in his hands all the way back to the truck.

With Edwardson's point-blank testimony and the cougar's unmistakable tracks, it was no longer a question of what species they were following, but a question of ancestry. Fendry sent the samples to the USDA's Wildlife Genetics lab in Missoula, Montana. Genetic code from the samples could begin to distinguish between a lion of South American stock, typically sold by breeders, and a North American resident of wild descent. Although, soon enough, they would have more than a drop of blood to work with.

Wydeven forwarded the tentative news to his network, of a cougar in Milton, Wisconsin. Back east, Spatz addressed his ECF colleagues with a message of astonishment spiked with trepidation. "Milton is a good hundred miles east of the Mississippi; forty southeast of Madison. It's spitting distance to Milwaukee or Chicago."

The Milton lion was heading straight for the thickest mass of humanity on the Great Lakes, and he was already pushing his luck. "Getting chased out of someone's barn is getting pretty close to requiring a standard hazing or removal intervention, at minimum," said Spatz to his team. "And if the cat is injured, as it appears to be, you couldn't blame the DNR if they consider it a potential threat."

Over the next two months and more than fifty miles, the Milton lion continued on his southeastern slant across Wisconsin, leaving sign in Janesville, Clinton, and Elkhorn. On March 15 he left his tracks in a shady enclave of suburban estates surrounded by pastures and crop fields. He was little more than a mile from the Illinois line.

In the meantime, word had come back from Missoula. The drop of blood rescued by wildlife warden Richter in Milton revealed the cat as a male cougar of North American ancestry, his DNA profile most closely matching those from the Black Hills of South Dakota. He was nobody's pet. From his birthplace in the Hills, he had travelled eight hundred miles as the crow flies, easily tripling that as the cat meanders. He had vaulted the hostile plains, only to head for the ultimate wall.

When he reappeared two weeks later, he was another fifty-five miles southeast and a ten-minute jog from the shores of Lake Michigan. He had thus become Illinois' third mountain lion of the past century and a half, and its only current survivor. (His latest predecessor, in 2004, was stopped by a bow hunter's arrow.) Another two weeks down the road, on April 12, the lion was spotted in a neighborhood just yards from the Linden Avenue terminus of the Chicago L, the third-busiest mass transit rail in the United States. On the other side of the neighborhood ran the Chicago River, a forested corridor leading to two unfortunate ends. Northward, it emptied into the world's seventh-biggest lake and one hundred miles of open water. Four miles south lay the Midwest's largest city and nearly three million people. Of those two options, the lion took the latter. Two days later, all hell broke loose.

At nine in the morning, police began receiving calls from anxious residents in an upscale urban neighborhood on the North Side of Chicago. Apparently, there was a mountain lion roaming the brownstones and row houses of Roscoe Village. There was a mountain lion sleeping on somebody's porch. There was a mountain lion leaping from yard to yard.

Lion alerts flooded the neighborhood e-mail network. Animal control officers combed the streets. Cops converged in cars, on bicycles, on foot, some of them wearing flak jackets. There was yelling and chasing. Guns were drawn. The frightened cat leapt fences and scrambled helter-skelter down alleys. Pedestrians ran for cover into strangers' houses.

The chase escalated into live theater of high-tension melodrama spiced with slapstick humor. A precious clip of amateur video caught an officer of the law on the hunt, eyes keenly probing ahead while his quarry tiptoed across the path behind him. *The Great Escape* meets the Keystone Kops.

Late in the day, the dark comedy took its inevitable turn. Near 5:30 P.M., police officers spotted the cat going down an alley. Megaphones blared, clearing the streets, warning all to stay inside. The police saw a clear shot, and fired. The wounded lion struggled over a fence and into another alley, where four officers finally cornered him. They would later claim the lion turned on them.

Inside the adjoining house, resident Ben Greene heard what he thought was a gun battle erupting on the street. He gathered his two young sons and wife, and huddled the family in a back room. The shooting ended quickly. Greene crept downstairs and peeked out the window to see a line of policemen gathered on his lawn, guns still drawn and aiming into the alley. He opened the door. "We got him!" they said. "We got him!"

In the alley lay the huge, incongruous form of a mountain lion, its body pierced by at least six bullets. Chicago police captain Mike Ryan later said the cougar had tried to attack his officers when they approached. There was no way to take it into custody, he told reporters. There was no choice but to gun it down.

Next morning the dead cat appeared on page 1 of the *Chicago Tribune*, its body curled up on the concrete and cordoned off with police tape like a vanquished gangster. A necropsy identified the victim as a young adult male, 122 pounds, his stomach empty. All telltale signs of captivity were lacking: no missing claws, no tattoos or microchips, his genitalia intact. At Wydeven's suggestion, Illinois officials sent a tissue sample to the genetics lab in Missoula, where it would eventually confirm the biologists' suspicions. The Chicago cougar and the Milton cougar were the same young prospecting male from the Black Hills of South Dakota.

From there the Chicago cougar's story gathered momentum. The morning following his *Tribune* debut, his photo appeared again on the front page, elbowing for space with the U.S. arrival of the Pope. Within two days, the online photo gallery of the cougar crime scene had registered more than half a million views, his story inciting thousands of comments, few of them flattering.

"One of nature's most beautiful creatures, in the wrong place at the wrong time, and our immediate response is to kill it."

"The question is, why not with a tranquilizer gun? And why, according to the article, did it take 10 shots?"

"Shame on the individual from the Illinois Department of Natural Resources for commenting that the cougar isn't protected by the state because it's not part of our ecosystem."

"Shame on us!"

Defenders of the shooting returned fire.

"The responsibility of the CPD was to eliminate the immediate threat to the safety of others, [and] they did a commendable job."

"I guess to animal activists, the life of a wild cougar is more important than the residents of Chicago."

Chicago's mayor Daley chimed in, dutifully backing his officers: "If a cougar attacked a child, you'd be suing the city, you'd be filing lawsuits because the police officer didn't do his job." Chicagoans attacked their mayor in turn: "Daley is full of it when he said the reason to kill the cougar was for the safety of children in the area." One citizen sent a letter threatening to burn down Daley's house, with a follow-up note addressed to his police force: "Dear Cougar Killers . . . Prepare to DIE like the Cougars you killed." Soon thereafter, with obvious suspicions, the house next door to Daley's vacation home went down in flames.

So went the public catfight over the shooting of the Chicago cougar. He was an innocent creature gunned down by trigger-happy cops. He was a child stalker stopped in his murderous tracks by Chicago's finest. But for those who understood his true intent, he was a bracing reminder of the towering barriers still standing between a lion simply looking to find a mate, and a society seeded with people simply wanting him dead. For those who better knew the lion, any blame was ultimately overcome by disappointment over what could have been.

"A big ambassador opportunity was blown," said Spatz. "Problem is, just showing up gets them shot."

"I don't blame the cops," said Wydeven. "People don't realize there's five minutes between the tranquilizer dart and the animal lying on the ground. So much can go wrong. You don't want a half-tranquilized cougar running through a big urban area. But there are situations where they should be left alone."

"I'm hesitant to second-guess the Chicago shooting," said Tischendorf. "But keep in mind the Chicago suburbs had no anticipation of a situation like this. The SWAT team's training—none of it involves what to do if a mountain lion comes to town."

Not that Tischendorf hadn't tried. Both he and Wydeven had been independently developing protocols in anticipation of just such chaos as Chicago. Wydeven had suggested to his superiors in Wisconsin a checklist for handling the inevitable wayward cougar, based on the cat's behavior and surroundings, something to replace the bullet as first and last resort. Not long before the Milton cougar came through on his way to Chicago, higher-ups in Wydeven's department had jettisoned his proposal. "They didn't want guidelines," is all the diplomatic Wydeven could say.

Tischendorf, for his part, had parlayed his cougar-catching experience in Yellowstone into a first-responder course for those law officers and game agents who, if the Midwest movement played out as he'd predicted, for the first times in their careers would be meeting the cougar on their home turf. He had formally offered his service to wildlife agencies across the Midwest, including Illinois. He'd put himself and other select houndsmen and biologists on call. As of April 15, 2008, the day the Chicago cougar came to town, he'd had no takers.

"The cops went into it, sadly, without a lot of prior experience," said Tischendorf. "They might have been comfortable around burglars or gunmen, but they didn't understand large carnivore behavior. So when they say they shot in self-defense, I can understand that. It's a wrong perception they had, but a real perception."

FIVE Attack

To him who is in fear, everything rustles.

—SOPHOCLES

FOR ALL THE OPPOSING howls of injustice, the perception that had sanctioned the killing of the Chicago cougar and a crushing share of his fellow Midwest pioneers was a perception that may well have been honestly earned—if in large part by creatures half a world away and a million years departed. Those creatures ultimately responsible were lions and leopards and saber-toothed cats, packs of wild dogs and roving hyenas, from an ancient era of sub-Saharan Africa. In their time, they had been the apex predators of a grand Old World menagerie, monkey to elephant, aardvark to zebra. And with particular relevance to those fearful humans who would one day open fire on America's comeback lion, they had made meat of walking apes.

From the first teetering steps to the inimitable cocky stride in humanity's six-million-year journey—from tree-dwelling, knuckle-walking offshoot of an African ape, to bipedal globe-trotting pedestrian of the world—had come uncounted sidetracks and detours through the bellies of big cats. Being hunted was a fact of early life that forever shaped the growing brains and bodies of the people who would come to be.

Flashbacks of that humbling era first came to light from a complex of limestone caves in the Sterkfontein Valley of South Africa. It was there, beginning in the early 1900s, that anthropologists began unearthing a rich bone-yard of African wildlife—of antelope, baboon, hippo, giraffe, jackal, hyena, leopard, and, of particular interest, an unusual collection of early humans and their australopithecine predecessors, some of them two million years

104

old. And of those protohumans, a certain curious number were represented by skull parts bearing odd holes and indentations.

A feisty South African paleontologist named Raymond Dart was the first and most prominent to venture a guess as to the fate of the skulls' original owners. Dart figured those dents to be the impact craters left by antelope leg bones, wielded as clubs by fellow ape-men. Dart's killer ape-men came to fame thanks in good part to a dramatic rendering of his hypothesis by the author Robert Ardrey in his 1960s bestselling book *African Genesis*.

Until along came another South African paleontologist, named Charles Kimberlin "Bob" Brain, who offered up a more tranquil purpose for the bones, with some hands-on demonstrations to back him up. The leg bones that Dart had seen as head-bashing clubs were rather worn and scratched; Brain easily reproduced similar scratches on modern leg bones by digging for roots in the Swartkrans hillside. Dart's skull-crushing bludgeons thus became Brain's gardening tools.

As for the victims' killers, Brain found a more fitting suspect to blame than a murderous ape-man. Into a pair of perfectly round holes in a child's fossil skull, Brain neatly inserted the fangs of a fossil leopard's jaws.

From where Brain stood, the victims' skulls had been bitten, not beaten. Brain figured the cave as both refuge and deathtrap for early humans, a place to shelter out of the winter chill, but occasionally, too, a place to be ambushed by lurking beasts. The cave in Brain's view was no longer an ancient crime scene exposing the homicidal roots of human nature. More likely, it was a picnic spot for big cats looking to eat their human meat in peace.

The terrors visited upon those little bands of ape-men—huddled naked and blind in the blackness, hunted by fanged monsters with night-vision eyes—would come to haunt the human mind forever after. Those terrors would come to reside in the amygdala, a nugget of neurons buried deep in the forebrain. The amygdala had evolved as a bodily command center programmed to act with uncompromising haste upon the sight of life-threatening danger. Upon receiving the eye's image of, say, a crouching saber-tooth, the amygdala would fire. In roughly enough time for a housefly to flap a wing, the alarm would be delivered and the response executed, by way of widened pupils, hurried breath, racing heart. Adrenaline would flood the bloodstream, priming the muscles for what the amygdala was assuming was the most pivotal fight or flight of the creature's life.

The amygdala and its five-alarm urgencies had with good reason been granted priority over the conscious control of the cerebral brain. The sight of a saber-tooth springing from close quarters was perhaps not the best time to analyze the animal's intent or admire its gleaming fangs. Over the long haul of time, those who stood to ponder such situations tended not to leave as many descendants as those who let their legs do their thinking.

Crisis averted, the amygdala's knee jerks and high anxieties would dissolve into yawning periods of repose and contemplation, but inevitably, too, the pervasive whisperings of hunger. While not getting eaten may have been the amygdala's foremost duty, getting something to eat, on the other hand, demanded a more calculated strategy. That task fell to the gray matter of the cerebral cortex, processor of complex thought, problem solving, and speech. Though the amygdala's basic design had become a standard of brain architecture across the animal kingdom, the human cerebral cortex would stand out, ballooning to freakish proportions. Over the final third of Homo sapiens' evolutionary arc, the volume of the brain doubled. And like the amygdala, it, too, had the tracks of big cats treading all over it.

The billowing human brain came with a ferocious appetite. It would come to consume 20 percent of the resting body's energy needs, a heavy caloric burden for a big ape foraging strictly on vegetarian fare. It seems the growing brain had, through a crucial shift in diet and lifestyle, come to periodically feed on generous infusions of animal flesh. And it seems that in the human's Pleistocene birthplace of eastern Africa, substantial helpings of such meat and marrow had become available for the taking.

Meat of Man

The African savanna where the human prototype emerged nearly two million years ago was busy with big predators. There were lions and leopards, a wolflike canid, and a cast of hyenas, one of them with long legs built for chasing. There were at least three lines of saber-toothed cats. Often enough, the predators bit off more than they could chew in one feeding, and wandered away, leaving piles of flesh and bone momentarily unguarded. Such temptations offered great reward, if you dared. Enter the upright ape.

The human form arose during the ecological upheaval that was to become the Pleistocene epoch, as the African continent cooled and dried, and forests gave way to woodland islands, and the woodlands to savanna and grassy plains. The great apes' world was shrinking and expanding at once. They came down from their trees and started foraging on two legs, like no ape ever had, and venturing to the forest edges and beyond, along the riverside woods snaking out upon the plains. Entering upon the land of giant beasts, they found themselves rather slow of foot and dull of tooth and, not too uncommonly, food for fierce predators.

The first humans were, among other things, prey. But they were also survivors, if barely, on an enormous talent for one-upmanship. The first humans eked through their Pleistocene trial, in no small part, by eating their predators' lunch.

By night the little people listened from their trees for the roar of lions and cackling of hyenas and the braying of zebras, and charted their prospects for fresh carcasses in the morning. By day they took to stretching their legs and searching for the kills of the carnivores that had haunted them the night before. Human eyes, perched high atop a vertical torso, scanned the skies for circling vultures, peering over tall grasses for lions in wait. They zeroed in on the meat and bone left by the professional hunters. And for the occasional steep price of getting caught, they often enough came away free with the spoils.

Such was the hypothesis of a growing cadre of paleoanthropologists who, by the latter half of the twentieth century, had begun formally disrobing the popular macho persona of man the hunter, re-dressing him in the more humbling guise of scavenger. A few with bolder curiosities had come to test the hypothesis themselves. For eight days in 1968, renowned wildlife biologist George Schaller and his anthropologist colleague Gordon Lowther, while camped in the beastly heart of Africa's Serengeti Plains and savannas, set out into a land of lions and Cape buffalo and elephants, in search of edible meat, unarmed.

In just one thirty-three-hour stint canvassing the plains, the two amateur ape-men came upon the equivalent of nearly eighty pounds of flesh and skin. They found what would have been free lunch in a Thomson's gazelle lying dead from disease, and in another abandoned with only its stomach missing. They watched others falling to cheetahs and wild dogs, and figuratively helped themselves to those, too. Happening upon a zebra leg bone, Lowther selected a handy stone from a creek bed and crushed his way into the marrow. Schaller took the same stone and bashed in the zebra's skull, "exposing the brain, potentially a nice snack."

Not only scavengers, Schaller and Lowther played the predator, too. They chased and caught (and released) a sick little zebra; they cornered and imagined clubbing a blind giraffe—the two of them symbolically bagging some three hundred pounds of meat in one outing. It was not so far a stretch, after all, to imagine how such seemingly helpless waifs of humanity's childhood had crept into Africa's Pleistocene badlands and emerged with the keys to the world.

Yet for all its adventurous spirit and palpable risk, Schaller and Lowther's meat-seeking stint on the African veldt amounted to a walk in the park compared to the outings their ancestors navigated on the mean streets of the Pleistocene. Stone Age Africa was a far more dangerous place for a naked human to be walking about. The dedicated carnivores roaming the Pleistocene terrain outnumbered the modern Serengeti's celebrated assemblage by two to three times. Chief among them was a suite of saber-toothed cats.

The saber-tooth featured enormous maws and oversize fangs. Its chassis more resembled that of a heavyweight hyena, with squat hindquarters and long, powerful forelimbs. Its skull and skeleton tagged it as a hunter of thick-skinned behemoths—young elephants, hippos, buffalo, and tank-bodied giraffes called sivatheres—wrestling its victims into position with those massive forearms, stabbing and slicing vital organs and arteries with those infamous scimitars.

The saber-tooth was quite likely the most fearsome icon of carnivory ever met by man. And in the scenario first championed by paleoanthropologist Curtis Marean, that same icon was among the evolving human's most vital benefactors. Marean noted how, in the give-and-take of adaptive design, the saber-tooth's outsize canines had been fashioned at the expense of its cheek teeth, leaving the jaws somewhat less equipped for cracking and crushing bone; and how the saber-tooth's stocky hindquarters suggested something less of an open-field-pursuit specialist and more of an ambush predator to be found lurking under woodland cover. All this was to say that the saber-tooth, with its apparent preference for enormous prey and its untidy habits of butchering, likely left big stashes lying hidden and preserved in the cool of the forest to whatever, or whoever, in an unguarded moment should dare to dart in first.

And over time, those stashes more commonly went to the little bands of dashing thieves with their hungry brains, racing to beat the hyenas and jackals, free hands working fast with crude cutters and scrapers and hammerstones to sever limbs and smash bones into portable packages of meat and marrow, with sentinels standing by to bark alarms of the owner's return, and feet ready to scramble for the nearest tree.

Leopards also figured large in explaining the early human's meat-stealing vocation. Of moderate size but inordinate strength, leopards commonly hauled whole gazelles and other hoofed prey into the branches of trees. They hung them there while they left to gather their cubs or wait for the cool of night to feed. They hung them well out of reach of the ponderous saber-tooths and lions and hyenas, but not well enough to thwart the lithe, bipedal primates who could still climb like monkeys.

The big cats of Africa apparently provided a critical boost of relatively easy calories for the first people willing to exploit it. But those calories would come harder with time. With the Pleistocene's drying, the forests continued to shrink. With the shrinking forests went the forest-dwelling saber-tooth and its larders. The scavenging trade grew more competitive and hazardous. Foraging humans would be forced more often into the grassland domains of lions and hyenas, and farther from the nearest climbable tree.

Yet that which didn't quite kill the would-be humans eventually made them stronger. As the risks heightened, noted Marean, body and mind responded. The legs and stride lengthened, the arms shortened—more the runner, less the climber. The raids became bolder, the tiptoeing approaches turning to full-frontal assaults. The people who had once crept like jackals to steal untended carcasses began confronting their owners straight on, brandishing sticks and rocks, hooting and waving arms. Anthropologists would later observe chimpanzees and baboons executing such bluff and bravado upon cheetahs and leopards. They would find tribes of modern people across sub-Saharan Africa performing similar dances, regularly stealing meat and bone from beneath the big cats' noses.

Some would further surmise that the newest meat seekers on the block had become not only competent at their craft, but inordinately good at it, perhaps to the point of driving both their closest competitors and most generous benefactors out of business. Within half a million years of the first appearance of handcrafted butchering stones, emulating the teeth of the protohumans' competitors, several hyena species disappeared. Another half a million years later, the saber-tooth they'd been robbing disappeared, too.

The newcomers eventually completed their carnivore's apprenticeship by mastering the classic weapons of the trade. They added fangs and claws in the form of pointed sticks, to be followed eventually by darts and spears tipped with wicked stone points flaked to the sharpness of broken glass. If they could not ambush their quarry, they would sometimes run it to exhaustion, in marathon chases lasting hours. They became hunters of big game. No longer tethered to the leftovers of others, they ascended to the pantheon of apex predators.

Viewed through the anthropologist's ten-million-year hindsight, so many of the hallmarks of humanity were more easily explained, at least in part, by a long life-and-death dance with big cats. The training for such a lifestyle was demanding, the weeding process brutal, lavishing eternal rewards on the winners, exacting capital punishment upon the losers. To the bold and the brainy, to the quick of foot and sharp of eye and mindful of team play, went the spoils. To the rash, the greedy, and the careless came one-way trips into the big cats' bone piles.

What continued to stymie those assembling pieces of the story was why the contest still did not more often go to the cat. It wasn't for lack of opportunity. Seven times during Schaller and Lowther's ape-man reenactment in the Serengeti, the unarmed men came upon prides of lions. Seven times the lions fled. The most troublesome bites either man received were from tsetse flies.

"To my puzzlement, man is not an important food item of lions even though no other large mammal is as defenseless and easy to kill," wrote Schaller, still scraping for explanations. Perhaps it was the odd upright stance, so foreign and confusing to a creature programmed to dispatch four-footed prey. Perhaps it was the humans' ability to strike back with those free hands. "Perhaps man's ancient ability and predilection to defend himself has imbued lions with caution."

But for all the untold reasons the cats so seldom made meat of such easy pickings as people, there remained the sobering fact that, with statistical rarity but indelible imprint, they nonetheless still did. And some of them notoriously so.

Reigns of Terror

The Tsavo lions of Kenya were two maneless males who terrorized a construction crew trying to build a railroad bridge for the British Empire over the Tsavo River. The construction had begun in March of 1898, under the supervision of Lt. Col. John Henry Patterson, who soon started losing his workers to lions, who had taken to dragging them from their tents by night and eating them. During the last three months of what Patterson described as "the reign of terror," one of the Tsavo lions was figured to be filling half his daily dietary needs with human flesh. The terrified workers fled in droves; the British Empire was stopped in its tracks—by a pair of lions.

Patterson set out to kill the lions. After nine months of chasing, he finally shot the Tsavo man-eaters to death, the second lion dying after receiving nine bullets over eleven days. Not to let a good story go unembellished, Patterson wrote a book of his exploits, crediting the Tsavo lions with killing 135 humans. A century later, biologists analyzing the chemical signatures of human flesh in the dead lions' bone and hair downgraded Patterson's exuberant estimate by one hundred.

Thirty-five or 135—either way, it was the most celebrated take for any two lions that had ever terrorized any pocket of humanity. Various theories would be offered to explain the motives of the aberrant Tsavo man-eaters.

Several of them centered on a theme of desperation. It turned out one of the killers, the one credited with the most deaths, had a misshapen skull with crooked jaws and a missing tooth. Moreover, drought and viral plagues had recently decimated Tsavo's buffalo and cattle and other staples of lion sustenance. Perhaps the lions of Tsavo were already desperate for easy prey when, lo, the unwitting windfall of bridge builders came conveniently traipsing into their territory.

Or perhaps the lions' taste for human flesh had been learned. Tsavo had for centuries funneled Arab slave caravans en route to the coastal port of Mombasa. Passing through Tsavo, the slaves died in droves from sleeping sickness or from drowning at the river's crossing. The bodies, in those times, were commonly left where they fell. Outbreaks of smallpox and sieges of drought added more corpses for the lions' consideration.

That the man-eating did not end with the Tsavo man-eaters—people there would continue to fall prey through the following century—suggested several other disquieting possibilities. Perhaps the lions of Tsavo had been taught the vocation of man-eating as cubs or, worse, had been born with it. Perhaps the entire culture of Tsavo lions had become predisposed to bipedal prey: a culture of people-eating lions.

Monsters reminiscent of the Tsavo lions would crop up through the modern ages, and always with lurid tales and legends to follow. A village in eastern Zambia was terrorized in 1991 by the Man-Eater of Mfume, who dragged his sixth victim of the year from her hut in the middle of the day and then retrieved a bag of her clothes and paraded it through the street, roaring. Villagers witnessing the sight believed themselves in the presence of a demonic sorcerer.

Certain tigers in Asia would make the atrocities of the Tsavo and Mfume man-eaters seem trivial by comparison. The Champawat Tigress of India supposedly killed 436 people before Jim Corbett, renowned slayer of man-eaters, shot her.

And for sheer audacity and lethal resolve, no cat's actions matched the people-killing exploits of the leopard. The biggest of them less than half the size of a robust male lion, the leopard was a compact but versatile predator. The leopard hunted day or night, concealed behind its cryptic coat of spots.

It was an agile climber with Olympic strength, able to haul the dead weight of prey twice its size high into the trees, or drag a corpse miles across rugged country. The cryptic leopard was inconspicuous enough to crouch invisibly on the village edge by day, and come slipping seamlessly through the alleys by night. The leopard was known to snatch roaming dogs off the streets and people out of bed. The leopard hunted humans where they lived.

A handful of man-eating leopards grew notorious as supernatural serial killers and escape artists, and none was more feared than the outlaw known as the Leopard of Rudraprayag. The Leopard of Rudraprayag was estimated to have killed more than 125 people in Uttarakhand, India, before the cat hunter Corbett came looking to kill him.

The Leopard of Rudraprayag was not statistically the most lethal of leopards. The Leopard of Panar, also of northern India, was credited with killing at least four hundred people. But the Leopard of Rudraprayag was by far the most infamous. Toward the end of his eight-year reign of terror, his exploits from rural India were being carried by dailies around the world, from the United Kingdom to the United States, Hong Kong to New Zealand. He was a particularly bold and intelligent leopard, with the reputation for stalking villagers in their huts, leaping through windows, and slipping through doors left ajar. If the homes were not sufficiently fortified, he would force his way in. If he could not break down the door, he would dig a hole through the wall.

This leopard also exhibited a modus operandi reminiscent of the Tsavo lions, in that he hunted along a route feeding him a steady supply of prey. Rudraprayag was on the pilgrim's path to the Hindu shrines of Kedarnath and Badrinath, each year traversed by tens of thousands. For the barefoot throngs passing through the leopard's domain, nightfall was a time to huddle together in shelters and count the hours until dawn.

For the better part of eight years, the Leopard of Rudraprayag cast a cloud of paralytic fear over the countryside. And over the last two years of that span, his would-be assassin, Jim Corbett, came to stand in awe.

I should like therefore to give you some idea of what terror—real terror— meant to the fifty thousand inhabitants living in the five hundred square miles of Garhwal in which the man-eater was operating, and to the sixty thousand pilgrims who annually passed through that area between the years 1918 and 1926. No curfew order has ever been more strictly enforced, and more implicitly obeyed, than the curfew imposed by the man-eating leopard of Rudraprayag.

As the sun approached the western horizon and the shadows lengthened, the behaviour of the entire population of the area underwent a very sudden and very noticeable change. Men who had sauntered to the bazaar or to outlying villages were hurrying home; women carrying great bundles of grass were stumbling down the steep mountain-sides; children who had loitered on their way from school, or who were late in bringing in their flocks of goats or the dry sticks they had been sent out to collect, were being called by anxious mothers, and the weary pilgrims were being urged by any local inhabitant who passed them to hurry to shelter.

When night came, an ominous silence brooded over the whole area—no movement and no sound anywhere. The entire local population was behind fast-closed doors and, in many cases, had sought further protection by building additional doors. Those of the pilgrims who had not been fortunate enough to find accommodation inside houses were huddled close together in pilgrim shelters. And all, whether in house or shelter, were silent for fear of attracting the dread man-eater.

The Leopard of Rudraprayag survived armies of bounty hunters plied with offers of ten thousand rupees for his body. Professional hunters were employed full time to destroy the leopard. Special licenses were granted expressly for shooting him. Soldiers on leave were encouraged to carry their rifles home with them; if they did not own one, they were provided one. Roads leading into villages were mined by traps baited with goats. Government officials planted poisons in human corpses.

For all the effort, the leopard remained all but unscathed. He shrugged off a bullet that took a piece of a hind toe, and seemed to relish the poisoned corpses left as bait. A leopard believed to be the killer was twice trapped, only to escape before his executioners arrived. In the battle of thousands versus the leopard, the leopard continued racking up his score.

Corbett came to know the cat better than anybody who lived. He would sit by night in trees above baited carcasses, and in towers overlooking bridges where the leopard was likely to cross. He would walk the abandoned roads at night, searching. Mornings, he would find his traps unsprung, his bait stolen, and the tracks he'd supposedly been following tracing his own footsteps from behind. Even after managing to poison a leopard, Corbett knew from the victim's carelessness that he'd killed the wrong cat. "I had not fully realized the degree of cunning that a man-eating leopard can acquire after eight years of close association with human beings."

In the end, after an eleven-night vigil waiting in the branches of a mango tree above a tethered goat, Corbett finally got a decent shot at the Rudraprayag leopard (through the beam of a flashlight) and killed him. When word got out, thousands flocked to see the demon where he lay.

Examining the body afterward, Corbett took note of the old bullet wound in the cat's foot, along with several partly healed cuts from head to tail, likely received in a fight with a rival. He was an old cat. His teeth were worn from age. One of his canines was broken. And there was a small memento hinting as to when and why the leopard may have taken up manhunting. Wrote Corbett, "I found a pellet of buckshot embedded in the skin of his chest which an Indian Christian—years later—claimed he had fired at the leopard the year it became a man-eater."

In his years of hunting man-eaters, Corbett would come to suggest certain patterns of the trade, patterns describing the Tsavo lions as well. Advanced age and disabilities often led the big cats to seek easier, two-legged prey. They may, too, have learned the taste of human flesh through the windfalls of plague. Corbett connected outbreaks of man-eating in rural India to outbreaks of cholera and flu that overwhelmed the cremators and left human bodies unburied. "A leopard, in an area in which his natural food is scarce, finding these bodies very soon acquires a taste for human flesh," Corbett explained, "and when the disease dies down and normal conditions are established, he very naturally, on finding his food supply cut off, takes to killing human beings."

More pervasive ingredients for manufacturing man-eaters would proliferate over time. In a pattern repeated around the world, humans swarmed over once-wild landscapes, razing forests and obliterating cover, displacing the wild herds of cat prey with the domestic herds of pastoralists. Swept before the human tide, a few of the cornered cats would fight back. Faced with diminishing options, they would come to glean their sustenance from the trespassers.

In the swampy Sundarbans forest overlapping Bangladesh and India, where woodcutters, honey harvesters, and fishermen had come to make their daily living, tigers had taken to killing them by the dozens each year. (The dangers escalated to the point that Sundarbans woodsmen took to wearing face masks on the back of their heads, fooling the surprise-attack tigers into believing they were forever being watched.) Scores of farmers and herders of rural Africa were still being hunted by lions. Seventy years after Jim Corbett ended the career of the Leopard of Rudraprayag, newspapers in the India Himalaya were still running familiar headlines (KILLERS ON THE PROWL) and leopards were still dispatching roughly ten humans per year, the toll rising with time.

But in North America, a more mysterious uptick in man-eating had begun to stir fears, from the creature historically better known for fleeing unarmed men and tiny terriers alike. Beginning in the 1970s, it seemed America's mountain lion had, with rare but accelerating frequency, begun attacking and killing humans.

It was a strange turn to an otherwise lopsided history of the mountain lion's slaughter by American people. It may well have been that mountain lions had been eating people on occasion for fourteen thousand years, at least since the country was invaded by the Stone Age spearmen from Siberia. But for most of the two species' time together, the record all but lacked evidence of human casualties. There was no archaeological blood trail remotely resembling the carnage on Africa's first people by its resident big cats. There were no American caves littered with ancient human skulls bearing fang holes of mountain lions. Nor did modern times and written records reveal any smoking guns. There was no Leopard of Rudraprayag or Lions of Tsavo or any reigns of terror in the history of American mountain lions. America's only predatory monsters worthy of the title had come armed with guns and traps and names such as Ben Lilly.

The mountain lions who met the first Americans had never seen such an odd creature. The human life-form contradicted the quadruped search image they'd been chasing through the ages: two legs, not four; neck held vertically, not horizontally. How to tackle this strange fur-clad thing more resembling a bipedal bear? This odd upright bear also happened to utter strange barks and fling pointed sticks that could kill or maim a mountain lion venturing too close. And in time the talking bear came with hunting dogs and firearms, too.

North America's post-Columbian history of lion attacks, as written and recorded by white men, would amount to a murky rendering of campfire accounts and lurid yarns, spiced just often enough with believable scenarios of real people in vital struggles against authentic mountain lions sincerely looking to eat them. The chronicle begins in 1751, with a sawmill owner named Philip Tanner, who was inexplicably attacked and killed by a cougar on the edge of the woods near Lewisville, Pennsylvania. Tanner's tombstone was chiseled with the image of a crouching cougar.

Into the early 1800s the trail goes cold, the records so infrequent as to be tallied not by the year but by the decade. Dates and victims' names go missing: two brothers in the swamplands of Mississippi, both killed by a cougar in their cabin; a plantation slave defending himself with a knife in the swamps of Georgia, both combatants found mangled and dead.

Certain attacks stretch the bounds of gullibility. From the Catskills of Upstate New York comes a report of a cougar stashing his human prey in a tree, while another victim is leapt upon from the branches. Neither arboreal behavior, of cougars caching prey or attacking from trees, would ever be verified by modern cougar biologists.

Some attacks at least seem plausible. In 1844, in Lycoming County, Pennsylvania, a Dr. Reinwald is "found lying in the snow with the back of his neck bitten through; medical instruments scattered about, large cougar tracks all around." Why he was not fed upon, nobody explains. Nevertheless, it remains among the records as the last eastern casualty by what was likely one of the last eastern mountain lions.

The pioneers push westward; the spotty chronicle of cougar attacks follows them. Sometime in the 1860s, a luckless survivor of an Apache ambush in Arizona is then stalked and killed by a cougar. In 1876, in the Edwards Plateau region of Texas, a man named Henry Ramsey opens his door to a disturbance in his front yard, is sprung upon by a large panther, and later dies an agonizing death by what is suspected to be rabies. In 1882, a five-year-old boy named Gussie Graves from the state of Washington dies of wounds from a cougar; and eight years later, a seven-year-old California boy named Arthur Dangle is out playing among the oaks when killed by two lions, both of them later treed and shot.

Through the first three centuries of European occupation, attacks by cougars in North America remained an anomaly far outnumbered by solar eclipses. The twentieth century began the same. Through the 1960s, records amounted to fewer than twenty attacks and just four deaths. But there developed a twist. More than half the attacks inexplicably came from one tiny outpost off the Pacific coast, on British Columbia's Vancouver Island.

That was to say, for the first five decades of the 1900s, more than half of all attacks credited to cougars came from less than 1 percent of the creature's North American range, from a Pacific Northwest island slightly smaller than the state of Maryland.

Vancouver Island defied tidy explanations. Bruce Wright, eastern cougar evangelist of the 1950s, puzzled over Vancouver Island from afar. In an observation that would gain a certain resonance in the decades to come, Wright noted that "Many of these attacks have been made by young animals that have just been deserted by the mother, and there is evidence in some cases of mistaken identity on the part of the attacker. Some attacks have also been made by very old or crippled individuals."

In another observation that would regrettably not survive the test of time, Wright observed, "Such a situation is not known ever to have existed anywhere else in North America, and it might be expected to reach acute proportions only in an insular fauna with few prey species, such as that of Vancouver Island."

Whatever dark magic had cursed Vancouver Island, cougar attack capital of the world, would hold sway for decades to come. In the meantime, other little islands of trouble would surface on the mainland. In the 1970s, twenty people were attacked (three to death), most of them again in British

Columbia, but now including six attacks in the United States. Another thirteen attacks and two deaths were recorded in the 1980s. It was hardly an explosion of fresh violence, but the attacks had developed a new parameter. As on Vancouver Island, they came with the first hints of repetition and pattern. And suddenly, the American public began to take it personally.

In April 1984 a ranger for Big Bend National Park in west Texas was out hiking when she was bowled over by a young cougar, who ran away without biting. Four months later, same park, an eight-year-old boy was tackled and gripped by the head in a mountain lion's jaws, until the boy's father fought the cat off with a stick. The boy would survive to undergo rounds of reconstructive surgery; the mountain lion, a young, eighty-five-pound male, was later treed and shot.

In 1986 a semblance of serial trouble started likewise in California, when a five-year-old girl named Laura Small was ambushed in the Ronald W. Caspers Wilderness Park in the Santa Ana Mountains southeast of Los Angeles. The little girl was grabbed by a cougar from under her mother's watch, and dragged into the bushes. A heroic stranger named Gregory Ysais arrived in time to repel the cougar with a stick, but not before Laura Small suffered a crushed skull that paralyzed her right leg and arm, and a lacerated eye that would never see again. It was California's first documented lion attack in more than seventy years. The suspected attacker, soon shot, turned out to be a two-year-old lion. But contrary to the standard profile of a starving wretch, he was strong and well fed.

Seven months later, Small's parents sued Orange County and the California Department of Fish and Game for not warning them of the danger, in a park where a couple of dicey encounters with cougars had been reported in the weeks preceding their daughter's attack. One hiker said she'd been forced to pelt a particularly bold lion with rocks.

Within two weeks of the Smalls' filing suit, six-year-old Justin Mellon was playing in the same park when he was snatched off the trail, his head in the jaws of a cougar. Mellon's father fought off the cougar with a knife, and Justin was later sewn back together with more than a hundred stitches. The Mellons joined the Smalls in suing.

With news of the Orange County attacks going national, every game agency and its lawyers operating in cougar country of America had been served notice. Trailheads began sprouting warning signs. The mountain lion was on its way from highlight of natural history to looming threat and legal liability.

The attacks sent scientists back to the books to reconsider America's cowardly lion of legend. In 1988, wildlife biologist Lee Fitzhugh from the University of California at Davis was among the first to draw his colleagues' attention to what seemed a different beast in the making. At a mountain lion workshop in Prescott, Arizona, Fitzhugh addressed a roomful of colleagues with the message that their profession had been seriously underestimating the lethal potential of America's lion.

Citing the recent attacks at Caspers Park, and the ensuing lawsuits that had blindsided the parks managers, Fitzhugh admonished his colleagues: "Mountain lions are no animal to consider lightly, and people should be told forcefully that lions are dangerous. There seems to be a public impression that they are not."

Fitzhugh pointed to the California cats' behavior in the moments before the attacks—the stalking and crouching, the sweeping tails. These were something other than the posture and twitching of a playful cat. These were traits universally recognized in the cat family as those of a predator contemplating its prey, said Fitzhugh. More disconcerting, suggested Fitzhugh, the attackers were learning the habit.

"Prey recognition is a learned behavior in cats, and knowledge of what constitutes prey may be gained in several ways," said Fitzhugh. "Several encounters with 'strange' species lead the cat to identify the species. Once identified, felids typically treat the 'strange' species as a conspecific or as prey."

Fitzhugh had raised the unsettling possibility that whatever taboos or matters of taste had kept human beings largely off the mountain lion's menu over their first fourteen thousand years together were now, in a more civilized and crowded world, beginning to fade. With more people funneling into the parks and wildlands where lions lived came more opportunities for the lion to reconsider its aversion to human prey—and worse yet, argued Fitzhugh, to spread that boldness to its fellow lions.

Fitzhugh hypothesized that certain lions could be learning to hunt humans. Which begged two fundamental questions: Was it true? And if so, what to do?

Science on the subject was scarce, though some had already formed their own conclusions. Near the closing of the 1988 cougar conference, a wildlife biologist and predator-control specialist named Walter E. Howard addressed the audience with a plea for killing more mountain lions. "Anti-hunting organizations who oppose the hunting of the mountain lion are, through their short-sightedness, causing much unnecessary suffering amongst lions," said Howard. "Protection from harassment and pain from humans and increased friendly exposure to people will cause them to lose some of their innate fear of people."

Howard continued: "Whenever a lion ventures beyond the geographic boundaries of its designated management range, it should automatically lose all protective status. It will have become an unneeded surplus individual that should he dispatched at the first opportunity before it creates bad propaganda for its species."

Howard's speculations of emboldened cats, and curious panacea of shooting them for the good of people and cougars alike, would come to approximate those of most western game agencies toward their lions. Over the following decades, the cougar-killing prescription would serve as well for wildlife managers of the Midwest, as the first pioneering cougars of the prairie were with rare exception being dispatched on sight.

In Denver three years later, at yet another national meeting on mountain lions, the theme of dangerous lions was raised to marquee status, officially encrypted to read LION-HUMAN INTERACTIONS. Among the headliners was the conservation biologist Paul Beier from Berkeley, who had just finished compiling the closest look yet at the bizarre new spike in lion attacks.

Beier had examined a century's worth of reports back to 1890, searching through the scientific journals and files of wildlife agencies, through hunting magazines and newspapers. He recounted the long quiet spell through the early decades, the first fifty years revealing all of six verified accounts of cougar attacks and three deaths. There came a minor spurt in the 1950s, with five attacks, none of them lethal, and the statistic was repeated in the 1960s.

Then came the 1970s, when the figures leapt. Sixteen people were attacked in the 1970s, three to death. (Eight of the offending cougars were subsequently hunted down and shot.) The upswing continued through the 1980s, the attacks now including the front-page tragedies of little Laura Small and Justin Mellon.

Beier's tallies confirmed the impressions that something slightly new was afoot, that as of December 31, 1990, there had been more fatal cougar attacks in the last twenty years than in the previous eighty. That the century's death toll could still be counted on only two hands mattered little. That these were people being killed in the most ungodly way, by a big cat in a nation that had supposedly vanquished its forest-dwelling demons at least a century ago, mattered much.

Patterns emerged from Beier's analysis, few of them adding measurably to what Bruce Wright had surmised forty years before. More than half the attacks and all the human deaths were suffered by the young and the weak, most of them children between the ages of five and nine. All who died were beyond sight of adults when the cougar struck. The lions who attacked them were generally youngsters, less than two years old and not long on their own. Most were described as underweight and apparently struggling to feed themselves. Two of the attackers had porcupine quills lodged in their throats.

Most of the attacks came during the spring and summer, when people tended to be outside, with a few bizarre exceptions. One lion leapt through a cabin window in rural British Columbia to attack a man who fought himself free with a butcher knife. The cat was later killed. In Lewis, Colorado, a two-year-old boy went to pet what he mistook for a big yellow dog in the garage when the lion swatted him and bit his leg. The boy recovered; the cat was later killed.

Beier found that those who most consistently survived were those who fought back or feigned courage, waving their arms, brandishing sticks, throwing stones, and shouting like banshees—channeling their inner primate from Pleistocene Africa. Those who fled or played dead were typically treated like prey and dispatched accordingly.

All the people-eating lions recorded in American history had apparently stopped at one human, after which they either were hunted down or moved on to less anomalous prey. None continued long enough to earn nicknames for their exploits. No single mountain lion ever bored its way into the psyche of a people as had the serial killers among African lions and Asian leopards.

Beier concluded with a dose of perspective for any panicky bystanders now fleeing in fear of a mountain lion Armageddon. The decades of the 1970s and '80s had on average left one person dead by mountain lion every four years—compared to twelve per year from rattlesnake bites, forty due to bee stings, three from black widow spider bites, and upward of twenty from attacks by dogs. In 1979, lightning killed eighty-six people in the United States.

What remained was a much simpler tale, of the rare but unfortunate reality that along with more people crowding into cougar country were bound to come more deadly encounters.

But perhaps there was a bit more to it than that. Beier was followed at the podium by the naturalist James Halfpenny. Halfpenny, a Ph.D. mammalogist and master tracker, had since 1985 been soliciting and gathering reports of mountain lions in the city and surroundings of Boulder, Colorado, with a growing sense of concern. The reports led Halfpenny to believe that the cougars of Boulder were growing bolder.

It seemed, from what Halfpenny's informants were reporting, that the mountain lions of the Colorado Front Range, and Boulder County in particular, were running into each other with increasing frequency and impending tragedy. Lions were reported walking city streets, sitting on rooftops, bearing litters of cubs under porches. Lions were supposedly attacking horses. In 1990 a young woman had been chased up a tree by two young cougars, and harried for half an hour before the cats lost interest and left.

Halfpenny surmised that the lions of Boulder were being drawn by a herd of pampered deer protected from hunting and growing fat on Boulder's green landscaping. The citizens' sightings led Halfpenny to believe that the cougars of Boulder were meeting people more regularly and, more ominously, growing comfortable in their presence. The lions, in Halfpenny's assessment, had grown dangerously habituated to humans.

Halfpenny laid out his hypothesis by way of Boulder's boomtown history and the time-worn pattern of plunder that followed. The settlement of Boulder in the 1850s began with a rush of precious metal miners. With the sprouting of mining camps came a spree of market hunting to feed them, followed in rapid fashion by wholesale disappearance of the elk and deer and forests, from foothills to mountain peaks. By the first decade of the 1900s, the hoofed prey and whatever mountain lions might have once subsisted on them were gone from Boulder's Front Range. Eventually the ruins came under repair. Deer and elk were reintroduced, and proliferated in what had since become a game refuge over much of Boulder County. Their native predator followed. Tall pines had grown up on the open flanks of the hills overlooking the city, lawns and hedges had sprouted across town, the whole of it amounting to good habitat for deer to feed, and therefore good places for lions to hunt.

Boulder, perched a mile high in a picturesque fold between the short-grass prairies of the Great Plains and the glacier-tipped peaks of the Colorado Rockies, by the 1980s was fast becoming a Lycra-clad mecca of world-class endurance athletes and endorphin junkies, of runners and mountain bikers, rock climbers and skiers, and their trailing legions of amateur wannabes and weekend trail hikers. This was the ultimate outdoor culture coming to share its playground with a billowing swarm of deer, and their ever-attendant lions. In such a mixing bowl there were bound to be more collisions, more cougars seeing people as moving protein, warned Halfpenny.

As had Beier, Halfpenny dutifully calculated and recited the minuscule odds of a cougar attack—which for a resident of Boulder County amounted to seven times less likely than winning the lottery. ("I'm much more afraid of cars and dogs," Halfpenny would say.) But such odds mattered little to those people demanding guarantees, or to the unlucky one in thirty-five million drawing the winning ticket.

"Will another mountain lion attack occur possibly along the Front Range?" asked Halfpenny. "The answer seems to be yes. And it's not an 'if' question, it's a 'when' question. It'll probably be pretty soon."

Leading lion scholars, for their part, scratched their heads. The habituation hypothesis remained just that. Nobody had yet rigorously tested the intuitively tempting notion of modern lions in a crowded world losing their fear of people; nor the lions' inclination to take the crucial next step, toward eyeing those ever-ubiquitous bipeds as prey. The lion's occasional appearance of boldness around humans was nothing new. There had always been certain mountain lions who just didn't seem prone to flee upon detection. The biologists Stanley Young and Edward Goldman, who in 1946 wrote the first major natural history of the American puma, noted its harmless habit of following people. They found themselves amused by the cougar's benign sense of curiosity. They told of a purring puma sleeping beneath an occupied hammock in the wilds of British Guiana; they shared Goldman's personal story of a hunting trip in the mountains of Nevada where he circled to learn a mountain lion was tracking him. "I discovered the fresh track of the animal persistently following each bend in my course."

Theodore Roosevelt—legendary for his love of killing cougars—had a hard time imagining the cat as much of a threat to humans. "It is true, as I have said, that a cougar will follow a man; but then a weasel will sometimes do the same thing. Whatever the cougar's motive, it is certain that in the immense majority of cases there is not the slightest danger of his attacking the man he follows."

Linda Sweanor and her husband Ken Logan, too, who during the 1990s had handled hundreds of the cats in their seminal study of desert lions in the San Andres Mountains of southern New Mexico, had recorded a certain disinclination of their study subjects to run when approached. Their study area lay inside the U.S. Air Force's White Sands Missile Range, a heavily guarded bombing ground where drones were occasionally blasted out of the sky by live warheads. Few cougars lived lives less frequented by human crowds than the lions of the San Andres Mountains. Yet upon approach, the San Andres lions commonly exhibited what Sweanor and Logan came to call "staying behavior." Instead of running, they simply stayed. Perhaps such lions were defending nearby cubs. Some might have been imagining themselves hidden. Certain lions would stay or flee, depending on the day. By no means did staying herald an imminent attack. "Thus, staying behavior does not necessarily indicate a puma has become 'habituated' or lost fear of humans," concluded Sweanor and Logan. No matter. It was the cougar caught staying, the cougar found treed in town or hiding under porches, who so typically took the bullets.

Mat Alldredge, the biologist who would lead Colorado's first Front Range lion study, launched in the wake of Boulder's ramped up fears, spied repeatedly on trailside lions that by all rights should have had a field day bagging hapless hikers. "I'd have cats bedded right off common hiking trails, just hunkering down and pretending people can't see them," said Alldredge. "If lions were becoming habituated toward people, or if lions did put people into their search image for prey, we'd have a lot more serious encounters."

One of the most prominent ambassadors of the urban lion—and unwitting assassin of the habituation hypothesis—was a particular female lion living on the edge of Prescott, Arizona, a city of about forty thousand people one hundred miles north of Phoenix. In 2006, wildlife managers from the Arizona Game and Fish Department had fitted a radio collar to a lion they had trapped on the edge of town. Upon release from her captors, the Prescott lion settled back into the territory in which she had been trapped, which included the backyard where she had been hunting the local house cat. She was otherwise found to be feeding large on the deer and javelina and other local wildlife that had come to commandeer the friendly streets of Prescott by night. She hunted and bedded and hid at the feet of so many of Prescott's pedestrians, who never had a clue. She became the silent star of an ongoing documentary, her followers tracking the blips of her radio signal day after day, night after night, as she mingled invisibly among the people of Prescott. She was followed for the last three of what were estimated to be the eleven years of her life—an unheard-of longevity for a wild lion, attributed in part to the savvy choice of Prescott as her all-night supermarket.

The show eventually ended one day in July 2009, when the Prescott lion's followers found her stumbling to the ground as they approached. She would not survive her injuries—it seemed she had been hit by a car—but her life would serve to reconfigure the assumptions behind Arizona's official problem-lion protocol. No longer did the mere appearance of an urban cat automatically register a death warrant from Arizona authorities.

"She was really a spectacular animal," said Ron Thompson, Arizona's chief carnivore biologist and leading fan of the Prescott lion. "She was the crack in the door, through our myopic view of how we perceive mountain lions. They don't see us as natural prey. They're named Puma concolor—cat of a single color—for a good reason. You just cannot see them. We're at the interface with them far more than we realize."

Yet for all the Prescott lions treading so discreetly through backyard America, it was the aberrant aggressor here and there who would dominate the public discourse. Through the 1990s, the record of lion attacks continued to rise, the casualties peaking at nearly one human death per year. And along with the numbers came new heights of notoriety.

Soon into the new millennium appeared several mainstream books on the subject of lion attacks, their covers adorned with stalking cougars and bared fangs, their themes of danger salted with graphic carnage. But no book would so rivet the country's fears as the one attack that took place on January 8, 2004, in a mountain park outside Los Angeles.

It was there in the Whiting Ranch Wilderness Park that Anne Hjelle, a lithe, thirty-year-old fitness instructor, former marine, and on this day a free-wheeling mountain biker, was plummeting down the trail when something reddish flashed over her shoulder and struck her to the ground. "Jesus, help me," cried Hjelle, the back of her neck gripped in the jaws of a mountain lion.

Hjelle punched and flailed, the lion's fangs stabbing for vertebrae and vital arteries. With bloodied hands, Hjelle pried the lion off her neck; he reattached himself to her face. Hjelle felt no pain, only the horrific premonitions of her own death, or a life with no face.

Her cycling companion, Debi Nicholls, jumped from her bike and came running to find Hjelle being dragged down a ravine. Nicholls threw her bike at the cat, screaming all the while, and grabbed tight to one of Hjelle's legs.

The lion continued dragging Hjelle by her face, Nicholls in tow. "I remember the feeling," Hjelle later recounted, "just the strength of him. Ten guys wouldn't be any match for it."

Other riders came running to Nicholls's screaming, and started pelting the lion with rocks. Said one later, "It took three rocks the size of almost soccer balls to get this thing to move, and we hit it square with those rocks."

The lion had by now shifted his grip back to Hjelle's neck, squeezing her windpipe, suffocating his prey. Hjelle blacked out. Another rock hit the cat square in the face, and finally he let go and bounded into the brush. Hjelle sat up, the flesh of her face hanging, blinded in the cascade of her own blood.

She was airlifted out of the hills to a trauma center where the doctors reattached her face and mended her shredded neck with two hundred stitches and staples. Five years later, plastic surgeons would still be repairing the lion's damage. In the meantime, though the gracious Hjelle would never utter a bad word against her attacker, her savage disfigurement by lion rang alarms across the country, from front pages to the nightly news to national radio—and not just on account of her own ordeal.

The day of the attack, Hjelle had actually been luckier than one other. Just seconds before meeting her attacker, she had passed an abandoned bicycle, a bicycle that had belonged to another young cyclist, named Mark Reynolds, who would be found to have had his heart, lung, and liver eaten by the same lion. That night, within fifty yards of where Reynolds's half-buried body was found, an Orange County deputy wielding a flashlight and a shotgun killed a three- to four-year-old male lion, upward of 120 pounds and by all appearances healthy.

The double attack was without precedent, the details baffling. The attacker was neither a starving orphan nor a crippled geriatric, and his targets were not defenseless children, but vigorous, athletic adults. Speculation ruled. Apparently Reynolds had stopped to fix a chain on his bicycle, and in the crouched position more fitting the cougar's quadruped prey, he was ambushed. Perhaps the lion was still in a hair-trigger state of predation when, by a supreme case of bad timing, Hjelle came bouncing by. Or perhaps the lion was guarding his kill. Then again, maybe he'd not killed Reynolds after all.

The autopsy would reveal no damage to Reynolds's neck, no wounds or obvious indications of death by lion. Some suggested that Reynolds had died from a heart attack rather than a lion attack. Was the lion merely preparing to scavenge Reynolds's already dead body when another creature came threatening to steal his prize, a creature in the unfortunate form of Anne Hjelle? Reynolds's heart, the evidence that might have answered that speculation, had unfortunately been eaten.

Reynolds's parents later sued Orange County for not warning their son of such danger in the park, a suit they would drop after Reynolds's cycling friends prevailed upon them. Those living and playing among the mountains had come to accept the risks, which had now come to include the rare but tragic possibility of attack by mountain lion.

Between the child-snatching cougars of Big Bend, the dramatized lion's den of Boulder, and now the cyclist slayer of Orange County, the American mountain lion's fleeting age of innocence had passed. The blowup over Hjelle's and Reynolds's attacks would otherwise obscure less sensational statistics that by the mid-2000s marked a downward trend in lion aggressions against people. The Prescott lion and her fellow legions of good-neighbor exemplars were to remain back-page filler of modern media and victims of preemptive executions. The first decade of the twenty-first century had dramatically inverted the lion's tagline from conservation triumph to cautionary tale.

So it was that the Chicago lion had become a martyr by way of mistaken identity. He was a 125-pound feline that roughly fit the mold of the creature that had buried its fangs in the nascent psyche of humanity. He was the saber-tooth who had terrorized the cave people of ancient Africa. He was the Tsavo lions, the Rudraprayag leopard, the California cougar that had killed Mark Reynolds and left Anne Hjelle all but dead. He was very much like the Twin Cities lion now following his ill-fated path.

SIX Northbound

Do not go where the path may lead, go instead where there is no path and leave a trail.

—RALPH WALDO EMERSON

THE FRONT-PAGE IMAGE of the Chicago cat leaking blood upon the slab was still fresh in mind and looming larger with every eastward step as the Twin Cities lion made his way across Wisconsin. On December 27, barely four days after hamming for the camera on the edge of Jason Weber's cornfield in Downsville, the lion was spotted again, another nineteen miles east, in farm country outside Eau Claire. Three weeks later, at 3:20 A.M. on January 18, he was caught stepping in front of another trail camera, leaving a stunning broadside view of a mountain lion padding through the evening snow, his golden coat faintly mottled with the fading spots of a grown kitten coming into adulthood. Of more urgent note for those following was his location. This sighting was forty-four miles southeast of the last. The lion was by all appearances headed for the Lake Michigan megalopolis and the firing squads.

The lion's bearing, in the unlikelihood he should survive the inner-city SWAT teams or eight-lane beltways of Milwaukee or Chicago, would eventually have him rounding the southern bend of Lake Michigan and into agro-industrial moonscapes of corn, soy, and pig farms, and beyond to the next urban deadends of Toledo and Cleveland. There was nothing promising and everything foreboding about the southeastern route he seemed so bent on tracking.

At which point, as if smelling the dangers ahead, the cat turned away. Two days later, yet another trail cam captured his image. To his champions' relief, the latest picture pegged him twelve miles north of the last.

The turn would amount to no minor detour. Little more than a week later, he was seen crossing a road and tracked in rural Price County, another sixty miles north. Wydeven forwarded the news: "This is the first time we have seen a major shift in direction of movement." Back east, Spatz and fellow followers exhaled. Their lion was pointed at what seemed the least suicidal of his remaining options. After nearly seven hundred eastbound miles, he had suddenly changed course. He was heading toward the ever-green forests and glacier-carved lakes of Wisconsin's Northwoods.

The lion that Wydeven had been remotely chasing from his office in the northern reaches of the state was now coming to him. He drove the half hour to the Price County sighting, eager again to get a houndsman working the trail and a collar on the cat. But the tracks were two days old. And the search was now entering upon the territory of a wolf pack with a reputation for killing dogs who trespassed. The houndsman backed out. Wydeven went home.

The lion apparently followed. On the morning of February 15, 2010, Wydeven answered a call from Larry Baldus, a friend who lived just south of the village of Cable, seventeen miles from Wydeven's home. Baldus had been out for his morning walk with his chocolate lab, Bubba, when the two came upon a line of giant tracks beside the road. Baldus in his daily constitutionals had grown accustomed to crossing paths with the resident wolves who occasionally trotted down the country roads of Cable. These new tracks broke the mold. The imprints were rounder, the toes skewed to one side, the typical canid claw marks missing. *My god, that has to be one hell of a huge wolf,* thought Baldus. *Or a cougar.*

Cable was a town conceived by trappers during the fur rush of the 1600s, when beavers of the northern waterways were liquidated to supply the headwear of European royalty. The town evolved through the centuries in fits and starts: a boomtown of railroad workers and lumberjacks, with their boardinghouses and saloons; a way station for sport fishermen and tourists; a backwoods mecca of outdoor enthusiasts and endurance athletes. And Cable, like every little outpost of the Northwoods, had its own cougar lore, rife with sightings of big cats lurking here and there and loping across roads. Local rumor held that there were hundreds, maybe thousands.

Larry Baldus was not among the believers. "The way people were reporting them, it was like cougars were being thrown out of a bus." But there was no denying the tracks at his feet. Baldus stared some more. He hesitated to call in the experts, for fear of embarrassing himself over a stray dog. Instead, he called his brother-in-law, a hunting guide in cougar country of Wyoming. Sounds like a cougar, replied his brother-in-law. Baldus went back and stared some more before finally phoning his friend Wydeven. Baldus protected a couple of the tracks with an overturned bucket. Wydeven hurried over, lifted the bucket, and expertly declared, "Wow!"

The two backtracked the lion through twenty inches of snow, through a neighboring yard and across the highway, down a snowmobile track leading to the end of a driveway. The lion was availing himself of packed trails and ready shelters. His tracks emerged from beneath a school bus parked in the woods, where he'd bedded down out of the arctic winds.

He'd then gone for food, wandering through a winter deer yard in a dense grove of evergreens, his tracks disappearing amid a stampede of hoof-prints. Before losing his trail, Wydeven gathered a scat.

Rumor of the Cable cougar all but beat the trackers home. Baldus walked into the Sawmill Saloon for a beer, to the greeting, "Hey, Larry, I heard you saw a cougar." A neighbor later confronted Baldus about not having sounded the alarm.

"Was that really a cougar?"

"Yes, it was a cougar," answered Baldus.

"You endangered me."

"What?"

"It could've attacked me."

Wydeven, in the meantime, sent the scat off to Missoula for testing, and posted his latest field notes to the network. He assumed the lion had headed on his way to parts unknown, where, with luck, he'd hear from him again.

Two weeks later, at 8:30 A.M., while Wydeven was away, his wife, Sarah Boles, took the call. It was Larry Baldus, announcing in a singsong voice: "He's BAA-ack."

Baldus and Bubba had again come upon those enormous cat prints following the shoulder of the road. Judging from their freshness, they'd been left that morning.

Boles, a certified tracker herself, joined Baldus on the lion's new trail, which all but retraced his old trail, wending through alder thickets along the Namakagon River and up the banks under canopy of spruce and fir, where the deer had been bedding.

The date was Saturday, February 27, 2010—"Birkie Saturday" to the locals, otherwise distinguished in the universe of snow sports as the thirty-seventh running of the American Birkebeiner. At that moment, just two miles east of the lion's tracks, the woods were a-clamor with the clanging of cowbells and the cheers of bundled spectators rooting onward some eight thousand skiers from around the world gliding and poling their way forty miles through the forest in the largest ski race of North America. The skiers' starting line lay within five hundred feet of the same Namakagon River whose banks Boles and Baldus were now searching. From the westernmost jog in the racecourse angled the clear-cut swath of a power line running straight as a city boulevard to within six hundred meters of where Boles and Baldus were now standing. With such obvious corridors for a lion commuting through Cable, it took little to imagine the precious image of a mountain lion sashaying across the trail just moments in advance of an oncoming stampede of skiers rounding the bend.

More to Wydeven's curiosity, this was new behavioral territory for the lion. It seemed that, for the first time in his recorded journey, he had doubled back. Perhaps he'd been harried round in a big loop by the local wolf pack. Or perhaps he'd grown hungry down the trail and remembered the deer yard back in Baldus's neighborhood. The one certainty arising from the lion's latest hitch was that of a new uncertainty. After eleven weeks of a steady eastward bearing, the lion had begun throwing his followers the curve.

He'd also been good about checking in; that, too, was about to change. Since his emergence in Champlin in the first week of December, the lion had yet to go more than fifteen days without tripping a camera or leaving fresh sign of himself. So it was that after apparently coming home to roost in the deer yards of Cable, the lion disappeared as if never to be seen again.

On the Perception of Threat

As the lion vanished into the stillness of the Wisconsin Northcountry, the gunfire had just finished echoing from his home port nearly eight hundred miles behind. Midway through the second week of February, the 2010 hunting season in South Dakota's Black Hills ended with the killing of the fortieth mountain lion, a four-year-old female weighing ninety-six pounds. Snow in the Hills had made for good tracking, and the hunters had reached their limit six weeks ahead of schedule, averaging one dead cougar a day. Landowners on the plains would later take advantage of their endless season, bagging three more cats, one of them a prospecting young male already three hundred miles into the eastern prairie, nearing Iowa. Before the year was out, another twenty-three Black Hills lions would be killed by agency gunmen and private citizens on complaints of pet-snatching, loitering near town, or otherwise inciting fear. Fifteen more were hit on the roads. Three were caught and killed in traps set for other animals. Five were killed by other lions, or were found starving to death. All counted, ninety-four mountain lions from the Black Hills—nearly half of all the lions estimated to be living there—were recorded dead in 2010.

For some, that number was not high enough. By August 2010, the state's game biologists were back, recommending that an extra five lions be added to the kill quota for the upcoming hunt. Soon thereafter, the game commission overseeing them overstepped the biologists' recommendations by another five female lions. The 2011 hunt was set at fifty lions.

A pattern had taken shape, continuing the trend toward more lions bagged and less science considered in their killing. Similar politics had intervened in advance of the 2010 hunt. Back then, wildlife professor Jon Jenks from South Dakota State University and biologists from the game agency started by suggesting that another five females be added to the year's kill quota, on their contention that the population could sustain the loss without harm. In the meantime, Black Hills hunters had started grumbling about lions taking too many of their deer and elk. They came armed with wild declarations of some twelve hundred of the big cats swarming over the Black Hills (amounting to five or six times the biologists' best guesses). More than five hundred of the hunters had signed a petition requesting that the game commission allow them to kill yet more lions. The commission obliged.

Wildlife commissioner Tim Kessler, a local businessman who also operated a pheasant-hunting farm, had emerged as chief champion of the hunters' cause. Kessler had been a consistent voice for fewer lions since the lead-up to the first hunt in 2005, citing danger as a chief concern. "Never before in the history of this state has the commission had to deal with an animal that can kill people."

Kessler had commended the state's game biologists for "being good, conservative conservationists. But you maybe want to be more aggressive on this one." In 2009 he again motioned to override the biologists' recommendations, to allow an extra five females to be killed in the hunt. The vote carried.

Pressure mounted as well from the state legislature, to see the lions not only throttled at their source, but chased down everywhere else they might flee beyond the Black Hills. The prairie campaign had begun in early 2008, when state representative Betty Olson presented a bill to have any lion found outside the Black Hills of South Dakota declared a predator, to be legally shot by anyone possessing either a fifteen-dollar license or a fear that the lion might harm them or their property, which in practical application sanctioned the killing of lions by just about anyone, anytime, for any reason. The mountain lion, under Olson's bill, would be lumped in with prairie dogs, coyotes, skunks, crows, porcupines, and jackrabbits, among others in the state's official class of undesirable varmints, to be shot on sight. It was the beginning of an anti-lion crusade that Olson would carry forth with unflagging dedication.

Olson owned a ranch on the plains far north of the Black Hills, near the dusty little one-stop of Prairie City, which lay a few miles outside Slim Buttes, where at least two of the Hills' dispersing lions had made pit stops over recent years. One was the young male M-32, wearing Dan Thompson's radio collar, who came through in 2006 on his way to Canada. Another wanderer was later struck and killed there on the highway. Olson believed these to be vanguards of a sinister plague. Mountain lions were devouring their deer and their antelope. Mountain lions were spooking and mauling their cattle and horses. Olson at every opportunity told the story of unseen mountain lions eyeing her and her grandchildren.

"Attacks on humans and domestic livestock are increasing at alarming rates as they run out of food resources," Olson told her fellow representatives at a hearing in the House.

Like Kessler and his commission, Olson and her ranching constituents were at distant odds from biologists about the fundamental facts of mountain lions in South Dakota. Biologists knew of no lion populations within a hundred miles of Olson's ranch. They had yet to confirm a single head of livestock attacked by a mountain lion in all of Harding County, where Olson lived. Biologists had yet to confirm a single attack on a human in South Dakota's history.

Yet there was imminent danger, insisted Olson, pushing for easier killing of lions. Never mind that state policy had already made it as easy as pulling a trigger; Tony Leif, the director of the game agency's wildlife division, had admitted as much: "We have a number of instances where a landowner has elected to kill a mountain lion because it was on their property in close proximity to their livestock or close proximity to their home or buildings. And in no case have we ever prosecuted any of those landowners for doing that."

Olson nonetheless wanted the policy stamped into law. "They are very large, very dangerous predators, and it is only a matter of time before somebody is eaten in South Dakota."

Olson's bill was voted down in 2008. In 2009 she was back, with a new bill bolstered with yet another perk for lion killers. She again wanted it legal for any landowner fearing any prairie lion to shoot it—and to keep the pelt, too.

"I've only seen one, and I didn't have a rifle with me when I saw it," Olson explained. "I would have shot it then and I would have lost the pelt."

She was not nearly alone in her contempt for the lion:

"Now, we have groups of people whose sole objective is to protect the rights of mountain lions," said state representative Nick Moser. "I assure you I'm not one of those people. I would be hard pressed to find a single good reason why we would want any mountain lions roaming the state of South Dakota."

State representative Charles Hoffman: "If you see a mountain lion, according to federal fish and wildlife, that mountain lion is hungry. It's no different than when you see a skunk. Over ninety percent of skunks have rabies. They're a threat to you and your families. Take care of it. Take action."

Nor was the lion entirely devoid of defenders:

"The mountain lion has become this yearly bogeyman that comes up, and for some reason it's perceived as this huge threat," said state representative Brian Dreyer. "Betty Olson, in talking to her, she said, 'You know, Brian, you live in Rapid City and you have kids there. It is a threat. You should look it up on Google.' So I did. Three hundred eighty-two thousand hits for mountain lion attacks. Five hundred sixty-three thousand hits for Bigfoot attacks. Two hundred seventy-four thousand for bogeyman attacks. New York City: Sixteen hundred people per year bitten by other humans. Two people per year die from vending machine accidents. I haven't seen anybody get killed by a mountain lion and I've got them living in my backyard."

State representative Chuck Turbiville: "Make no mistake about it, the intent of this bill, the intent of the sponsors, is to eradicate the mountain lion from the face of this state. The part of this bill that really bothers me is the perceived threat or imminent threat. For those people who absolutely want to rid this area of mountain lions, any time they see one can be a perceived threat. A mountain lion crossing the highway fifteen miles from your property can be a threat because it can end up in your farmyard and eat Sparky, or mountain lion cubs that you see along a creek bed can grow up and destroy livestock."

Representative Ed Iron Cloud: "It is really a sad day when an animal is perceived as a threat and shot on sight."

When the votes were cast, Olson failed to get her pelt, but gained the more lethal dagger of her bill in writing. In March 2009, South Dakota governor Mike Rounds signed into law the killing of prairie lions on the perception of threat.

With the conclusion of the 2010 Black Hills mountain lion hunt, the results were tallied, and the ongoing concerns of the lions' advocates rekindled. There'd been twenty-four female lions killed in the hunt. That was too many, said veterinarian Sharon Seneczko, speaking on behalf of her Black Hills Mountain Lion Foundation and herself.

Those killings, by Seneczko's estimation, had left at least thirty kittens and awkward teens orphaned and likely to die by slow starvation, if not before wandering into trouble among the backyards and city streets.

"We saw this play out across the street from where I live," said Seneczko, after a mother lion had been shot nearby. "The kittens were playing on the lawn. Some turkeys walked right by them. They didn't have the slightest idea what to do. I just cringe. I'm not normally afraid of mountain lions, but for the first six to eight months after the hunting season, I'm paranoid. I'm watching my dogs, because we have hungry youngsters out there and they're not doing well."

Seneczko had noticed lions regularly crossing through her property, more readily since the hunters had taken to the Hills. She had a neighbor who'd had to hire a Great Pyrenees dog to guard her goats. Another neighbor had lost a corgi puppy off her porch to a cougar—a cougar, it turned out, who had lost part of a foot in the trap of a state wildlife agent. From where Seneczko stood, all that shooting certainly wasn't making matters safer for anybody or any deer in the Hills.

Seneczko was arguing from more than anecdote. She had the weight of a mounting body of science behind her. Maurice Hornocker and a dozen fellow blue-chip lion experts had summed it up in no uncertain terms in their seminal *Cougar Management Guidelines*. Neither the health of humans nor herds of deer and cattle were being served by selling more licenses to shoot mountain lions.

There was also the glaring paradox of California. Thirty-nine years had passed since its citizens outlawed sport hunting of cougars in their state.

California had more people and more unhunted cougars than any state in the country, yet it ranked near the bottom in numbers of cougar attacks per capita. (While Vancouver Island, which hammered its lions, retained its dubious ranking as cougar attack capital of North America.) California also harbored several times more cattle and sheep than any western state outside Texas, yet California farmers were losing fewer livestock to lions than their counterparts in about half the states that hunted them.

In the decade leading up to Mark Reynolds's death and Anne Hjelle's attack on that singular day of cougar infamy, more than thirty thousand mountain lions had been killed by sport hunters in the United States. Yet the trickle of attacks kept trickling. The South Dakota party line that mountain lions needed killing for the common good—indeed, for their own good—was an assumption being sold by wildlife managers across the lions' North American range. It seemed intuitive—kill more lions, make life safer for humanity and its chosen animals—until serious scientists tested the assumption.

Juvenile Delinquents
After two heavily publicized lion attacks on children in northeastern Washington in the 1990s, the state's game agency reacted with a vengeance, ramping up the hunt. An ecologist at Washington State University named Robert Wielgus stood ready to gauge the results. Wielgus and his students took to examining sport hunts across the state of Washington and over its northeastern borders with Idaho and British Columbia. By the spring of 2010, he and his team had begun publishing their findings, and with them laying siege to the cherished rationales of most every sanctioned lion hunt in America.

Where the state imagined its hunters imparting control, Wielgus and company found chaos: The more cougars were shot, the more livestock were attacked, the more pets were lost, the more complaints were lodged. The more cougars were shot, the louder the demands for shooting more cougars.

The hunters were shooting holes in an otherwise stable community of lions, the holes in turn filling with more reckless youths, in particular young toms drifting in from afar. As Wielgus liked to say, "Every time you kill a dominant male, three juvenile delinquents show up for the funeral. With the grown-ups gone, the young hooligans run wild. You don't get to be an old cougar by doing stupid stuff like hanging out in backyards and eating cats."

"Remedial hunting," concluded Wielgus, "was actually the problem."

The findings of Wielgus and crew shone a hard, unflattering light on South Dakota's cougar-killing rationale. An unarmed John Kanta gamely defended his department: "We're able to say the hunting season is ... reducing the number of problem lions," said Kanta, citing no evidence. South Dakota governor Mike Rounds seconded Kanta's guess as fact, while blithely dismissing Wielgus's science. In a letter responding to Seneczko's complaints, Rounds answered, "I do not agree that sport hunting disrupts important dynamics within the lion population."

Oddly enough, more damning evidence that it did was soon to come directly out of the Black Hills, in a study funded in part by the state's own Game, Fish and Parks Department. A young scientist from South Dakota University was just then finishing his dissertation, a good part of it focused on the effect of the Black Hills' new sport hunt on complaints and problem lions. Brian Jansen, who began following collared cats around the Hills in the years after the first hunt of 2005, had found young lions disproportionately involved in pet snatchings and town appearances. And lots of roaming young lions, as Wielgus and students had repeatedly shown, were what game managers got in Washington when they attacked their lions as hard as the South Dakota hunters were attacking theirs.

"The number of mountain lions lethally removed by state personnel continued to increase in years of sport-hunting, despite apparent numerical stability in the mountain lion population," wrote Jansen in his dissertation.

In light of the mounting evidence that South Dakota was shooting both its cougars and its own foot with the same bullet, Seneczko graciously defended her opponent John Kanta as a messenger caught in the crossfire. "He wants to keep his job," she said. "He has a family to feed. He's under tremendous pressure not only from his own department, but from ranchers and hunters and people like me."

Kanta had stood repeatedly before the wildlife commission to hear his department's recommendations shot down by political appointees lacking biological training. Said Seneczko, "Why are we spending so much money on research if the commission's going to ignore its own biologists? They threw John under the bus."

Seneczko was sporting bruises of her own. In her years of speaking up at town meetings and lion hearings, she'd been ridiculed and patronized. The petite Seneczko had been surrounded by lion-hating hunters, bullied by big men poking fingers in her face. One threatened a reporter for wanting to speak with her. Seneczko thereafter resolved to bring a bodyguard. "It was like an ugly mob," she said. "These are people on a mission. There's a good many here who want lions gone. There's Betty Olson, testifying that children are going to be at risk, that you charge too much for lion tags, that you should be handing them out on the streets."

As time went on, Seneczko and the lions' allies grew weary of their beatings in the political ring. Those fighting the escalations sought their little victories where they could find them. Tom Huhnerkoch, a semiretired veterinarian and outspoken lion ally from the Black Hills town of Lead, had fought to have one of his chief adversaries, Tim Kessler, removed from the wildlife commission. South Dakota law limited a citizen's service on the commission to eight years; Kessler had served seventeen. Huhnerkoch threatened suit; Kessler surrendered and quit.

The battle went to Huhnerkoch, though the war was going to the lions' killers. The political powers indeed wanted the big cats gone. Back in 2008, Huhnerkoch had put up his own money to post a billboard in Rapid City, a mountain lion's giant face announcing a lecture in Rapid City hosted by Seneczko and the Black Hills Mountain Lion Foundation. The lecturers were two young researchers from Rob Wielgus's lab in Washington State, bringing some of the first news of their scientific findings on the waste and futility of hunting lions for human safety. In light of that new information, the South Dakota wildlife commission went on to raise the Black Hills' kill quota in each of the next two hunting seasons.

Three months after Adrian Wydeven recorded the last tracks of the Cable lion, another trail camera went off one hundred seventy-nine miles away, in

the northeast corner of Wisconsin, portraying a familiar figure. At 10:40
P.M. on May 20, in the backyard of a country home outside the village of
Lena, the camera captured the hind view of a cougar strolling through the
dark toward a toddler's two-story jungle gym. A spot beneath the base of the
cat's tail suggested the genital patch of a male.

Wydeven could not help but suspect. The new cat's relative proximity to
the lion of Cable in space and time suggested that the two were one and the
same. It seemed unlikely that yet another cougar could so suddenly have
entered Wisconsin and crossed the state unseen—without once tripping
either the beam of a trail camera or a headlight, or leaving a set of snow
tracks across somebody's path—as the Cable cat had done a dozen times
since showing up in the Twin Cities some five months earlier. It seemed
Wydeven's winter visitor from Cable was back on the radar, his bearing
again eastbound.

The lion was now thirty miles north of the city of Green Bay, back in the
checkerboard fields and woods of farm country, and apparently striking out
for the shores of Lake Michigan. He continued northeast, covering another
twenty-five miles over the next six days, and after making an easy swim over
the meandering Menominee River, he walked into a farmer's woods, where
he tripped another shutter. The picture came out blurry, the flash glaring,
the head of the animal missing beyond the left edge of the frame. But with
the rest of him sprawled across three-quarters of the screen, there was no
mistaking the obvious life-form—the massive paws and elevated haunches
and tail like a furred python. Experts confirmed the identity, and the press
release followed. He was the first mountain lion ever photographed in
Menominee County. The lion had just entered the Upper Peninsula of
Michigan, where no lions had been known to live and breed since 1906.

Forces of Evil

The former cougar of Michigan had fallen in the usual way, its demise
following soon upon the arrival of white settlers with their saws and guns,
hounds and bounties. But unlike the comeback cougar of the Rockies,
Michigan's cougar had yet to return, the state only rarely serving as temporary

quarters for loose pets and lone strays passing through. That, at least, was the official position of the Michigan Department of Natural Resources.

A counterculture position on the Michigan cougar professed undying faith in the survival of the great ghost cat. The cougar was still roaming Michigan by the score, as seen by many, in fields and woods and backyards, through headlights and flashlights in myriad fleeting glimpses.

The Michigan cougar rift made for the liveliest drama. Beginning in 2001, an organization calling itself the Michigan Wildlife Conservancy and, more specifically, its executive director, Dennis Fijalkowski, and director of wildlife programs, Pat Rusz, had made it their mission to convince all nonbelievers that Michigan's mountain lion had never actually been extinguished—that it had held on in small but reproducing numbers, amounting to some twenty to one hundred cougars still inhabiting Michigan. Fijalkowski and Rusz, both of whom held doctorates in wildlife science, over the years had gathered sightings and secondhand accounts from across the state, ferreting reports of tracks, bagging samples of scat, and promoting as their clincher homemade video of two live cougars—little of which, to their eternal ire, passed muster with either state authorities or seasoned cougar biologists.

"We're in the majority," grumbled Rusz. "Stop in any roadside coffee shop or bar, and everybody has seen them. When you dig deep, what you find, even at the top level, is this message of 'Well, we don't have many breeding, if at all.' How this gets translated, from media to the people, is they're all coming from South Dakota. I don't think any of them really believe that. But it's a hell of a narrative. It gets everybody off their back. It translates to, 'We don't have to do anything. These are alien cats coming in and right back out.'"

"It's about money, ego, power—all the forces of evil," said Fijalkowski.

Rusz and Fijalkowski cheer-led their fellow believers, delivering lectures far and wide on Michigan's unofficial population of mountain lions, while charging the authorities with willful neglect. "These people cannot be trusted," said Fijalkowski. "Somebody at the levels above the Wildlife Division is the architect of a campaign of deceit to fool the public here."

Among the Conservancy's smoking guns was a 1997 roadside photo from Alcona County depicting a close-up of a cougar reposing in a bed of ferns—at which DNR authorities had done a double take. The Alcona cougar had apparently just lain there while a motorist sidled up to take its picture? Beyond the subject's suspect demeanor, there was something not quite right with its anatomy—the way one of the cat's front legs so abruptly disappeared beneath the vegetation, as if edited by a straightedge and X-acto knife; the very gaze of the creature, the creepy slotted stare of its eyes, suggesting to some the work of an amateur taxidermist. All agreed it was a cougar; not all agreed it wasn't stuffed.

Among the few shards of hard evidence came a skull found in 2001 by woodcutters in the Upper Peninsula's Chippewa County. The skull was indeed that of a cougar. But how it had gotten there was to become the bone of contention. After a bit of poking around, it turned out the skull had been found lying three hundred yards from the shop of a taxidermist. When questioned, he readily confided it had once belonged to somebody's pet cougar, an eleven-year-old declawed cat named Sasha. The taxidermist had skinned the cat and thrown its skull in a heap out the back door, where some surmised a dog then dragged it away. The DNR's official record of wild cougars in Michigan remained at zero.

In 2006 the indefatigable Rusz coauthored a paper with Bradley Swanson from the conservation genetics laboratory at Central Michigan University, a paper that appeared in the peer-reviewed journal *American Midland Naturalist*, proclaiming scientific proof of cougars living in Michigan. Rusz and a small team had collected some three hundred samples of scat from a dozen sites across Michigan and had the DNA extracted to identify their sources. Ten came back tagged as cougar. Judging from the distance between the samples, Rusz and Swanson estimated that at least eight cougars were roaming Michigan over the three-year span of their surveys.

Within a year came a rebuttal in the same journal, from three scientists, one of them Michael Schwartz, molecular geneticist at the U.S. Forest Service's national lab in Missoula, Montana. Schwartz and company fairly well savaged Swanson and Rusz's field methods and genetic analyses, throwing out all but one cougar sample as invalid. They rated Rusz's extrapolations of at least eight Michigan cougars as "pure speculation." Why, they wondered in print, over the last century had not one cougar in Michigan been killed by train, truck, or automobile; or just once been captured in a land all but mined by fur trappers; or shot or treed in a countryside swarming with hunters and hounds; or tracked in any one of the state's annual winter wildlife surveys canvassing thousands of miles of Michigan wildland?

"Thus, all that we would feel comfortable in stating, is that the number of cougars documented in the scientific literature in Michigan since the early 1900s is now one," they concluded, adding a dash more salt for the wound. "Whether that sample represents a released pet, a dispersing individual or a planted sample is not something that we can assess."

But the most entertaining flap over the Michigan cougar came in July 2004, when the Michigan Wildlife Conservancy dropped its bombshell to end the war. It released a professionally produced video, introduced by Fijalkowski and featuring "unmistakeable" footage, captured by a landowner in Monroe County of southern Michigan. The landowner, Carol Stokes, had filmed a pair of felines walking along the wooded edge of her cornfield about one hundred yards away. Anticipating the skeptics and naysayers, Fijalkowski had hired two experts to verify the video and reconstruct the scene. A video producer cut and pasted figures of deer and people for comparison, calculating the cats at five to six feet long. A retired forensics cop with the Michigan State Police swore to the authenticity of the video. Neither, unfortunately, had spent much time watching live mountain lions walk.

Skeptics asked five biologists and two zookeepers with more than a century of cougar experience among them to watch the video. Each immediately saw two house cats. Each saw the dainty little steps, the hunched backs, the wispy tails raised like pennants—all mannerisms and morphologies common to house cats and antithetical to mountain lions. None had ever seen or known of a mountain lion walking with such a vertical tail. None was buying the video wizardry that had somehow figured the cats stretching as long as a six-foot man was tall.

But a funny thing emerged from the rubble of the Conservancy's discredited claims. Soon after the scientific dustup over Swanson and Rusz's scat study, the Michigan DNR sent four staff biologists to New Mexico for field training under the mountain lion guru Harley Shaw. They returned as a team of first responders, Michigan's new unofficial Cougar Team, to be ready, just in case, for that rare transient from the edge of the Rockies to come walking their way. It was the Cougar Team that in June 2010 examined the photo of the Twin-Cities-via-Wisconsin lion, fresh over the Michigan line, and pronounced him the state's first authentic lion photographed in a century.

The lion was now heading into a country of farm and forest, rich with deer and scarce of roads. He was travelling east through the peninsula, bound north and south by the Great Lakes Superior and Huron. Straight ahead, flowing between the twin cities of Sault Ste. Marie, Canada, and Sault Ste. Marie, USA, was the St. Marys River.

Sault is Old French for "rapids." Here the St. Marys River dropped twenty-one feet, the water rushing and tumbling in violent cataracts that had the first daring Indians and French explorers portaging their canoes. That treacherous stretch of water would entail the eventual construction in 1855 of the Soo Locks, to sidestep the rapids. The locks would tame the wild St. Marys into the busiest shipping canal in the world, where tourists gathered to the daily parades of superfreighters stretching a thousand feet long.

Either the twin cities of Sault Ste. Marie or the Soo Locks was a lion accident waiting to happen. But there was a natural way around the rapids and across the river, and a certain parade of wildlife had over time figured it out. Twenty miles southeast of the Soo Locks, the river braided itself around a cluster of islands, all of them partially forested, some of the crossings measuring no more than half a mile. Biologists flying over the winter archipelago had recorded the tracks of a host of big mammals not uncommonly fording the gaps. Whitetail deer, coyotes, and red foxes had been using the islands as international stepping stones. Over the years, eyewitnesses had seen all the great northern mammals (moose, elk, deer, bear, and wolf) commuting here between countries. It was here also that some half a century earlier, the coyote, the archetypal song dog of the western plains and prairies, was suspected of first helping himself into the forests of the East, on his way toward famously colonizing every state in the Lower 48. And soon it appeared that at least one lion was attempting the same thing.

That the lion could and would negotiate great waters had been hinted by his trips across the rivers Missouri, Mississippi, and St. Croix. History suggested he was not particularly unusual in this respect. Young and Goldman, in their 1946 overview of cougar natural history, had found records of swimming cougars far and wide.

"A steamboat descending the Columbia River met with one swimming across where the river was at least a mile and a half wide, and without difficulty the men succeeded in capturing it, by means of a noose thrown over it." In 1930 a biologist intercepted a puma swimming midstream across a mile's width of the Orinoco River of Brazil, at which point the puma "became confused and tried to climb aboard."

Cougars have since been discovered island hopping in Lago Guri of Venezuela, a lake the size of Connecticut, and off the coast of British Columbia's Vancouver Island. A young female mountain lion wearing a radio collar went from the South Rim to the North Rim of the Grand Canyon in eight hours, swimming the Colorado River en route. In March 2009, biologist Mark Elbroch tracked a big tom puma making regular forays across open stretches of water exceeding half a mile in Lago Cochrane of Patagonia. Elbroch found the puma had been visiting an island to dine on sheep by night, and then swimming back to spend his days hiding on the mainland. It was in similar fashion that the lone lion from the Black Hills likely island-hopped his way over the rushing St. Marys River in the summer of 2010, and took his first steps into Canada.

SEVEN The Deer Shepherd

And the trouble is, if you don't risk anything, you risk even more.

—ERICA JONG

BACK IN THE SUMMER of 2008, the Eastern Cougar Foundation had formally begun its transition from hopeful little rumor-response team to hardened crew of science-based recovery advocates. It had finally abandoned the search for the cat that was no longer there. Its advisory board met; the hard facts were swallowed. For all the years of searching, with its cougar maps populated by pinpoints of trail-cam selfies and slain wanderers from the West, not a single wild female had been found among them. Except for the beleaguered little colony of panthers in South Florida, progressively strangled in a noose of land development and political giveaways of their habitat, there remained no wild breeding populations east of the Mississippi. In November, incoming president Chris Spatz announced the new course the foundation was striking, away from the false leads and metaphysical phantoms. It would soon thereafter be calling itself the Cougar Rewilding Foundation, its new charge to educate and advocate, and to see its missing namesake safely home.

The landscape of cougar conservation was shifting amid a series of seismic tremors. From the western front came news of more mountain lions returning to forested islands north and south of the Black Hills. From the Cypress Hills bordering Alberta and Saskatchewan to the Pine Ridge of northwestern Nebraska came new sightings and evidence of reproduction, confirming not only the occasional wanderlusting male, but a rare female or two that had forded the gaps. These amounted to what had become a handful of little satellite colonies of lions lined up along the prairie edge of the Rockies, each colony a potential launching point for scouts pushing east.

Meanwhile, the Chicago cougar had demonstrated both promise and improbability. His DNA trail leading back to the Black Hills had shown that a determined cat with more than a little luck was capable of making the Midwest leap. And that the most towering obstacle to the cougar's repatriation of America was neither open space nor asphalt nor rushing river, but a certain intolerant segment of society with lethal weaponry.

The southern approach for the cougar's return was further confirming the most desperate odds. In November a man was hunting deer from a tree stand along Georgia's western border when a cougar came strolling below. Georgia had no resident cougars, and hence no laws against killing them. The man shot the cougar dead. What authorities immediately dismissed as an escaped captive would later be revealed, through genetic analysis, as a wild young wanderer from southern Florida. He was the first Florida panther ever known to escape the state, however briefly. He was within striking distance of the southern Appalachians, and with them an elevated expressway of passable lion habitat running two thousand miles to the Great North Woods of Maine. He was also, by right of his birthplace, supposedly afforded the federal protection of the U.S. Endangered Species Act. No one was charged for his killing.

Whether eastward from the Rockies or northward from the Florida swamps, the exiled eastern cougar would need help coming home. The rewilders' pleas for civility and compassion obviously weren't cutting it. But their cause had lately embraced yet a more ecological rationale for why the East so needed its big cat back.

The murmur had been gathering from field sites and conference halls, formally surfacing in academic journals and publicized in mainstream media. Researchers from around the world were returning with disquieting reports of forests dying, coral reefs collapsing, pests and plagues irrupting. Beyond the bulldozers and the polluters and the usual cast of suspects, a more insidious factor had entered the equation. It was becoming ever more apparent that the extermination of the earth's apex predators—the lions and wolves of the land, the great sharks and big fish of the sea, all so vehemently swept aside in humanity's global swarming—had triggered a cascade of ecological consequences. Where the predators no longer hunted, their prey had run amok, amassing at freakish densities, crowding out competing species, denuding landscapes and seascapes as they went.

Spatz needed only to step outside to field-test this new theoretical jargon of ecological cascades to witness yet another New York forest withering under an invading army of deer. "Alpha predator recovery is no longer a matter of redemption; it is an ecological imperative," he wrote to his followers. "The East's forests are dying without them." By fate of strange convergence, that summer, as he began shifting to the new warnings from science, Spatz was also welcoming a new adviser to his team—an ecologist, it turned out, who was more than a bit familiar with the burning topic at hand.

Landscape of Fear

John Laundré, with his colleague and wife, Lucina Hernández, had recently relocated to New York's Oswego State University, near the shores of Lake Ontario. Laundré had spent more than twenty years tracking mountain lions, from Coahuila, Mexico, to eastern Idaho. Over that time, he had witnessed a certain unheralded power in his subject, a power beyond its superpredator's verve for bringing down big strong animals as food. It was a power to alter the very landscape on which it hunted. It was a power, more to Laundré's point, often imparted without drawing a drop of blood.

Laundré grew up on a farm in Green Bay, Wisconsin, hunting and fishing, watching *Wild Kingdom* on TV, and imagining himself a wildlife biologist. He went on to earn his doctorate tracking coyotes in eastern Idaho, and in 1986 he signed on to lead a new project studying mountain lions there. Laundré's subject fairly well conformed to the standard lion profile. His study site did not. Eastern Idaho, as viewed from the outskirts of Pocatello, was a fragmented landscape of modest mountains separated by potato fields. From one of the southern peaks, Laundré could see to the Salt Lake Valley of Utah, with a million people crowding against the flanks of the Wasatch Range. Up to that time, the mountain lion had more commonly been pegged as a beast typically beholden to the wildest of places—in academic parlance, a wilderness obligate. Laundré's subjects buried that notion in the lion-haunted potato fields and suburbs of Pocatello. He found his cats commuting through cattle pastures on their way to work, chasing deer. He came to know a big cat combining great stealth with surprising tolerance, wending its way seamlessly through human territory.

Laundré grew particularly fascinated by the lion's hunt. The mountain lion was an ambush specialist, jumping deer from the borders of forest and outcrops of rock, a hunter of the edges. On the flip side of that equation, the lion's long-legged prey remained safest in the open, where there was time to react and run like the blazes. The lion was quicker; the deer was faster. The closer to the edge, where the hiding places lay, the better for the lion. The farther out into the open, where head starts and top speeds ruled the day, the better for the deer.

Those were the basic parameters of the contestants' life-and-death playing field. But it was more than a physical contest, Laundré came to suspect, that determined the outcomes. "It was more than just a bunch of marbles rolling around, and if one bumps into another, you remove one of the marbles," said Laundré, as the classic old models of predator-prey dynamics had long held. There was a lot more going on than death by random collision. There was a psychological factor that permeated all, a familiar factor that laypeople more simply called fear.

Fear was an emotional term seldom bandied about by high-minded students of predator-prey ecology. Laundré suffered no such qualms. "The biggest mistake was to divorce predation from behavior," he said. "Anthropomorphism raises its ugly head. We have no problem assigning aggression to animals. We accept that. And fear is the counterbalance to aggression."

It was fear, Laundré observed, that interrupted the deer's every nibble of flower or twig with a moment of heads-up caution; fear that kept the herds moving, feeding swiftly and consuming lightly. Laundré began to think of the lion-deer dynamic as a game of risk. For the deer, the edge was a place where the plant life was richest and the nutritional rewards the greatest. But it was also a place, in a land patrolled by lions, where an unguarded moment could cost the ultimate price. For a hungry deer in a land of lions, the eternal dilemma became a choice of enduring another day of hunger in the barrens or risking instant death in the garden. It was fear of lion, perhaps even more than death by lion, that lightened the herds' ecological hoofprint. And the phenomenon extended far beyond a few Idaho lions.

Laundré was among a throng of scientists who had flocked to Yellowstone National Park soon after the winter of 1995 to take part in what was to become one of the great ecological experiments of the century. Yellowstone, since its inception in 1872, the world's first national park, had established itself as the quintessential wildlife park of the Lower 48, with its herds of roadside elk, and grizzly bear traffic jams, and one-ton bison going nose-to-nose with suicidal tourists through open car windows. Yet for all its Edenic aura, Yellowstone had for seventy years been masking an unsightly wound. The wound, it turned out, had been inflicted with a final bullet in 1926, when a trapper eliminated the last two of some 136 of Yellowstone's native wolves. Soon thereafter, the park began to sag under the weight of what was to become the densest, most pampered herd of elk on the planet. Thirty-five thousand of the giant deer, weighing upward of seven hundred pounds apiece, came to appropriate Yellowstone as their private feedlot, bringing Yellowstone's future forests of cottonwood, willow, and aspen to their knees. The forests withered, their stream banks crumbled, Yellowstone's managers averted their eyes. For decades, conservationists railed, and eventually rallied for the return of the wolf. And after a long, bitter struggle against the rural politics of hatred, the conservationists won. In a defining moment of conservation history, the same U.S. government that had vanquished the wolf of Yellowstone brought the wolf back. In the winters of 1995 and 1996, thirty-four wolves were flown in from the Rockies of Alberta and released. And Laundré was soon among the scientists taking stock.

As he had watched the lions and deer in Idaho potato country, Laundré watched the wolves and elk of Yellowstone. Where the new wolves had yet to spread, Laundré observed the elk grazing to their hearts' content, heads in the proverbial trough, their calves bounding and frolicking with abandon. "It was a scene out of a Disney film," he said.

But where the wolves had come to roam, an air of anxiety fell over the herds. Heads were raised on high alert, calves were clinging to their mothers' sides. "Like a country at war," said Laundré.

Wolves and elk, or lions and deer—the principle was the same. Fear created a psychological terrain, with its forbidding peaks of anxiety and inviting valleys of peace. This was an emotional landscape invisible to the untrained eye, though eminently palpable to the creatures who lived and died by it—a "landscape of fear," Laundré named it.

Fear would be shown to affect the numbers, too, by similar telekinetic means. Another researcher, Scott Creel, from Montana State University, had come spying on the Yellowstone elk to find them doubling their time on guard when wolves were around. The elk were habitually giving up their choice grasslands for the less palatable but safer cover of the woods. Some of them grew stressed and weak; some stopped bearing young. For reasons only partly explained by their daily weedings by wolf, Yellowstone's bloated herd of elk began thinning to healthier numbers in the years following the wolves' return.

Laundré was not the first to venture into the forbidden ecology of fear. Fear had been reported in prey animals throughout the kingdom, from salamanders to marmots, deer mice to fruit bats. Australian researchers were measuring fear in dolphins and dugongs, who were forgoing better foraging in the shallows, where tiger sharks more often lurked. Researchers in Connecticut had famously documented fear in the psyches of grasshoppers—grasshoppers who worried more, ate less, and lived shorter lives in the presence of spiders, even harmless spiders, it turned out, who'd had their fangs glued shut. Laundré was not the first, but his ventures were among the boldest, parading the impact of fear upon the world's biggest wildlife stage.

Combining the ecology of fear with the actual act of killing, predation was, as Laundré often reminded others, "the strongest selective force in evolution." Which begged the obvious question: What happens when the force is no longer? The wolf and the elk, the lion and the deer, had developed a complementary set of stealth and evasion skills that had performed beautifully together for hundreds of thousands of years. But with the predator of late so commonly shot out of the picture, questions of consequences arose.

Soon into the Yellowstone wolf experiment, an odd pair of outsiders from Oregon State University entered the arena. Bill Ripple and Bob Beschta were not zoologists, but a landscape ecologist and forest hydrologist, respectively, who had come to decipher Yellowstone's reaction to wolves from the bottom up. They took measure of Yellowstone's ailing trees and streams, those cottonwoods and willows and aspens that had so long languished under the reign of the elk, those streams that had gone bare and eroded under too many hooves and mouths. Ripple and Beschta and a succession of students under them began documenting the first vigorous sprouting of saplings that had lain dormant for the seventy years that wolves had been absent from Yellowstone. They incorporated their botanical findings with those of their zoological colleagues, who were noting a resurgence in beaver to Yellowstone's northern range (beavers who fed chiefly on the resurging willow; beavers who provided oases of habitat for scores of aquatic creatures). The zoologists also noted windfalls of the wolves' carrion serving great gatherings of scavengers otherwise challenged by the scarcity of Yellowstone's brutal winters. Ripple and Beschta's eyes soon opened to the same landscape of fear that Laundré had first sketched. They began to recognize places where the cottonwoods and aspens were again growing, among gullies, logjams, dead-end sandbars, and other hindrances to a fleeing elk. They began to believe that these were trees that had taken root in places that the elk, lately living in a land of wolves, feared to linger.

Ripple and Beschta expanded their curiosities to a host of other national parks suspected of similar undoings. From the rainforests of Washington's Olympic National Park to the desert canyon lands of Utah's Zion, they found the correlations repeating through the last century, of predator annihilations followed by hoofed plagues and stunted forests and eroding streams. And no longer was it only wolves that had grown conspicuous by their absence. From the streamside forests of Zion, to the cottonwood draws of the Black Hills, to the hillside oaks of California's Yosemite, Ripple and Beschta timed the demise of their ecosystems to the disappearance of the resident lions and the subsequent swarming of deer.

Ripple and Beschta would continue their heretical tour, exposing America's crown jewels of wilderness as impoverished facades for lack of lions and wolves. As they went, they came to note their tracks were repeatedly crossing those of a like-minded scientist from seventy years before.

Already by the mid-1930s, a wildlife biologist named Aldo Leopold had begun documenting the damages and ringing the alarms of too many deer and elk amassing in a land of vanquished predators. It was an odd message coming from the man who had once preached death to the predators, and who had just written the book on how to grow bigger deer herds. In what was to become the classic text of a new profession, Leopold's *Game Management* offered among other things a five-step prescription for more deer, which would prove enormously potent. And in what was to become the classic parable of a man coming to face the fallacy of his most sacred values, within two years of the book's 1933 publication, Leopold would set out to slay the monster he had helped create.

Leopold's deer formula called for sanctuaries, game farming, habitat manipulations, hunting restrictions, and predator control. The last two ingredients, when added to the mix, produced a runaway reaction that its chemist hadn't counted on.

The avid hunter Leopold had long sold the antipredator solution as a roadside barker would sell snake oil. Soon after his graduation from the Yale School of Forestry, Leopold had shipped out as a new recruit of the U.S. Forest Service, to the southwestern forests of Arizona and New Mexico, where he settled in and began preaching death to all predatory vermin. In a 1919 edition of *The Pine Cone*, a sportsmen's newsletter of his own founding, he wrote, "Good game laws well enforced will raise enough game either for sportsmen or for varmints, but not enough for both. It is most emphatically a reason for going out after the last lion scalp, and getting it."

In the name of game, Leopold rallied his fellow sportsmen to kill more predators. Among his hired hitmen was the Southwest's leading lion slayer, Ben Lilly, whom he sent to clean out the Gila National Forest in the New Mexico highlands. Leopold soon after led the charge culminating with the

Gila's designation in 1924 as the world's first official wilderness area. Years later he would add the Gila to his list of countrywide disaster areas, under assault by too many deer.

But it was most famously in the span of a single year that Leopold's anti-predator crusade came crashing down before his eyes. Between 1935 and 1936, he made two international trips. The first was to Germany, to tour the famous Dauerwald, Germany's "permanent forests," meticulously engineered for maximum yields of timber and game, and minimum numbers of native carnivores. The second was a pack trip to the Rio Gavilán in the Sierra Madre of northern Mexico, a paradisiacal netherworld running thick with lions, wolves, and deer. Rio Gavilán's reputation for lurking Apaches and Pancho Villa's bandits had fended off civilization's typical tramplings: an ecology of human fear.

Leopold came away from the Dauerwald with a sense of cold, soulless sterility: "One cannot travel many days in the German forests, either public or private, without being overwhelmed by the fact that artificialized game management and artificialized forestry tend to destroy each other." He came away from the Rio Gavilán humbled to the core: "It was here that I first clearly realized that land is an organism, that all my life I had seen only sick land, whereas here was biota still in perfect aboriginal health. The term 'unspoiled wilderness' took on a new meaning." Between the two alternate universes, the one glaring distinction assaulting Leopold's eyes was predators. The managers of the Dauerwald had done away with theirs; the managers of the Rio Gavilán were the predators themselves. "I doubt whether the lion-deer ratio is much different from that of Coronado's time," Leopold wrote of the Rio Gavilán. During his nine-day stay there, he and his hunting partner saw 187 deer, in admirable condition. "At the very least the Sierras present to us an example of an abundant game population thriving in the midst of its natural enemies. Let those who habitually ascribe all game scarcity to predators or who prescribe predator control as the first and inevitable step in all game management take that to heart."

Leopold thereafter ditched his antipredator rhetoric and moved to forestall the fallout. In the early 1940s he and several colleagues began chronicling North America's deer disasters. They gathered histories of more than a hundred herds across the land, and in 1947 produced a countrywide map of "problem areas" marked in black, where the deer had outgrown the land's capacity to continue feeding them. From California to New York, the black marks spattered the map. The surveys were replete with tales of swelling herds, tattered forests, beaten rangelands, and mass starvation. The problem areas were embarrassingly familiar: Yosemite National Park of California; Rocky Mountain National Park of Colorado; Algonquin Provincial Park of Ontario; Nantucket Island, Massachusetts; Glacier National Park, Montana; the Adirondacks of New York; the Pisgah National Game Preserve of North Carolina; the Black Hills of South Dakota. Great swaths of black marred the map of Pennsylvania. The Upper Peninsula of Michigan, the Northwoods of Wisconsin—solid black. And all the marks came with a common denominator: "We have found no record of a deer irruption in North America antedating the removal of deer predators," Leopold wrote.

Wisconsin was an especial embarrassment. Wisconsin was where Leopold in 1933 had accepted a university position at Madison as the country's first professor of wildlife management. In the winter of 1940/41, the state sent crews into the northern woods to examine Wisconsin's deer yards. In all but a handful of the eighty-one yards surveyed, they found trees heavily browsed as high as a deer could reach. In more than a third of the yards, they found starving deer. The crews estimated that fully half the year's fawns were dead. Two years later, the survivors were hit by a hard winter, severe even by Wisconsin standards. Thousands more died.

Leopold employed the tragedy as a teachable moment. He arranged a tour to the famous Flagg deeryard of northern Bayfield County, for his fellow wildlife commissioners, and for a reporter named Gordon MacQuarrie from the Milwaukee Journal, who caught the eyeful Leopold had shrewdly intended.

One falls, unable to move. The other runs a few yards, is easily captured. It is so thin that Buss says, "you could shave your face with his backbone." He's a little buck, nobs barely protruding on his head.

Nasty story? Ask Mrs. Harry Thomas of Sheboygan, one of the committee, who went out with the rest through the snow. Ask her if she was able to take it when husky young Mr. Buss picked up that dying baby deer and, already in a coma of death, it tried to raise its head and look about. And if you ask her, tell her there were those among the throng who saw that she couldn't take it, because deer are not supposed to die the hard way.

Nasty story? Every whipstitch of that trip through the Flagg yards was that and worse.

To Leopold's mind, the Flagg yard was not by a long stretch the worst. The worst had already happened, a decade before and fifteen hundred miles south, in a high pine forest bordering the North Rim of the Grand Canyon, upon the Kaibab Plateau. The Kaibab had come to stand as the most notorious twin catastrophe of forest and deer on record, in large part from many eloquent retellings of the tale, the most famous of them Leopold's. And in those tales, the mountain lion featured heavily.

On the Kaibab Plateau once grew a crisp, cool parkland of ponderosa pines and flowering meadows that harbored deer and mountain lions and wolves aplenty. In 1906, President Theodore Roosevelt decreed the forest a federal game reserve. The Kaibab deer became a national treasure; the Kaibab predators became pariahs. Hunting of the Kaibab deer was banned, and government marksmen were called in to annihilate the resident enemy. Over the next twenty-five years, they killed 554 bobcats, 4,889 coyotes, uncounted eagles, and the Kaibab's last 30 wolves. The extermination of some eight hundred Kaibab mountain lions was credited to a single human.

Uncle Jim Owens was a wiry, graying man in his sixties, with a storied résumé as cowman, buffalo hunter, Indian fighter, and of late, chief executioner of Kaibab's remaining predators. Owens's lion-killing reputation had come to precede him. People paid to shoot lions with him. Outside his cabin hung a sign: COUGARS CAUGHT TO ORDER. RATES REASONABLE. His clientele included the likes of the Western novelist Zane Grey, and in 1913 came knocking a former U.S. president named Theodore Roosevelt.

Roosevelt had left office in 1909 as the most heavily lauded conservationist ever to inhabit the Executive Mansion. In a flurry of presidential decrees, many of them flying in the face of his political opponents, Roosevelt had salted away 230 million acres of untrammeled land as national park and forest. He had established fifty-one federal bird reserves, four national game reserves, 150 national forests, five national parks, and eighteen national monuments, among them the Grand Canyon and its Kaibab deer herd. And Roosevelt, an ardent hunter in step with the times, saw no good reason for mountain lions inhabiting any of them in any appreciable numbers. From those new national parks and forests of his, Roosevelt's U.S. Bureau of the Biological Survey and its militia of professional exterminators began erasing the resident vermin by the tens of thousands each year.

Uncle Jim Owens was Roosevelt's kind of guy, a man "to put a stop to the senseless and wanton destruction of our wild life," wrote Roosevelt without a hint of irony. "One important feature of his work is to keep down the larger beasts and birds of prey, the arch-enemies of the deer, mountain-sheep, and grouse; and the most formidable among these foes of the harm-less wild life are the cougars."

By the time Roosevelt visited to check out his administrative handiwork, Uncle Jim's body count of lions was nearing three hundred. And with the help of his hounds, he was fast after the remaining renegades of the Kaibab forest, chasing the survivors over the edge and down into the most impossible reaches of the great canyon.

Roosevelt was pleased with the product. As of July 1913, with deer hunters banned and the lions running for their lives, the Kaibab deer were on the rise, populating the plateau like lawn ornaments. They gathered in curious, carefree herds, staring as Roosevelt's lion-hunting party rode past. Roosevelt wrote, "Sometimes we roused the pretty spotted fawns, and watched them dart away, the embodiments of delicate grace." A defiant buck stood nose to nose with one of Owens's charging hounds.

Roosevelt wrote wistfully, too, of the lions, as "strange and interesting creatures . . . Their every movement is so lithe and stealthy, they move with such sinuous and noiseless caution, and are such past masters in the art of concealment, that they are hardly ever seen unless roused by dogs."

Owens's dogs eventually roused a lion for Roosevelt's party, flushing a big male off the rim and down upon the terraces of the inner canyon. The hunters came stumbling and sliding down, chasing the echoes of the hounds through thorn and scrub, and reuniting finally beneath a lone pine clinging to the edge of a thousand-foot cliff.

"It was a wild sight," wrote Roosevelt. "The maddened hounds bayed at the foot of the pine. Above them, in the lower branches, stood the big horse-killing cat, the destroyer of the deer, the lord of stealthy murder, facing his doom with a heart both craven and cruel."

Roosevelt's nephew drew the winning straw and shot the lion through the neck.

Before departing the Kaibab, the hunters would bag another two lions, the last a young female for which Roosevelt himself took the honors. He first marvelled at how blithely the fleeing cat had ascended the tree, legs extended, "as if she had been walking on the ground," before he took aim. "As she faced us among the branches I could only get a clear shot into her chest where the neck joins the shoulder; down she came, but on the ground she jumped to her feet, ran fifty yards with the dogs at her heels, turned to bay in some fallen timber, and dropped dead." Roosevelt wrote nothing more of the cat.

Roosevelt died in 1919, five years too soon to witness his beloved house of cards come crashing down. In the winters of 1924 and 1925, the stupendous herd of some 100,000 deer that had swarmed upon the Kaibab, swarmed for the last time. Having emptied the last of the Kaibab's emergency rations, the deer began starving en masse. The news and ensuing outrage reached the far ends of the country. Professional hunters were called in as an act of mercy. When the smoke cleared, one of every ten deer was left sifting through the smoldering wreckage of the great Kaibab deer range, and the legend was born.

Over the years, Leopold would parade the Kaibab catastrophe as a cautionary tale for the ages, of lands disfigured for lack of predators and the ensuing siege of prey, where the mountains looked "as if someone had given God a new pruning shears, and forbidden Him all other exercise." The Kaibab was a tale that would take several turns through history, from gospel to disgraced myth to gospel again. Leopold, too, whose name would one day accompany those of Muir and Thoreau in the pantheon of wilderness prophets, would also for a time in Wisconsin play the pariah.

For preaching that more deer, and particularly more does, needed shooting for their forests' own good; for suggesting that fewer wolves and lions needed annihilating, Leopold found himself the sportsmen's new target, the butt of snide editorials. And in the nationalistic climate following World War II, Leopold, the predator's new ally, was nothing less than an enemy sympathizer.

"The wolf is the Nazi of the forest," began a letter from a sportsmen's club to Wisconsin's wildlife commission. "He takes the deer and some small fry. The fox is the sly Jap who takes the choice morsels of game and the song birds. Can Professor Leopold justify their existence because deer meant for human consumption should be fed to the Nazi because we must have that protection for the trees?"

Leopold died of a heart attack in 1948, and in that morbid sense was spared watching his warnings so thoroughly ignored over the next half century. When those carrying on his work updated the tallies, Leopold's sporadic floodings of deer had come to better approximate tsunamis. A string of scientific papers began detailing what one of the authors would sum up as a "slow moving catastrophe." Across the forests of northern Wisconsin, one out of five species of wildflower, all of them relished by deer, had gone missing in the latter half of the twentieth century. In a famous sprawling meadow of Great Smoky Mountains National Park of Tennessee, missing lions and massive deer herds had amounted to forty-two species of wildflowers extirpated since 1970. In Shenandoah National Park of Virginia, forests fenced against deer were sprouting jungles inside, while those outside were falling bleak and barren, with their attendant cast of squirrels and ground-nesting songbirds disappearing in step.

From the land of Leopold to Long Island, deer were amassing at densities higher than any recorded since Columbus. Local herds were censused at tens of times higher than the forests could sustain. Wildflowers and saplings were disappearing, replaced by monoculture fields of ferns and aggressive weeds with names such as garlic mustard and Japanese stiltgrass. Native plants were being driven asunder; as early as 1992, botanists had identified nearly a hundred species of rare plants being made rarer by deer. Birds nesting in deer-favored shrubs began vanishing. Tree saplings, those previously destined to replace the forest overstory, had stopped growing beyond knee height of a deer. State foresters warned of timber failures. The U.S.

Forest Service in 2008 labelled the deer issue as "serious" in twenty states of the Northeast and Midwest. Two thirds of Pennsylvania's and New York's leading commercial timber species were dying off for too many deer.

Stephen Horsley, a veteran U.S. Forest Service ecologist working out of Pennsylvania, summed up the wreckage: "It doesn't matter what forest values you want to preserve or enhance—whether deer hunting, animal rights, timber, recreation, or ecological integrity—deer are having dramatic, negative effects on all the values everyone holds dear."

The once-fearsome landscapes of America were being overrun by prey, which included a suite of species other than deer. With its top dogs and big cats missing, America had also become a playground filling with little predators such as foxes and raccoons and footloose house cats. Mesopredator release, as the scientists named it, was a siege of midsize predators freed of those who would otherwise eat them. Among them, the house cat had become the most abundant mesopredator of all, some thirty to eighty million of them roaming backyards and local woods, revealing a track record of carnivory that stunned biologists and drove leagues of cat lovers to denial.

House cats were found helping themselves to wild birds by the billions each year, along with ten times as many rabbits and voles and other little native mammals, certain kinds of them rare and endangered. House cats were also, in lands more frequented by top-order predators, far less common and destructive. House cats roaming suburban patches of Southern California chaparral had been found to be eating the resident chaparral birds to extinction—except where cat-eating coyotes also roamed.

Mountain lions were famously fond of house cats, too. With backing from the South Dakota Department of Game, Fish and Parks, Dan Thompson had removed thirteen stomachs from Black Hills lions shot for wandering upon the prairie, to begin looking for all those missing cattle and sheep claimed by South Dakota ranchers. Thompson found no cattle at all, but among the more typical remains of wild deer and jackrabbit, he also found house cat.

Such was the sickness spreading across the lands of missing lions. And it had certainly not escaped John Laundré, freshly removed from his western landscapes of fear. Having settled into the deer-plagued forests of the Northeast, Laundré began wondering about their missing cougars. He heard word of the Cougar Rewilding Foundation and offered his assistance.

Laundré hadn't come east on account of cougars. He'd come to study coyotes, which, unlike the cougars now getting gunned down on the trip across, had forty years ago mastered the same leap, crossing from western plains to eastern forests. In the span of a human generation, the song dog of the prairie had quite comfortably settled into the green jungles of the East. The eastern coyote had made camp in forest, coastal dunes, mountains, and swamps, in suburbs and the country's biggest cities. Coyotes had taken up common residence in Chicago, been chased through New York's Central Park, and dug dens in Washington, D.C. They'd even once mingled with the lonely Canadian wolf, and incorporated some wolf genes, the better to chase eastern deer with.

Much like the lion, the coyote was heavily hunted, and then some, shot and trapped and gassed at every turn; it was open season year-round in most places. But unlike the lion, the coyote had fecundity in its corner, bearing an average five pups every year, with the maddening ability of upping the production to match the escalated shootings and poisonings. America's coyote had withstood yearly killings of half a million individuals, and kept coming.

The lion—producing one to four kittens every two to three years— couldn't begin to match the coyote's reproductive pace. But Laundré saw hope in its habitat plasticity. Lions had come to lurk the outskirts of San Diego, Los Angeles, San Francisco, Seattle, Boise, Reno, Salt Lake City, Phoenix, Tucson, El Paso, Albuquerque, Denver, and Boulder. They had proven their ability to survive a certain number of roads, a certain density of humans, and still feed and reproduce themselves. And if the urban outskirts of the West, why not those of the East?

As Laundré started exploring his new home in the Northeast, he grew impressed with how much wildness remained, but also how much of it had become a feedlot for white-tailed deer. He began to recognize the repeating patterns, from trees trimmed to the molar height of a deer, to forest floors carpeted in unpalatable ferns and prolific weeds. "From the southern forests of Georgia through West Virginia to the northern forests of New England, deer are instigating probably the most massive change in forest habitat since uncontrolled logging in our early history," he wrote in his first essay as science adviser for the Cougar Rewilding Foundation. This was a land under attack. And Laundré was not shy about the most obvious prescription.

"Can it happen here?" he asked. "Can the return of cougars, or even wolves, recreate this landscape of fear and save our eastern forests?" Laundré recalled his experiences in the Idaho landscapes of lion fear, and Yellowstone's recent greening under the new rule of the wolf. "Can they do what our fences, our repellents, and our hunting have failed to do? Given the results we are seeing in other areas, the resounding answer is YES."

Looking for someplace to start, Laundré didn't need to look far. Two hours east of his new home spread the largest park in the United States. Adirondack Park was an enormous dome of Precambrian uplift, a land of lakes and rushing rivers and forested mountains, forty-six of them rising higher than four thousand feet. The Adirondacks spread twice as wide as Yellowstone National Park. The park could swallow not only Yellowstone, but its fellow national parks of Grand Canyon, Glacier, and Great Smoky Mountains, too.

Laundré began working up the numbers. He tallied the Adirondacks' mileage of roads, its area of towns and houses, and borrowed a conservative estimate of its white-tailed deer population. He factored in known densities of lions living in other isolated populations of similar wildness, in the Black Hills of South Dakota and the Big Cypress Swamp of southern Florida. Laundré figured the Adirondacks could support as many as 350 mountain lions.

Laundré submitted his paper to the scientific journal Oryx. In the meantime, he and Spatz teamed up on an essay for the Wildlands newsletter, laying it all out in layman's terms. It wasn't just the Adirondacks that were lacking for cougars; it was much of New York, with more than a million deer and failing forests. It was the White Mountains of New Hampshire and the Green Mountains of Vermont, the great northern woods of Maine. It was the entire Appalachian Mountain chain, the Shenandoahs of Virginia through the Great Smoky Mountains straddling North Carolina and Tennessee, to the

Okefenokee Swamp of Georgia and the Osceola National Forest of Florida. These lands needed lions "as shepherds of the wild ungulate flocks. Eastern ecosystems are in jeopardy. The landscape of fear needs to be re-established for deer in the eastern forests. We need the shepherds back."

But where were the shepherds to come from? The options for western cougars walking their way east remained scant, and the pace glacial. As Spatz was quick to remind, "It took 20 years of dispersal from the South Dakota Black Hills to establish a source population 120 miles southeast in the Nebraska panhandle. Projected eastward, under ideal conditions, cougars won't be breeding in Minnesota, let alone further east, until 2050."

In May 2011, at the Tenth Mountain Lion Workshop in Bozeman, Montana, Laundré unveiled his preliminary findings. He pulled no punches: Not only was the lion able and fit for life in the eastern forest, the forest wasn't fit without the lion.

By the summer of 2010 the Twin Cities lion had entered the boreal forest of Canada. From Sault Ste. Marie eastward to the next significant city of Sudbury, population 160,000, was more than two hours by car, with few roads or towns in between. The next after that was North Bay, population fifty thousand. There were great stretches of Ontario lacking crowds and traffic, towns and roads, where the people most likely to be found were paddling canoes upon wilderness ponds. Winter left many stretches of Ontario deserted. It was big moose country, hunting camp and summer cottage country.

Eastward lay Algonquin Provincial Park, nearly three thousand square miles of North Country wilderness, home of moose and wolves and the lion's little snowshoed cousin, the lynx. If the lion could avoid the wolves, the Algonquin wilds would provide plenty of prey and cover. Eastward still came the Saint Lawrence Seaway, connecting the Atlantic Ocean to the Great Lakes, a fording formidably vast for a land-bound mammal thinking to swim it. But there arose in the seaway an archipelago called the Thousand Islands, the distance between islands swimmably short. The Thousand Islands had indeed once served as stepping-stones for the western coyote in his conquering of the East a half century earlier. In 2001 the islands had been famously used by a seven-hundred-pound moose named Alice, who went from the Adirondacks of New York to Algonquin Provincial Park of Ontario, 220 miles between. It appeared the lion, sometime around the early winter of 2010, completed the moose's trip in reverse.

On the evening of December 16, about 8:00 P.M., Cindy Eggleston was washing dishes in front of the kitchen window in her home in the woods near Lake George, New York, when a motion-sensing floodlight suddenly lit up her backyard. There, passing through, was a mountain lion.

"Dave, come quick!"

In the few seconds it took her husband to reach the window, the cat was gone.

"I just saw a big cat," said Cindy.

"It was probably a bobcat," said David Eggleston, a retired conservation officer for the New York State Department of Environmental Conservation.

"It was not a bobcat. It had a long tail."

Eggleston went outside into a dusting of fresh snow and found big cat tracks leading around the house, down the driveway, and onto the shoulder of the road, where they disappeared in a muddle of dog paws and boot prints. The next morning, he called Louis Gerrain, his neighbor and succeeding conservation officer.

"Louis, you're going to think I'm crazy, but Cindy saw a big cat last night."

The two started backtracking the cat through the woods behind the Egglestons' yard. Gerrain had been working the area for twenty years; Eggleston, much longer. Both were cougar skeptics, hardened from experience. But both—considering the size of the tracks they were now following— were budding converts by the minute.

They went about a hundred yards on the cat's trail. "Boy, it would be nice if we found where it rubbed up against a tree or a rock to get some hair," said Gerrain, the moment before he and Eggleston found themselves looking down at the cat's bed. The lion had curled up and napped in the snow, leaving an obvious outline of himself, appended with a perfect impression of his magnificent tail. With tweezers, Gerrain plucked some twenty-five hairs from the animal's bed.

The hairs ended up in the state pathology lab at Delmar, where wildlife biologist Kevin Hynes keyed them out as some sort of cat, then sent them to Melanie Culver's genetics lab in Arizona for finer identification. All parties were by now pretty sure they had a mountain lion walking loose in New York State. The last wild catamounts of New York had been shot out by 1900, which raised the usual suspicions as to the newcomer's origin.

The Lake George lion left without fanfare or followers. When the New York State Department of Conservation let him go quietly on his way, they did so on the belief they'd been visited by a half-tame, imminently doomed escapee from somebody's private collection, a pet that would probably show up dead soon enough. It didn't quite work out that way.

EIGHT The Gold Coast

ON MARCH 2, 2011, came a 110-page report bearing the somber news the rewilders were expecting. Four years earlier, the U.S. Fish and Wildlife Service had undertaken a formal review, to gather all the facts, answer all the rumors, and at last lay to rest the question as to whether the endangered species known as the eastern cougar, apparently still seen and sworn to by so many, still lived. The service's lead investigator, Mark McCollough, had pored over the literature and queried the leading cougar experts in twenty-one eastern states and provinces, fielding 573 responses along the way. McCollough had asked if any had proof of a reproducing population of cougars. Not one document or authority could honestly answer yes.

The service's report was accompanied by an old photo of Bruce Wright, pioneering cougar sleuth of the 1950s, posing beside a sorry stuffed specimen of the supposed last eastern cougar, trapped in northern Maine in 1938. McCollough was announcing that the search had failed. More to the point, that it was finished. There would be no federal recovery plan, no critical habitat designated, no more time or money spent to save an endangered species that was in fact extinct.

More than a few were not happy with McCollough's conclusions. In the Eastern Puma Research Network's next newsletter, John Lutz, evangelical president of the Network and patriarch of true believers and conspiracy theorists, ran the headline 5-YEAR USF & WS SURVEY ENDS AS A FARCE. It was as delicate as Lutz would get:

The survey also claimed to be, a [sic] "evaluation of current cougars in the east"! IT was NOT!!! What it turned out to be, was a deliberate WITCH-HUNT full of negative comments on all current WILD NATIVE pumas who continue to roam the eastern U.S. . . . [T]he "new" survey had nothing to do with "finding evidence of native wild cougars, but only concealing proof from the taxpaying public", thus ending as a farce to all Americans who will foot the estimated $3-Million cost.

Lutz went on:

The Survey was so upsetting to Vermont's Resident Squirrel Colonies, who generates fresh protein to the native wild in-state cougars/catamounts roaming the Marble State, they began attacking a "few persons" in some neighborhoods . . .

And finally:

Do YOU honestly believe these agencies who have DENIED any presence of WILD cougars/panthers for decades would suddenly change directions & admit: TO HAVING WILD COUGARS?? GET REAL!!!

Officials from Ontario's Ministry of Natural Resources would also object to McCollough's conclusions, telling reporters they had hard evidence of cougars in their province. The hard evidence amounted to nearly five hundred sightings reported over the prior twenty years, plus fifteen tracks, a sample of hair, and two deposits of scat.

Rick Rosatte, the Ministry's lead cougar investigator, privately contested McCollough's conclusions, citing a scientific paper he was then preparing, his findings replete with those aforementioned footprints, strong sightings, and a few physical samples of lion spoor. Stuart Kenn, Ontario's leading amateur cougar seeker, had even pinned a number to the guesswork, claiming 550 cougars living and breeding across the province.

McCollough shrugged. "There is no credible scientific evidence to back up these claims," he said. "Every state and province in the East has the same information—alleged cougar dots on a map and a few reports with a higher level of validity. Does this kind of information warrant publication in a scientific journal?"

Ontario had no record of females, no kittens, no bodies in hand. By way of contrast, McCollough cited biologists presiding over the tiniest of cougar populations—from the Black Hills and Badlands of the Dakotas, to the Pine Ridge of Nebraska to the cypress swamps of southern Florida—all of them repeatedly and predictably coming upon tracks in the snow, tracks in the mud, photos on trail cameras, and eventually, dead bodies one could touch. Cougars in the flesh, wherever they might be, eventually wound up caught by trappers, shot by hunters, struck by cars.

"We have no doubt cougars occur in Ontario from time to time," McCollough conceded. "However, we believe there is no convincing scientific evidence of cougars breeding in Ontario. We conclude that cougars that show up from time to time in Ontario, eastern Canada, and the eastern U.S. are either released or escaped pets or animals migrating from the West."

For Spatz and the rewilders, McCollough's basic findings offered nothing to fault. All agreed there was yet no science to back any claims of big cats breeding anywhere north of the Caloosahatchee River of Florida, and unfortunately so. But there was plenty of fault in the failure of McCollough's bosses to suggest doing anything about it.

"The eastern deciduous forest is dying before our eyes, on our watch because the cougar is gone," said Spatz in a press release. "Endangered bald eagles and peregrine falcons were restored successfully to the East from western sources. By failing to provide an action plan for the recovery of a species critical to eastern ecosystems using western cougars, the Interior Department is abdicating its responsibility to conserve this ecosystem."

The eastern cougar was gone, and the odds against its coming home on its own were stacking higher by the month. Lions of the Rockies were getting hammered ever harder; the Midwest crossing had become a shooting gallery. By the end of March, the Black Hills hunt had concluded its 2011 season with the killing of a record fifty lions—following which, South Dakota's wildlife commission would jump the 2012 limit another 40 percent, to seventy cats. Across the West, anti-lion administrations were turning up the heat. In May, at the Tenth Mountain Lion Workshop in Bozeman, Montana, where Laundré was delivering the first public presentation of his Adirondack lion feasibility study, there came news of Montana Fish, Wildlife, and Parks having just raised its lion-hunting quota by 37 percent over the last three years, without biological justification.

To that Bozeman gathering came two biologists from the Nevada Department of Wildlife with a status report that would make Montana's lion hunt look like a model of conservation by comparison. Nevada's Wildlife Commission had raised its 2011 mountain lion hunting quota to five hundred, more than twice the number of lions ever taken in a single season. In a rare display of candor and courage from civil servants, the agency biologists reported that "since 2003 harvest limit recommendations . . . have been indiscriminately chosen with little input from Department biologists by the Wildlife Commission."

Nevada, moreover, was funding a grab bag of expensive eradication projects, none backed by scientific rationale, some with bald-faced conflicts of interest. Nevada, its own biologists testified, had a rancher and his family under contract to receive eighteen hundred dollars for each cougar killed, his job to "maintain a balance between mountain lions and their prey." The authority supposedly monitoring that balance was the rancher himself, "as I guide clients for hunts and run my ranch in the area."

Missouri, meanwhile, was rapidly distinguishing itself as a black hole for eastward-leaning lions. In 2006 the Missouri Department of Conservation, on grounds of public safety and livestock protection—though no people or livestock had ever been harmed—had officially declared that "it is not desirable to allow the re-establishment of a mountain lion population in Missouri."

And in 2011, the state's official Unwelcome sign was emphatically confirmed and reconfirmed. On January 2, a coon hunter's dog treed a cougar in Ray County, in Missouri's northwest corner. The hunter shot the cougar out of the tree. A friend of the shooter covered for him, accepting responsibility for the shooting on the grounds that the cougar had been killing his cattle. He later confessed to lying on both counts. Neither shooter nor accomplice was prosecuted. The dead cougar was a young male, its DNA traced to South Dakota.

Three weeks later, some ninety armed Amish farmers in Macon County surrounded a field and started closing the circle, hunting for coyotes. They flushed, to their astonishment, a cougar. One man shot it; a second shooter brought it down. The wounded cougar jumped up, and a third killed it. The state, judging the cat a threat to his attackers, pressed no charges. The cougar was a young male, his genetic profile traced to Montana.

Before the year was out, a third Missouri pioneer, this one another young male from the Black Hills, would be shot by a landowner declaring fear as his defense. No charges were brought.

Thus three more colorful dots of Midwestern confirmation were added to the national map, to be paraded as proof of the cougar's historic comeback.

Yet, with the unfolding summer of 2011, at least one eastward lion was still alive on the trail. On the fifth of June, three months after the official pronouncement of the eastern cougar's extinction—six months after his unheralded appearance in the Egglestons' backyard of Upstate New York— the lion reemerged, with a statement. He was now twenty-three miles, northeast as the pigeon flies, from Manhattan's Central Park.

He had left Lake George on a southward bearing with untold detours, perhaps following the Hudson Valley. For all the apparent invitations of the Adirondacks—all the deer and mountains of wilderness and scarcity of cities—he had left the Adirondacks behind him, searching. And over the following six months, he had quietly made his way two hundred miles to within two nights' jaunt of New York City. He had come to a town of some sixty thousand people, reputed among other things as America's quintes- sential bastion of wealth, as prime habitat of hedge fund billionaires shel- tering in palatial estates on the beaches of Long Island Sound, a town with a hilltop view of the Manhattan skyline, a town seasonally tinted in country club green, named Greenwich, Connecticut. It was here, for peculiar reasons, that the lion suddenly exposed himself with a spat of recklessness unseen in the nearly two years since he'd left the Black Hills.

The lion made his appearance in Greenwich late on a lazy Sunday after- noon, sauntering past Brendan Gilsenan's kitchen window. Gilsenan was an

English professor at the all-boys Brunswick School, a prestigious college prep academy where he and his family of four lived in a cozy little cul-de-sac of faculty housing. The Gilsenans were relaxing at home watching a movie on the eve of their summer vacation in Cape Cod. At about 6:00 P.M., Brendan Gilsenan got up, walked to the kitchen, and happened to look out to see a huge tawny cat with a long thick tail strolling through his side yard.

"Mountain lion!" he yelled, and with his two young boys and wife scrambled outside for a better look. The lion crossed the Gilsenans' cul-de-sac and padded directly out onto King Street, where he was nearly hit by a car. He then turned back toward the house. Gilsenan herded his family inside.

The lion casually circled their house, the Gilsenans scurrying from one window to the next, following him as he went. The lion passed by the sliding glass door of the back porch, an arm's length and a pane of glass between him and the Gilsenans. The lion never so much as returned a gaze.

"It looked like something out of the zoo," said Gilsenan, "like a female African lion in the zoo. He was walking very nonchalantly, in a lion's sort of way. He wasn't spooked. He didn't look lost. He didn't look anxious. He was a beautiful animal. Absolutely beautiful. It just struck me how strong it looked, how really clean. The fur was so smooth and clean. It was a surreal moment."

Toward the end of the lion's tour, Gilsenan finally thought to get his camera. He fumbled to open the case, to point the lens as the lion angled away. Just before the lion disappeared down a trail at the edge of the yard, Gilsenan raised the camera high over his wife's head, took blind aim through the window, and clicked a digital image.

Gilsenan's son phoned the neighbors a hundred yards down the lion's path. The Burdetts, immersed in a movie of their own, let the phone ring through and half-listened to young Keegan Gilsenan leaving some sort of message in the background. Brendan Gilsenan simultaneously fired a text message to his pal Doug Burdett, and then led his family back outside to catch another look at the cat.

Meanwhile, an ambulance pulled up. Two paramedics, William Richards and Andrew Gottshall, had been passing by a few minutes earlier when the big cat stepped into the path of their truck, forcing Gottshall to slam on the brakes. Richards had called dispatch to report a mountain lion; dispatch hadn't believed him. He and Gottshall drove back and turned in to find the Gilsenans gathered outside. The conversation was frantic and fast. Nobody could quite believe what they'd seen. The lion had gone that way, said the Gilsenans, pointing down the walkway toward the Burdetts'.

Doug Burdett looked outside to see an ambulance pulling up, and went to the door.

"What's going on?"

Richards and Gottshall hesitated. Burdett cocked his head.

"We just saw a mountain lion run in front of our ambulance."

"You mean a bobcat?"

Richards and Gottshall meant mountain lion. They passed along their cautions and drove away, while Burdett pulled out his cell phone. There was Brendan Gilsenan's waiting text message: BIG FREAKING CAT HEADED YOUR WAY.

Burdett heard a commotion of crows out front. He followed a few yards down the walkway, where a creek emerged from a patch of woods. There, under dogged harassment by the crows, stood the lion.

Burdett's wife, Sarah, ran inside and grabbed the Nikon. She took special care to press the power switch on, then tossed it to her husband, standing three strides from the lion.

Burdett stared at the lion. The lion stared at Burdett. Burdett glanced back at his house. *How fast can I get to the door? How bad do I want this picture?* He looked through the camera, took special care to press the power switch—unwittingly undoing his wife's safeguard—and clicked away.

It was over in seconds. The lion started moving. He slinked beneath the footbridge and disappeared downstream into the creekside thicket.

Burdett went inside to verify what his mind was still struggling to comprehend. He looked into the viewfinder to confirm his *New York Times* cover shot, to find his camera asleep and the screen a crushing shade of black.

But Gilsenan's camera had been ready, and his aim had been true. His blind point-and-shoot from afar had somehow managed to frame the target. And there it was, albeit rather ghostlike in the distance, that unlikely feline trailing the long and tawny tail. Or so it seemed to Gilsenan, mentally projecting onto the fuzzy picture what he had just experienced with bracing clarity from arm's length.

Word got around, and first thing the next morning Gilsenan found an e-mail from the school's headmaster, asking about the rumored picture. Gilsenan hesitated. On second inspection, he wasn't sure the picture was even worth keeping. "It was the classic Loch Ness Monster picture," he said. "It was Sasquatch." The headmaster suggested Gilsenan share it with the school's head of security, Mike DeAngelo, who grew immediately concerned when he saw it. This was a boys' school whose summer camp was within one day of receiving fresh hordes of bite-size students gamboling about the trails and ballfields. DeAngelo forwarded the photo to the Connecticut Department of Energy and Environmental Protection (DEEP), and asked for help.

There hadn't been mountain lions known to be living in Connecticut for at least a century, and perhaps a good deal longer. The last bounty for a panther was paid in 1769. Townspeople of the early 1800s mentioned that the cats were still around, though few bodies were ever reported. In 1985 somebody's caged cougar got loose for a while before being rounded up. But that was all. The state's official line on Connecticut cougars, long before McCollough's federal pronouncement, listed them as extinct.

There had certainly been no shortage of claims to the contrary. Bill Betty, a Rhode Island resident representing John Lutz's Eastern Puma Research Network, had been making the lecture rounds, telling anybody who would listen that, by his estimate, thirty to fifty lions were still lurking about Connecticut. At his lectures, Betty would ask for a show of hands from those who'd seen the creature. He would nod at the number of hands. He routinely told reporters that he and his family had tallied thirty encounters with cougars, and that he himself had run across them fourteen times in the last forty years, some as close as ten feet away. "I've chased mountain lions away from kids," he said. "They are here. Those who say they are not are lying."

Betty had a local teammate in Bo Ottmann, founder of the Friends of Connecticut Mountain Lion, a coalition of seekers and believers with an Internet posting board populated almost weekly with various personal accounts of the cougar kind. Both men were otherwise well versed in their basic cougar biology, but markedly at odds with professional cougar biologists about the infinitesimal likelihood of such big cats bounding here and there across the nation's third-smallest and fourth-most densely populated state, while leaving neither hide nor hair of their existence. Neither Ottmann nor Betty found it particularly upsetting to his belief that for all the big cats so commonly seen crossing through the headlights and backyards, not one authentic photograph or body had yet to surface.

Paul Rego and Jason Hawley, the state's head carnivore biologists, were Betty and Ottmann's skeptical counterparts. Rego was a twenty-five-year veteran of the department; Hawley, his seven-year protégé. The walls of their office were festooned with furs from road-killed Connecticut carnivores: coyote, mink, bobcat, skunk, fisher, bear. And no cougars. Their work days were often spent responding to reports of mischievous coyotes or worrisome bobcats, or relocating Dumpster-diving bears. Over the years, they'd also found themselves more frequently fielding reports of mountain lions. They would respond to find the tracks of bobcats, coyotes, and dogs. They'd review breathlessly narrated videos of panthers on the prowl, only to find a house cat traipsing through a local meadow. For most of their investigations, they rarely had to leave their desks. They'd become self-trained forensics experts of phony cougar photos, a few keystrokes on Google producing within seconds the same stock image, originating from some other state, from some other month or year. Occasionally they'd magnify the image and see the steel bars of a cage in the background.

"The psychology is baffling to me," said Hawley. "You get an e-mail—'My brother just took this photo in his backyard'—you pull up the image and you find it's been online for three years. What's the psychology of that? That he has to fabricate the evidence to prove what he knows?"

As with their professional colleagues presiding across the cougar's uninhabited range, Rego and Hawley had developed an immunity to the common outbreaks of mountain lion mania and cougar chicanery. The job demanded a certain tact and diplomacy. "We can't tell people they're crazy, because they're not," said Hawley. "Sometimes it's easy to misidentify a wild animal. But even when we explain to them why it's not a mountain lion, they don't want to hear it." Rego and Hawley had been fielding the sightings week after week. As of June 2011, they'd fielded maybe a hundred sightings for the year, not "a single one of them having something we could definitively say was indeed a cougar," said Rego. Gilsenan's point-blank testimony notwithstanding, the Brunswick School picture was much too blurry for an all-points bulletin. Rego thought it might actually be a cougar; Hawley wasn't yet buying it. The definitive lion feature, that long trailing tail, as seen obliquely from behind, appeared to Hawley's eyes as a bobcat's left hind leg. The two agreed to sit tight. If it was a cougar, they'd soon hear more about it. They soon did.

By midmorning the day after the lion's Brunswick School appearance, the security man DeAngelo was joined at the scene by the Greenwich Police and Marcella Leone, founder and director of the Lionshare Zoological Conservation Center in Greenwich, a rare species breeding center housing lions and cheetahs, among others. The team searched the lion's getaway trail through a jungle of brush and prickers. The searchers soon found what was clearly a feline track, and a huge one, the breadth of which would have swallowed nearly two decent paw prints of a thirty-pound bobcat. Then appeared a scat, nine inches long and coarsely woven with the hair of deer.

These were signs on a scale beyond any native Connecticut cat. The doubts began to waver. At recess, the Brunswick School superintendents herded the kids close to the building with an air horn.

Next day, Sgt. Cynthia Schneider of the Connecticut Department of Energy and Environmental Protection arrived to investigate. Schneider recreated the scene, looking through the Gilsenans' window from which the blurry photo had been shot. She enlisted a neighborhood dog, a retriever mix notably bigger than a bobcat, and for comparison, stood him next to the tree where the suspect creature had been photographed. Two or three of the dogs would have fit inside the creature's frame. Gilsenan's Sasquatch photo had just taken on a new air of authenticity.

Tuesday night, the Greenwich Times broke the news of "a large cat" prowling King Street, with some counter-panic comments from city officials and the Connecticut Department of Energy and Environmental Protection.

"If there was a population, there would be carcasses, there would be paw prints," said Greenwich's conservation director Denise Savageau. "These are big animals, and there is just none of that."

"At this point, there have been reported sightings, but we don't have any confirmation yet as to what it is," said a DEEP spokesman, Dennis Schain, who threw in the possibility of a mistaken bobcat.

By the time the first public notice was printed on Tuesday night, it was out of date. The city and the DEEP had in the meantime been made aware of the investigation, of the tracks and the scat, and of how frightfully tiny that dog looked compared to the creature in Gilsenan's photo. As of 1:15 P.M., the Brunswick School was in lockdown.

The next morning, officials from the Brunswick School announced that they had closed the campus to all but faculty and staff. Its hiking trails had been posted. Soon after, the American Cancer Society abruptly cancelled a walk for charity that was to be held on campus that Friday, and hurriedly directed all seven hundred registered walkers down the road, to safer confines in a Norwalk gymnasium—the move, as it would turn out, placing the event squarely in the lion's path. "It's a pretty stunned community," said Keith Landesman, cochair of the charity walk and math teacher at Brunswick. "It's not a regular cat, that's for sure."

Savageau, speaking for Greenwich's conservation department, was working to quell the mounting hysteria, reminding all that the nearest population of cougars was in Florida, and with the next breath, hedging her bets: "If there is a mountain lion in the area, chances are it is a cat that was illegally captive and let go or it escaped." Just to be sure, Savageau instructed people what to do in case of a close encounter: "Act large. Stand up tall, wave your arms and make noises. Don't freeze. You don't want to act like a bunny."

Calls went out to local keepers of big cats across New York and Connecticut. One call ironically went to Lionshare, whose owner, Marcella Leone, had helped find the lion's scat. Neither Leone nor anybody else was reporting a missing mountain lion.

That day, the Greenwich Police released Gilsenan's photo, and the DEEP went public. "Although there is no population of mountain lions in the

Northeast," said Deputy Commissioner Susan Frechette, "we believe that this animal may very likely be a mountain lion that has been held in captivity and either escaped or was released."

By Thursday, Greenwich's local tremor had become a national rumble. CBS, Fox News, and the Associated Press picked up the story: UP TO 8-FOOT LONG, 160-POUND MOUNTAIN LION ON THE LOOSE IN GREENWICH, CONN. A local paper ran the tagline "Oh, the hazards of living amidst the fabulously wealthy. Nobody is reported to have been eaten. Yet."

The news was followed by the standard readers' feedback of scandal and conspiracy.

"It seems every time there is a potential cougar sighting in the Northeast, all the federal agencies are very quick to dismiss the sighting, or to explain it away . . . Is there some hidden political influence at work under the surface impacting these dismissals?"

"Probably . . . they are likely secretly re-introducing it, as they have openly done with red and grey wolf and wild turkey . . . It would be hilarious, how they always say first 'must have been somebody's pet' or 'the eastern cougar as a species is extinct'—pretending the possibility of their merely walking here is spurious . . . That makes me think THEY ARE re-introducing it."

Meanwhile, it came to light that the Greenwich mountain lion had already opened both a Facebook page and a Twitter account, with friends and followers flocking in by the minute.

"Depending on which social networking site you go by," reported the Greenwich Times, "the creature is either heading to Hartford to 'eat a politician' or hoping it can get into Greenwich Point without a beach pass."

There was an online poll asking, "Was this mountain lion looking for love?" Fifty-seven percent of the 586 voters responded yes.

There was no putting this cat back in the bag.

All Mountain Lion All the Time

Joe Cassone, a twenty-two-year-old conservation assistant with the Greenwich Conservation Commission, suddenly found himself at the center of the mountain lion maelstrom. His phone started ringing. It was the citizenry of Greenwich calling. "Is it okay to go jogging?" "Can I ride my bike?" "Can I leave my pet outside?" "What if I'm out hiking and I see one?" Cassone's basic media training hadn't, unfortunately, included that particular lesson on what to do when a mountain lion comes to town.

"I learned about mountain lions really fast," said Cassone.

The phone kept ringing. Reporters from National Public Radio, local newspapers, and national syndicates were calling, all of them forwarded to young Cassone. He handled more press calls in the week of the Greenwich lion than he had in his previous two years on the job. As the new de facto lion guy and PR front person, the sandal-clad Cassone had to start wearing shoes to work. Hardened beat reporters from New York City found themselves on equally uncomfortable footing. "Some of the questions were so bad," said Cassone. "One guy had me pull up an image of a mountain lion, and asked, 'When you look at that mountain lion, how's it make you feel?'"

When Cassone headed out to meet the press, security guards outside his office warned him to be careful. "They'd ask if I was going to bring a gun," said Cassone. To make them feel better, he would grab a stick. His office was positively abuzz. One of the secretaries had changed her jogging route. "It was all mountain lion all the time," said Cassone. "Everybody was talking about it. Everybody was worried about it. People wanted something done."

The Brunswick School was on high alert. Hired guards were patrolling the grounds, standing watch at lacrosse games. "We started looking at things differently—when you hear crows, or when the dog starts acting strangely," said Doug Burdett. "The kids couldn't play outside for a couple weeks."

"No doubt about it," said Brendan Gilsenan. "I was worried about my boys going out in the yard. To know that an animal that big is out and about. As a parent you'd be irresponsible to not be concerned."

Jason Hawley was watching the Greenwich circus with a strange sense of detachment. He still hadn't decided for himself the identity of the large tawny feline captured in the Gilsenan photograph, though someone in his own PR department apparently had. He and Rego, the two most experienced carnivore biologists of the DEEP, were still waiting for something of more substance to pop up.

While waiting, Hawley happened to pass by a pamphlet announcing a public talk on cougars—a talk sponsored by the Hartland Land Trust in northern Connecticut, on whose board of directors Hawley happened to serve. Hawley winced, imagining yet another wild-eyed storyteller weaving fantastic tales of Connecticut cougars crawling the countryside, with a surge of bogus sightings sure to follow. *Oh boy,* he thought. *Who are they bringing in?* Hawley arrived at the lecture hall in his civilian attire, a bearlike man standing six feet five, and sat quietly in back, gamely attempting his best impersonation of a fly on the wall.

The speaker was Chris Spatz. He'd driven east from his lair in the Shawangunks, ostensibly to deliver his standard lecture, "Bringing Back the Legend!" Three years into his presidency of the Cougar Rewilding Foundation, Spatz had been growing busier with time, hitting the road with his slide show, standing before local Audubon chapters, school groups, the Explorers Club of Manhattan. On this night he was facing a crowded room of well over a hundred, the turnout spurred by the outbreak of lion fever that had swept the newswires and social networks over the last two days. Spatz and his rewilders had been following as closely as anybody. He had received a copy of the Gilsenan photo on Wednesday, a few hours before the state went public with its warning. Spatz, the hardened cynic, remained ever wary.

As per his usual warm-up, he began with an informal survey, tailored on this night to accommodate the 160-pound lion in the room.

"How many have heard of, read about, or seen the photograph of the Greenwich cat?"

A roomful of raised hands.

"How many of you think this cat might be a former pet or captive?"

One in three raised their hands.

"How many of you think it might be a remnant wild, recently declared extinct eastern cougar?"

Another one in three raised their hands.

"And how many of you think it might be a cat clandestinely released by the Connecticut DEEP?"

Another third.

Spatz chuckled. "Looks like I've got my work cut out for me."

Greenwich lion or no, Spatz was there to show and tell the Hartland audience, as he had all the others, that their suspicions of a cougar behind every trash can were unfounded, that the cover-up had never happened—that if the cougar was going to reclaim the East in the lifetime of the present company, it was going to need more than sworn-to sightings and wishful thinking to complete the phenomenon.

Spatz went on to backfill the history of the missing cat and its seekers, from the birth of the Eastern Cougar Foundation via Todd Lester's meeting with the West Virginia lion, through federal biologist Bob Downing's first official search of the Southern Appalachians, to Spatz's own ghost chases with his hidden cameras and Crazy Horse visions.

He offered up a gallery of photos from the true believers and malicious frauds, of house cat cougars in cornfields, black panthers in the shadows. He flashed a photo of a sure cougar standing on somebody's deck in Cornwall, Connecticut. Aha! Proof of the Connecticut cougar! Except the background was forested in ponderosa pine, signature species of the Rockies. Cornwall, Connecticut, turned out to be Casper, Wyoming.

He ran through the last gasps of eastern cougar legends: The 1938 cougar killed in northern Maine; an escapee shot in Pennsylvania in 1967; another in West Virginia in 1973; the 1968 cougar of Saranac Lake, New York— which, as later confessed, was shot postmortem and paraded around as a wild trophy, after dying of old age in a zoo.

"This is our best evidence," Spatz said. "The best evidence is that there is no evidence. We've had twenty years of male dispersal, and no females. You can't have populations without females. And that's why we have to talk about recovery and reintroducing them."

Spatz listed all the once and future homes of the eastern cougar: The Superior National Forest of Minnesota; the Upper Peninsula of Michigan; the deer-bitten forests of northern Pennsylvania; the Adirondacks and Catskills of New York; the White Mountains of New Hampshire and the Green Mountains of Vermont; the Ozarks of Missouri and Arkansas; the Big Thicket of Texas; the Great Smokies of Tennessee; the Congaree Swamp of South Carolina.

He explained the cougar's return as ecological imperative, backed by the emerging science of top-down ecology, revealing the great predators as missing links in the broken chain of life. He delicately broached his own psychological hypothesis for the oh-so-many sightings of modern ghost cats. In these drab, suburban landscapes of New Jersey and Connecticut, "ghost cats continue to appear, and despite the record of misidentifications, I suggest something else is happening," Spatz said. "Like animals coming to us in dreams, perhaps these suburban sightings are a call to save, to restore, to reanimate in these impoverished landscapes the sense of beauty and awe felt by our ancestors, and by a young West Virginia coal miner on a mountain standing face-to-face with a mountain lion who departed with a piece of his soul. As cougars are guardians and shepherds of the forest and the desert and mountain ecosystems, so, too, are they shepherds of the soul."

Now it was the audience's turn. A man apparently frustrated with Spatz's failing eyesight asked again how many people in the room had ever seen a cougar in their eastern travels. A third of the audience again raised their hands. An animal control officer declared matter-of-factly that she knew the local whereabouts of a lions' den. Everybody in the room had a lion story or knew somebody who did.

Spatz, of course, had heard it all so many times before. He had once been sitting among them, pleading their case. But he had earned his cynicism honestly, through years of scholarship and dedicated dirt time, searching and not finding. So what was he to make of this supposed picture of a mountain lion strolling through the country estates of Greenwich?

"Dollars to donuts that cat gets shot," he said, "and it's going to be somebody's pet."

Spatz finished his talk. As the crowd filed out, Hawley walked up and privately introduced himself. "I must say, I'm pleasantly surprised." He thanked Spatz for siding with science. Not once had Spatz accused Hawley's department of cover-up or incompetence, or claimed that packs of the big cats were swarming before the biologists' blind eyes. Spatz had given the talk that Hawley—so busy chasing dead-end leads for chimerical cougars—wished he'd had more time for.

The conversation steered to the Gilsenan photo. Spatz suggested the picture looked pretty good to him—what with the creature's long tail and black tip—though he was waiting on the more technical analysis before betting his reputation on it. "What'd you think?" Spatz asked.

Despite what his PR department had otherwise announced, Hawley, their carnivore biologist, was still having trouble with that blurry tail that looked like a leg. Hawley was still leaning toward bobcat.

"Let's keep in touch," said Hawley.

Hawley's doubts had given the skeptical Spatz one more reservation about the miracle beast of Greenwich. Spatz packed his stuff and headed home to Rosendale. In his head he began composing an e-mail to his rewilding colleagues, to tell them that the Greenwich lion whose fate had so riveted the troops' attentions was maybe, after all, a mere bobcat.

The Greenwich lion, meanwhile, was on the move. In his fashion, he had skipped town soon after sending pulses racing, leaving the Greenwich citizenry watching their backsides. Even as schools and trails were closing, as the hundreds of charity fund-raisers were eternally circling an indoor track in their mortal fear of him, the lion was long gone.

After leaving Doug Burdett with an empty camera but a photographic memory of their meeting on the Brunswick School campus, the lion had disappeared into a tunnel of honeysuckle and rose briars, and hid until nightfall. From there he again headed east. Despite having been nearly struck on King Street, the lion likely tried the road again as soon as darkness descended. On the far side he entered a mile of easy going, through the woods and fairways of the Fairview Country Club, the golf course giving way to a verdant forest landscaped with private castles, swimming pools, and tennis courts, the forest finally giving way to the shoulders of the Merritt Parkway.

A Meeting on the Parkway

The Merritt Parkway is a divided four-lane thoroughfare of asphalt traversing a rare corridor of forested green through southwestern Connecticut. It is a survivor of a bygone era. The Merritt was conceived in the 1930s from a shotgun marriage of contrarian architectures. Engineers designed the parkway as a commuter road of Depression-era practicality, with a romantic nod to America's blossoming love affair with the automobile. The Merritt served as an inland relief valve for the coastal traffic that inevitably came to clog Route 1, the former Indian footpath–cum–principal automobile artery connecting the East's chief metropolises of Boston and New York City. It was, moreover, an aesthetic experiment offering motorists an artistic alternative to the ever-more-numbing experience of the daily commute. The parkway banned all trucks and skirted the stop-and-go of downtowns. It steered away from the straight and monotonous, its path curving and dipping to the natural flow of the Connecticut countryside. More than a hundred bridges spanned the sixty-seven miles of roadway, each unique in design and architectural style: art deco, art moderne, French renaissance, gothic, rustic, neoclassical—elegant archways variously ornamented with grapevines and fiddlehead ferns, griffins and butterflies. As works of art, they stood on their own.

But the greatest achievement of the Merritt was its imperviousness to the very change it had so seductively lured. The Merritt had somehow survived nearly eighty years swallowed inside the belly of the Northeast's burgeoning megalopolis. The parkway served a stretch of Connecticut harboring some of the nation's richest billionaires, most kingly estates, and expensive zip codes: the Gold Coast. And even as the crush of some eighty thousand cars a day eventually brought the parkway's rush-hour traffic to the same signature crawl of urban arteries everywhere, the "park" portion of the parkway had held its ground.

The road that invited the industries and cul-de-sac tentacles of exurbia had cunningly held them at bay, hiding nearly all manufactured eyesores behind a three-hundred-foot buffer of forest and meadow and ornamental plantings. The broad wooded shoulders of the parkway had become a demilitarized haven for wildlife, a no-hunting zone haunted by opossums and raccoons, coyotes and bobcats, and most conspicuously by deer. Grazing the meadows, browsing the tree lines, the parkway's deer had become predictable distractions to the daily grind, if to a fault. All too often the deer and the cars that struck them came to litter the breakdown lanes with mangled bodies of bone and steel. Such was the image that flashed before the eyes of a thirty-year-old commuter named Emarie Japitana, when shortly after midnight on Saturday, June 11, 2011, from the edge of her vision, she caught sight of something emerging from the dark and into her headlights.

Japitana had been working the Friday night shift as a nurse at the Bridgeport Hospital when her shift was suddenly cut short. Okay, she shrugged, and headed home for Berlin, forty miles up the road. She crossed from Bridgeport over the Housatonic River into the township of Milford, and picked up the Wilbur Cross Parkway, the Merritt Parkway's northeastern extension. But for the intermittent passing of headlights, the parkway was empty and dark. Japitana was barely five minutes upon the road, her SUV cruising free at sixty-five miles per hour, when she noticed a large brown animal—a deer, she assumed—loping toward her from the southbound lanes.

By the time Spatz was nearing home from his Hartland talk late that evening, the Greenwich lion was five days and thirty-five miles east of the town that was still seeing him everywhere. The lion had left Greenwich heading north-east, paralleling the shores of Long Island Sound. He may well have travelled the green corridor of the Merritt Parkway, tiptoeing by night through the sleeping citizenries of Stamford, Darien, Norwalk, Bridgeport, and Stratford.

Between the townships of Stratford and Milford the lion came to the Housatonic River, its banks spanned by six hundred yards of the Merritt Parkway and the Sikorsky Memorial Bridge. Across the Sikorsky ran the Merritt's four lanes of traffic, but also a walkway separated by a four-foot concrete barrier, easily tall enough to conceal a slinking lion passing in the dark. Upstream and down, the Housatonic came braided by sandbars and islands, making an otherwise vigorous swim more a simple series of short paddles.

By bridge or by water, the lion by midnight had gained the eastern bank of the Housatonic and put the river two miles behind him. The Merritt, continuing eastward of the bridge as the Wilbur Cross Parkway, began veering north. The lion emerged from the edge of the forest, the parkway now crossing his path. Two thousand meandering miles from his birthplace in the Black Hills, obeying a magnetic urge that had pulled and propelled him from the beginning, the lion pointed east.

The dimness of the parkway gave way to headlights passing in ephemeral flashes, the lights brightening, the humming of wheels and pistons rising to a peak, before fading into the darkness with its soothing chorus of crickets and frogs singing from the woods. The Doppler drone of another approaching car began overtaking the forest symphony, as the lion slipped downhill and onto the pavement. And in a routine he had practiced upon hundreds of uncounted parkways, superhighways, county drag strips, and country lanes in his two-year journey across America, he started across the road.

The whine of the machine ascended, approaching at ninety-five feet per second. The lion traversed the southbound lanes and continued across the median, his forward path growing brighter in the beam of the oncoming headlights. He slipped like smoke through the guardrail and again onto the road, where Emarie Japitana, heading north, caught her first sight of him.

Japitana had no time to react, no time to slow, only the wherewithal to keep from swerving. The lion accelerated at the sight of Japitana's looming headlights. In the instant before they met, he instinctively braced, claws gripping the asphalt. Japitana felt the heavy thud of her left front fender colliding with the animal, followed by the scream of her brakes. The lion, hit with an impact force of two tons, spun to a stop beside the guardrail.

NINE Resurrection

Rage, rage against the dying of the light.

—DYLAN THOMAS

JAPITANA STEERED HER SMOKING car to the breakdown lane and dialed 911. Within five minutes, a young Connecticut state trooper named Tamia Tucker pulled in behind and walked to her window. "You okay?"

"I hit something," said Japitana. "I'm sure it wasn't a person. I think it was a deer."

Tucker walked back and scanned the far side of the road with her flashlight. Japitana came sidling close behind her.

"I don't think it's a deer," said Tucker.

"What do you mean?"

The animal Tucker was illuminating had paws better fitting a bear, and a tail three feet long.

The next call went to Officer Todd Chemacki of the Connecticut Environmental Conservation Police, of a mountain lion lying dead near Exit 55 in Milford. Chemacki shook his head. He was busy responding to an airplane accident. (Earlier that day, a small prop plane had crashed into a southern Connecticut woods, killing one and seriously injuring another.) He was in no mood for an hour's drive at 1:00 A.M. to identify yet another roadkill bobcat. "Send a picture," said Chemacki. Seconds later, the picture popped up on his phone. Chemacki headed immediately for Milford.

He arrived to find the lion, incredibly as claimed, lying on the shoulder of the parkway, its blunt head leaking a pool of blood onto the asphalt. Chemacki knew well he was looking at an animal that had not roamed wild in Connecticut since the 1800s. He ran his eyes over the lion's neck, looking for the imprint of a missing collar. Chemacki, standing six foot one and weighing two hundred ten pounds, placed his big hand against one of the paws and realized how poorly the picture had captured the cat's enormity. He squeezed the paw, and a talon protruded from its sheath. *So unusual, he* thought, *for such a lethal pet not to have been declawed.*

Chemacki cinched a line around the animal's neck and hauled him as one would an oversize bag of cement into the bed of his pickup. The lion's nose touched the left wheel well, its haunches touched the right. Chemacki drove the lion to a state facility in Burlington, where he locked the body in a walk-in freezer, phoned in the particulars to headquarters, and went home for some overdue sleep.

Next morning, Chemacki's cell phone was frantic with calls from department supervisors and colleagues. There was disbelief in their tone, anxiety over the explanations. Beyond the professional circles stood a waiting citizenry of believers and worriers and government critics who would soon be claiming the body as proof of lions running wild in Connecticut. The lion's story needed explaining.

Paul Rego was among the first to get his wake-up call. It was conservation officer Paul Hilli: "You've gotta come down and check this out."

That same morning, oblivious to the sparks arcing across southern Connecticut, an unwitting Spatz was sending the e-mail to his rewilding colleagues, tossing cold water on any undue excitement over Gilsenan's Greenwich photo: "As I mentioned in an earlier note, one of the DEEP biologists came to my talk last night. They think this is a bobcat, told their PR department NOT to issue the press release that it was a cougar, but someone in PR screwed up, and others in the department are still perpetuating the possibility. So it goes."

At about the time Spatz was hitting Send, Rego, Hilli, and another conservation officer, Keith Schneider, were hauling the body out of the freezer. They laid the lion on a tarp and stood back. "Holy shit," said Rego. Even in death, the lion emanated an aura of physicality—how muscular, lean, and toned. "Almost athletic," remarked Rego, watching his captivity hypothesis crumble before his eyes. The men set about repeating Chemacki's cursory examination, to satisfy their most immediate suspicions. No tattoos on the animal's lips, no indications of a missing collar; his claws remained intact. The lion's teeth showed no chips or cracks from chewing a metal cage; his footpads, no unusual wear from a life confined to concrete. The men lifted the lion onto a scale. He was 63 kilograms (139 pounds) and fit. All the immediate indicators pointed to the same improbable conclusion that Chemacki had wrestled with: This lion was of the wild.

Anything with a Tail

Several hours later, the news hit the Internet, with the unmistakable image of a mountain lion lying dead on the shoulder of the Wilbur Cross Parkway. Believers and naysayers stormed Comments sections, as the mania returned to the Gold Coast with a fury.

> "Now this is hysterical. See DEP [sic] we the people know what we see. It is apparent you aren't so smart after all, and stop making us seem like we don't know what we are talking about. It is you guys that don't [know] what you're talking about. Perhaps a new animal book would come in handy."

> "I talked to someone the other day who said that early last week (June 6/7?) they saw a very large mountain lion cross Rte 53 around the Wilton/ Weston line. They reported the sighting to both Weston and Wilton officials."

> "Hey . . . I called the Wilton PD and Wilton Animal Control and they said they received no such reports."

> "All these 'sightings' and no photographs, in an age where nearly every person carries a cell phone with an integral camera? What's wrong with this (lack of) picture?"

The New York Times framed the lion's discovery as vindication of the voice-less masses, as "an undeniable told-you-so moment for all those whose accounts of encountering a mountain lion were ever questioned, laughed at or worse."

Believers were plied out of the woodwork, some dusting off stories years old. "Jeremy Joyell, 68, of Bristol, Conn., said he saw one in 2004. 'He ran right in front of the car. And I saw him. He was about eight feet long. Four feet of body and four feet of tail.'"

"Mr. Joyell said that even though his sighting was never officially verified, the news that an actual mountain lion was found left him feeling vindicated."

Reporters scrambled, and stumbled. In their haste to interview the driver of the car that struck the lion, they got the wrong driver. They started calling Japitana's sister, and publishing her name. Japitana's brother-in-law took to intercepting the calls, angrily defending his wife. "She was home sleeping at the time," he shot back. "People are making bad comments about my wife and she is very upset with the media right now."

On Sunday, the day after the lion's death, the lion began resurrecting himself right and left across southern Connecticut, starting in Greenwich. At 11:30 A.M., a family of five reported they'd seen a "large tan cat" scaling a twenty-five-foot retaining wall in their backyard. Their yard bordered a 280-acre sanctuary owned by Audubon Greenwich. That day, Audubon Greenwich closed its trails. "Closing the trails in Greenwich is like closing the beaches in Jaws," said Joe Cassone, who responded to the family's lion sighting. "They were weird about it," he said. "They didn't want to talk about it." A large scat was collected near the sighting, sent off for analysis, and later came back identified as a dog's.

Meanwhile, a motorist on the Merritt Parkway reported passing a lion in a tree. And on Friday, a Fairfield town official had reported seeing a lion dart in front of his car at one hundred feet. "There is absolutely no doubt in my mind that this is a mountain lion," he said, for lack of physical evidence. Newspapers and a local TV station carried his story.

At least one copy editor from Norwalk was finding good humor in all the hysteria. "So there have been sightings in Greenwich, New Canaan, Milford (where one died), and now Fairfield—in other words, Norwalk is surrounded." Four days later, the suggestion of another sighting closed a public pool in Trumbull.

Cassone started mapping the sightings. Greenwich grew cluttered with cougars. There were sightings from the golf course across from the Brunswick School; there was the sighting from the edge of the Audubon sanctuary that turned out to be canine. Said Audubon's land steward, Andy Chapin, "After the first report, everything got reported. Anything with a tail"—a sighting in Greenwich one hour, a sighting twenty miles away in Fairfield the next, and another in Greenwich soon after that. There was a new anonymous picture making the Internet rounds, of a Connecticut cougar reclining with hoaxlike clarity in the shade of a fenced yard. From another yard came a report of a dead fawn—obviously the work of a cougar, said the homeowner; in fact, the work of a coyote, said the inspecting biologist.

The ironies were endless. Jay Tischendorf, reformed believer and ranking board member of the Cougar Rewilding Foundation, immediately recognized one of the featured scenes in the lion's Greenwich drama. In 1985, during his vagabond days as freelance wildlife biologist and eastern cougar sleuth, Tischendorf had lived for a season on the grounds of the same Audubon sanctuary whose trails were now closed for fear of lions. "A local and well-known birder told me at the time that the Connecticut DEEP knew then of a denning mountain lion. I didn't know what to make of the tale."

On Monday, two days after the news broke of the dead lion on the parkway, Hawley checked in with Spatz for the first time since their meeting at the Hartland lecture. "Kind of ironic, the night of your talk, huh?" wrote Hawley. "I'm sure all those believers went 'I knew it!' all at once."

Hawley and Spatz traded ideas on nailing down the cat's origin. The easiest explanation of captivity had been summarily dispatched by the dead lion, tooth and nail. It was time to call in the specialists.

"I certainly won't presume how to do your job," wrote Spatz, "but if I were the DEP [sic] I'd have as exhaustive a necropsy done as possible . . . This incident is making international headlines; I'd want my ducks in a row."

Spatz, for his part, hurried to head off the rumors and runaway hopes among his own troops. "Whatever we learn of the origin of the Connecticut cat . . . it won't be the harbinger of recolonization so wistfully reported," he wrote in a letter to members of the Cougar Rewilding Foundation. "It won't change the fact that South Dakota lied about the number of cougars in the Black Hills to justify gutting its breeding population . . . It won't change the reality that anyone blessed to have an encounter with a pioneering cougar in the Midwest can claim self-defense and kill it without repercussion . . . It won't change that it's hell in 2011 to be a cougar in the United States."

On June 20, the U.S. Fish and Wildlife Service's chief pathologist arrived from the National Fish and Wildlife Forensics Laboratory in Ashland, Oregon, to perform the necropsy. Tabitha Viner's primary task was to find any bodily evidence of the lion's former captivity. The lion's origin had become a federal matter. Had he not come from somebody's local illicit collection, there remained a chance he'd been transported across state lines, perhaps a federal offense. Federal biologists keeping tabs on southern Florida's panthers, supposedly protected by the Endangered Species Act, were among those who couldn't help but wonder. The possibility that an endangered species had died with human help demanded investigation.

Viner, accompanied by U.S. special agent Tom Ricardi and Connecticut's Rego and Hawley, ran the lion through a set of X-rays, searching in vain for the microchips of a tagged pet. The lion's body was then driven to an examining room at the DEEP's Sessions Woods Wildlife Management offices in Burlington, where he was lifted onto a stainless-steel operating table. Even as Viner was running her gloved hands over the dead lion's body, sixty miles away, the police chief of Fairfield was announcing to reporters that his officers would have to shoot the lion if he didn't leave town. "If we can't contain the animal, the animal by its mere presence will have to be euthanized."

Viner stood before the Connecticut lion, reviewing the outward facts: all claws and genitals intact, the body lean and muscular, the footpads evenly calloused as those of a wild, wandering animal. She went over the lion's face, forepaws, and rump, noting the skin occasionally pierced by two-inch quills. At some point or two in his life, the lion had tussled with a porcupine—not exactly the commercial chow of a cage-fed cat, nor that of any southern Connecticut carnivore, where no porcupines lived. This lion was no local.

Yet, again, the claws: Their tips had been shredded, the tatters revealing to Viner the poignant moment of the lion's last heartbeat. The lion, in desperation, had clung to the asphalt before the impact blasted him loose. He had seen the hit coming.

Viner continued the examination with a blade. She began skinning the lion, looking for hidden cuts, abrasions, and bruises. The lion had them all. On the right side of his torso ran a string of fractured ribs, all in keeping with Japitana's recollection of the collision. In the lion's intestines, Viner found tapeworms, a harmless parasite of the sort rarely picked up in cages. The stomach, embedded with yet another porcupine quill, was otherwise empty. It had been as many as thirty-six hours since the lion ate. It was the stomach of a large carnivore on the move, seamlessly fitting the scenario of a cat marching the thirty-five miles from Greenwich over the previous five days.

Two such days of probing and slicing, and no longer were any among the examining team still asking themselves who'd let the lion loose. The question was now: Where on earth had this wild animal come from?

Nearly three weeks later, the answer came back, with thunder. Hawley and Rego had shipped a plug of flesh from the lion's tongue to Michael Schwartz and Kristy Pilgrim of the U.S. Forest Service's Wildlife Genetics Laboratory in Missoula, Montana. What the Montana scientists found was about to rewrite the natural history of mountain lions.

Schwartz and Pilgrim had become the leading forensic analysts of the country's biggest collection of mountain lion DNA. Over the years, they had gathered more than eight hundred samples of genetic code from lion researchers across the eastern Rockies. From a well-preserved sample of DNA—extracted from blood, hair, urine, feces, or flesh—they could match a wayward animal to its home population. With several such samples collected over time and space, they could trace its path, too, as they'd most famously done with Chicago's slain cougar of 2008, tracking him back through Wisconsin to his birthplace in the Black Hills.

Likewise now, Schwartz and Pilgrim compared the Connecticut cat's genetic signature to those of lion populations from across the Rockies—from Arizona, New Mexico, Colorado, Wyoming, Montana. They compared it to the new eastern satellite colonies on the prairie edge—the Pine Ridge of Nebraska, the Badlands of North Dakota, the Black Hills of South Dakota. Among them all, the lion's signature aligned only with that of the Black Hills. Schwartz and Pilgrim suddenly realized they were looking at the genetic trail of a creature who had walked from the edge of the Rockies to the Atlantic Ocean, two-thirds the width of North America.

Or had he? There remained that oddest possibility of somebody trucking a wild male lion from Black Hills to Gold Coast. (Then again, what better place for a lion prank than Greenwich, Connecticut?) That possibility was to be summarily squashed by the next round of inquiry.

From a molecular strand of the lion's DNA, the scientists had selected twenty chemical sequences, the arrangement of which is unique to every individual. This was the lion's genetic fingerprint. The likelihood of his fingerprint matching that of another lion was next to nil. Under such microscopic scrutiny, even parents and offspring, brothers and sisters, appeared as night and day.

Schwartz and Pilgrim fed the lion's fingerprint into the database among eight hundred others. The lion, to their astonishment, drew a direct hit. And then another. And another. And another. The Connecticut lion's fingerprint matched perfectly and repeatedly with Wydeven's Wisconsin lion: with the hairs gathered by Harvey Halvorsen at Anderson's hayfield in Spring Valley; with the scat bagged by Jess Carstens in Jason Weber's cornfield in Downsville; with the scat found by Wydeven himself in the deeryard of Cable. The Connecticut lion matched Dan Stark's sample of urine from the Willow Lake Preserve of Vadnais Heights, Minnesota. (One month later, the lab would receive yet another matching sample, of fur from the lion's December stopover in the Adirondacks.) The lion was suddenly the talk of the Missoula lab. This was an unprecedented forensic odyssey of a wild, uncollared mountain lion on a jaunt across America.

Anticipating the contrarians, Schwartz and Pilgrim calculated the likelihood of the samples having randomly matched—of the Connecticut lion, the Twin Cities lion, and the Wisconsin lion being different lions, but with identical fingerprints. That likelihood amounted to one in 854,000,000,000.

Once Schwartz and Pilgrim finished blinking and rechecking their math, they sent Hawley and Rego an intriguing e-mail from Missoula: WE'VE GOT SOME PRETTY INTERESTING INFORMATION ABOUT YOUR COUGAR. Next day, Rego took the call from Schwartz: "Are you sitting down?"

On July 26 the Connecticut DEEP held a press conference to announce the identity of the Milford lion. The lion was not the more easily imagined missing pet. He was a young male who had arrived in Connecticut via Wisconsin, and Minnesota, and most likely, the Black Hills of western South Dakota. He had walked more than half the width of North America, through an expanse of humanity that hadn't tolerated his kind for more than a century.

"The journey of this mountain lion is a testament to the wonders of nature and the tenacity and adaptability of this species," announced DEEP commissioner Daniel C. Esty. And with that, the eye-of-the-storm stillness that had descended in the weeks following the lion's death gave way again to freshening gales.

"Amazing news," trumpeted the New York Times. Milwaukee's Journal Sentinel gave the citizens of Wisconsin their amazing news, as did St. Paul's Pioneer Press to Minnesotans. "It's one of those amazing animal stories," Adrian Wydeven told reporters. "This probably represents one of the longest movements ever recorded for a terrestrial mammal." Albany's Times Union heralded the Connecticut cat as testimony "that someday they may be able to re-establish themselves there."

Columnists worked the cover-up angle, multiplying Connecticut's first sure lion of the century into hidden herds prowling the countryside. "If there's one mountain lion (albeit a dead one) in Connecticut, why can't there be others? . . . With a dead mountain lion on the hood of an SUV, it's a lot more difficult for the powers-that-be to ignore they are among us."

Another writer stretched the same stray logic to more fantastic lengths, suggesting that the lion's offspring were soon to follow. "Young male mountain lions are known to travel in search of a partner for mating. The South Dakota visitor could have met his match prior to being hit by the vehicle."

The chatter eventually gave way to serious contemplations. Several of the biologists the lion touched along the way, led by Jason Hawley, began drafting a scientific paper documenting the unparalleled odyssey. The details were astounding, the implications sweeping. The lion had wandered farther from his birthplace than any big cat ever tracked. He had exceeded the Chicago cougar's record run by half. His course had traversed three major biomes of North America and every manner of habitat between. He'd negotiated ponderosa pinelands of the Rockies, Great Plains prairie, Midwestern cornfields, Minneapolis exurbia, Wisconsin dairy country, Great Lakes boreal forest, Adirondack mountains, and eastern megalopolis. Allowing for his inevitable zigging and zagging and backtracking beneath the radar, he may have covered five times the beeline distance from the Black Hills to Connecticut. Had he straightened his path, the mileage would have carried him coast to coast three times.

Along the way, the lion had shredded the broadcloth arguments woven by those claiming clandestine societies of cougars operating in every eastern state and province. He had walked through states where armies of seekers and decades of field time and thousands of miles canvassed in search of his kind had failed to find the caliber of proof he alone had left in a single pass. His trail, blazed by a creature otherwise legendary for its invisibility, had been picked up at least fifteen times in the course of eighteen months. The lion had all but rained evidence of himself at every stop.

"We know the cougar's range in North America," declared Hawley. "It's not a question. It's not possible that there's a breeding population in the East. Look at the Dakotas—some of the lowest human densities in North America—yet they're getting three, four, five road kills per year. Imagine states like Connecticut, Vermont, New Hampshire. One animal shows up and look what happens to it. He's photographed all the way. In a state like Connecticut—with people, cars, trail cameras—these things just don't go undocumented."

Armchair experts would continue throwing their darts in the dark, dismissing the genetic analyses as somehow fundamentally flawed—to which a wearied Hawley could only shake his head.

"People are convicted of murder on less data," said Hawley. "This is the same science and technology that convicts murderers, on this evidence alone."

There was a good reason the young suitor from the Black Hills hadn't stopped until hitting the Atlantic—and probably would have continued on to Europe had there been an oceanic bridge with a few trees and deer planted on it. Never did he catch scent or sight of a female mountain lion. His passing was the proof. He had sampled a transect of eastern America for native lions as no hound or human ever could—and he had found it wanting.

Along the way the lion had quietly disarmed those who would grab for their guns. The presumed serial killer at large had passed through uncounted barnyards, pastures, and corrals, past all their ready offerings of easy meat, without incident. He had toured towns and cities swarming with two-legged enticements. He'd had the drop on officers Penney and Martin as they stood blind on the dark banks of the Mississippi; he may well have been watching as Dana Larsen-Ramsay unwittingly wandered past his dinner in the woods of Willow Lake. He had stood with only a lion's leap and a dead camera between himself and Doug Burdett. And he had walked on. Not one time in his two-year tour of America was the lion known to have threatened a human soul, though many were the times he would have been executed as a public enemy if so much as seen.

"This unequivocally repudiates any and all arguments of the fear mongers," wrote John Laundré in a retrospective tribute to the lion's extraordinary odyssey. "Cougars are NOT 'Beasts in the Garden.' Of all large wildlife species, they are one of the best and safest neighbors people could have."

Trail of Tears

The deepest wounds inflicted by the lion were those of a certain sorrow in his passing. Long after his death, in living rooms and lunchrooms and downtown taverns of southern Connecticut, his mention would reliably evoke bittersweet memories of that indelibly etched moment in one's life when the mountain lion came to town.

"The lion? He was the talk of the office."

"At first it was disbelief, then sadness."

"Everybody was sad."

"I was devastated."

Brendan Gilsenan had been driving his family home from vacation when he received the news of the lion's demise. "I was upset," said Gilsenan. "It was such a beautiful animal. Even when we came back to school in the fall, it was the talk of the summer."

"The kids were all rooting for him," recalled Doug Burdett. "One of mine came back from school in tears."

The lion's voyage had transcended mere mileage. The country he crossed, as seen from space, shone by night as an incandescent Milky Way of humanity, the glow gathering eastward and clustering here and there into brilliant urban constellations and megastars. A creature of twilight and shadows, the lion had embarked from the dark empty spaces of western mountains and plains and marched headlong into the hardening glare of an alien society. He was either a blind tourist of miraculous luck or a courageous explorer of incalculable resolve. Those among his closest followers had little doubt which of the alter egos had engineered the Olympian effort.

"He was an unfathomable genius at work," said Harvey Halvorsen, who had walked a mile in the lion's tracks through the snow of Spring Valley. "I wish it would have come to a different end."

"I think of those moments of fear and anxiety, and moments of sheer bravado and cockiness, and throwing caution to the wind," said Jay Tischendorf, a lionlike wanderer in his own youth. "The Connecticut lion is nothing short of a hero."

"The Connecticut cat's tale," said Chris Spatz, "is an epic of tragic love."

The lion would be revived with every anniversary essay of the Connecticut spectacle, with every new rumor of backyard cougars and metropolitan lions in the midst. The believers would go on believing. The rewilders would keep looking westward.

The lion's remains would eventually come to rest in Connecticut, in the state's wildlife offices in Burlington, his pallid skull gazing through the glass of a display case, his pelt hanging among those of the bears and bobcats in Jason Hawley's office. The great limbs that had carried him across the country would shrivel to empty sleeves of fur and parchment. The magnificent tail of muscle that had steadied the lion two years through the crosswinds would go limp, like the streamer of a fallen kite.

EPILOGUE Tolerance

But deliberate war on any species, especially species of such evolved beauty and precise function, diminishes, endangers, and brutalizes us.

—WALLACE STEGNER

As of THIRTY MINUTES past sundown, March 31, 2015, the latest hunt for lions in the Black Hills officially closed, as scheduled—sort of. Forty-three lions had been reported killed, from a limit set at 75. The next morning, Spatz sent a note to the rewilders, announcing yet another smashing of hope for eastward pioneers on the horizon. The hunters' kill in the Black Hills amounted to ten fewer than the year before, eight fewer than the year before that. It was the third consecutive year that the hunters hadn't found enough lions in the hills to meet the legal limit. The hunters' spokesman, John Kanta, would explain the undershot target by way of the weather. "A lot of that is due to some of the lack of snow," he said. "Snow is a great tool for hunters to use to track mountain lions." The lions' spokesman, Spatz, having listened to three consecutive years of such excuses, would explain it more simply as overkill. "They got what they wanted on both sides of the Black Hills when they started this five years ago," he said. "A cougar population sink in the Black Hills sending out fewer and fewer dispersers east."

The lions' defenders had suffered casualties among their own ranks. A disillusioned Sharon Seneczko, who had fought every advance of the anti-lion armies since the first murmurs of violence in 2003, by the summer of 2013 had shuttered her Black Hills Mountain Lion Foundation and retreated for cover. "I'm pulling out," she said. "I tried for ten years. We've had busloads of people go to hearings. But it doesn't seem to influence the power of the commissioners. When is enough going to be enough? I wouldn't be surprised if they increased the use of dogs."

Seneczko's cynicism would prove well founded. A year later, the South Dakota game commission—again pressed by state legislator Betty Olson citing dire threats to lives and livelihoods in the face of the lion's near-spotless safety record—legalized houndsmen to join the year-round prairie hunt, to chase and kill cougars to the far corners of the state.

The eastward cats were under state-sanctioned attack, cross-checked by snipers and sicced by dogs. And to Spatz's unending ire, the cats' most likely allies were all but looking the other way.

"There's a developing failure of nerve out there, of publications refusing to look honestly at cougar recovery," said Spatz, "and an equally disturbing failure by cougar biologists who wouldn't weigh in this year against the lies and prejudice masquerading as science in South Dakota and Wyoming. How, after these cats have given you a professional career and life, can you not show some gratitude to them, to try to stop the massacre?"

In 2012 the *Journal of Wildlife Management* had featured what would turn out to be a seminal report on the cougar's supposed comeback, if not its most crippling. Its authors, led by scientists from Southern Illinois University in Carbondale, had tallied evidence of prairie lions over the decades: tracks, photos, kill sites, videos, DNA, and bodies. Under the title "Cougars Are Recolonizing the Midwest," the report announced 178 confirmations between 1990 and 2008, the confirmations increasing with time.

Buried deep in the technical discussion lay a single vital sentence of caveat: "For a population to expand its range, both males and females need to disperse from the source (e.g., the Black Hills)." What hurried reporters instead took away was a big misleading map of the Great Plains swarming with cougars, mindless to the fact that not one female cat or kitten had been confirmed east of the prairie states, that not one wild cougar of any stripe had survived the gauntlet. COUGARS AGAIN SPREADING ACROSS THE MIDWEST, headlined one tale, replete with requisite rancher quotes of a mountain lion invasion—"They're so thick out here, it's unbelievable"—followed predictably by the apocalyptic decimation of the deer: "We have carcasses all over where they've been killed."

Spatz and company had a far darker account of the movement, minus the manufactured drama. Spatz's colleague and lead cougar archivist, Helen McGinnis, had, too, been tracking the Midwestern cats. Unlike the Illinois report inciting the hysterics, McGinnis had not stopped tracking in 2008, a distinction that would loom paramount.

Between the years 2000 and 2011, McGinnis had documented seventy-four dead cougars and two live captures upon the plains. Most, of course, were young males, and most had been shot. The closest approximation of true recolonization amounted to a single, young, eighty-pound female who, in a remarkable feat for her gender, had made her way more than eight hundred miles from the Black Hills to a backyard of Tulsa, Oklahoma—where she was tranquilized and eventually caged, to spend the rest of her life in a Kansas zoo.

Only one mountain lion had, to anyone's knowledge, made it eastward beyond Chicago. And his skull was now sitting in a display case in Connecticut. The numbers of dead pilgrims had been rising. Depending on perspective, the year 2011 had been either the emigrants' most productive year since the movement began, or its most deadly. Sixteen lions had been confirmed upon the prairies, fifteen of them dead, and the other, the Tulsa lioness, behind bars.

"One of the things we're not seeing in the Midwest is older cats," said Spatz. "We think, and Wydeven has also suggested, that many are being shot and not reported—you know, the old 'shoot, shovel, and shut up' adage—after their presence is confirmed. Many just disappear."

The rewilders wondered how soon the well would run dry. What with the mounting toll at their source, they feared the year 2011 would prove to be the last big crop of dispersers venturing upon the plains. Time would appear to bear them out. By 2014 the prairie casualties had fallen by half.

South Dakota, true to form, had been wielding a bigger hammer with every new season. During the Black Hills hunt of 2012, a record seventy-three lions were taken, three more than the legal limit. (The last casualty, coming a day after the season had supposedly ended, was a kitten.) It was a limit that had been upped from fifty cats the year before, and would be upped again in 2013, to one hundred. It was a limit that would not be nearly reached again.

"With the source colonies being pounded into population sinks, prairie states bent on stopping eastern pioneers dead in their tracks are slamming the door on the most promising alpha predator recovery story in the world," Spatz railed in a 2013 essay. He was preaching to a small choir. Mainstream news editors still preferred their lion stories spiked with impending danger. On the second anniversary of the Connecticut lion's death, the New York Times ran yet another lions-are-coming story, A GLAMOROUS KILLER RETURNS, top-heavy with portents of mayhem: "Left free for an evening, [the emigrants] were capable of killing a dozen domestic sheep before dawn, eating their fill and leaving the rest for the buzzards. They were also known to attack humans on occasion." Spatz fired off a grumpy letter of corrections to the Times. He would grow busy with such letters.

Nebraska had taken to emulating South Dakota's hard line against lions. Nebraska, which had only recently confirmed a nascent breeding population of as few as fifteen adult cats huddled in the state's northwest corner, passed a law in 2012 clearing the way for hunters to begin shooting them.

"The time is now," said a Nebraska county commissioner, Stacey Swinney, at a public hearing. "This is a predator with no natural enemies. We need to chase these animals and make them afraid of us . . ."

And chase them they would, though the rhetoric about making them afraid was conveniently jettisoned in favor of simply killing them. In May 2015 a young lion wandered into metropolitan Omaha, where he curled up in a shady corner outside an office building. (He was later found to have suffered a broken leg.) City cops, after consulting with the Omaha Humane Society, opened fire with shotguns and pistols. They kept shooting. They fired sixteen shots into the crippled lion.

Nebraska's brand of welcome echoed the Midwest's. In 2013 a lion from one of the prairie colonies wound up on an Illinois farm where he was found cowering beneath a corncrib. A conservation officer, declaring the lion a threat to public safety, shot him where he hid. Missouri, which also harbored no resident mountain lions, had a state senator named Bill Stouffer intent on declaring them an invasive species. To which a spokesman for the state's Department of Conservation all but concurred: "The animals are considered too dangerous to just let the population grow." In 2014 a mountain lion showed up in Kentucky, apparently the first such cat to cross the Mississippi since the Connecticut lion, the first such cat to make it to Kentucky since the Civil War. An officer with the Kentucky Department of Fish and Wildlife, deeming the lion a threat to people in a nearby town, shot him out of a tree, earning himself one of Spatz's letters.

The Midwest's lion offensive would reach its moral nadir in December 2013, fifty-five miles east of the Black Hills, when a young tom came walking unseen into the roadside town of Wall, of Wall Drug fame. The visiting lion failed to escape town before sunrise, and at 8:00 A.M. somebody spotted him ducking for cover into a crevice. Officers of South Dakota's Game, Fish and Parks therewith set about killing him. They dropped smoke bombs into his hideout. The lion clung tight. A city employee arrived and started digging—with a backhoe. The cat staggered out. "It was still very much alive," confirmed the game department's Mike Kintigh. "So they dispatched it with firearms and removed it." The backhoe lion was officially tallied as the 724th killed in South Dakota since the lions' Black Hills homecoming, the casualties equaling roughly the human population of Wall. Twenty-four hours later, the head of South Dakota's game department and the editors of the *Rapid City Journal* each received their letter from Spatz.

Through all the killing, Spatz and company would take their encouragements with every bullet dodged and ally enlisted. One heroic defense came by odd way of a senator with the Nebraska legislature, a savvy, tenacious, lion-backing badger named Ernie Chambers. Soon after Nebraska took to shooting its tiny colony of cats, Chambers shot back: "There is no need or justification whatsoever to hunt these animals. It's cruelty. It's barbaric. I will do what I can to stop it."

Chambers introduced a bill to repeal the hunt, gathered enough votes, and in March 2014, after the inaugural season that killed three of Nebraska's few lions, the Nebraska legislature banned the hunt. Nebraska governor Dave Heineman vetoed Chambers's bill. Chambers rallied his fellow legislators to override Heineman's veto. The vote failed, twice. Chambers would not let go. He appended his hunting repeal to more popular bills. The bills stalled, piling up Nebraska's legislative docket behind them. Chambers's one-man stand for the lion finally received reinforcements, by way of more dead lions. Before the year was over, thirteen more Nebraska cats were recorded shot, trapped, or run over. Ten of them were females. It was a jarring toll, even by the standards of Nebraska Game and Parks, which, while otherwise retaining its zero-tolerance policy toward town cougars, put a hold on the 2015 sport hunt.

But from where Spatz sat, witnessing the Midwest slaughter from his eastern foxhole, the most hopeful light on the cougar's horizon was gathering farther west. California, which had long ago distanced itself from every other western state with lions—by not hunting them—had recently upped its commitment to the cats another leap. As of the first day of 2014, California's new law declared that state wildlife agents were to "use only nonlethal procedures when responding to reports of mountain lions near residences that do not involve an imminent threat to human life." Meaning that the sort of well-intentioned cats automatically executed in the Dakotas or Nebraska would instead be respected in California.

Mingling the most lions and most people of any state in the union, California had offered itself up as the nation's grandest experiment in coexistence. One month later, Spatz was on a plane headed west, to see for himself what such tolerance looked like on the ground.

He toured mountain parks overlooking Silicon Valley and San Francisco, the parks busy with walkers, joggers, cyclists, and mountain lions. He passed notices at the trailheads offering the obligatory warnings and practical advice on behaving in lion country, the messages capped with a refreshing twist of compassion: PLEASE PROTECT THEM BY PROTECTING YOUR- SELF! He visited a cougar den within a quarter mile of a housing development. He stepped over lion scat in the middle of a well-beaten hiking trail. He chatted with fellow pedestrians, many of them walking solo, none of them mentioning any fear for their grandchildren. The utter absence of paranoia was palpable. "There's no policy of treating a cat who enters town boundaries—as we see in the Dakotas and Nebraska—like marauding invaders with automatic, lethal force. No one I talk to appears to feel besieged, as we hear in accounts and testimony from residents of the Prairie States . . . who live with a fraction of the cats in far emptier landscapes."

Spatz returned from California with renewed resolve to bring the eastern lion home, and armed with a new quiver of barbs for those intent on stopping them. He collected news clips of residential cougars handled under California's brightening climate of compassion: a young lost male hiding in the garage of an apartment complex south of San Francisco; a young female lioness (named Mable by one of the residents) spotted in a gated community of Mission Viejo; another young male cornered in a yard on the east side of Sacramento—all of them tranquilized without trouble and released to the wild. With every new clipping of coexistence from California, Spatz began mailing the lion's Midwest executioners. He peppered Nebraska Game and Fish, the Omaha Humane Society and police department, Kentucky's Fish and Wildlife Department. For good measure, he attached to each missive a copy of California's official nonlethal protocol.

One particular California cat would provide Spatz his lion's share of lecture points. In February 2012, to the amusement of greater Los Angeles, an infrared-triggered trail camera captured a flash-lit photo of a mountain lion taking a nighttime stroll through the chaparral of the city's Griffith Park. Griffith Park is an eight-square-mile mountain playground housing two museums, two golf courses, an equestrian center, the Los Angeles Zoo and Botanical Gardens (with one and a half million visitors each year), the Greek Theater (with seating for nearly six thousand), the Griffith Park Observatory, sundry playgrounds, camping sites, tennis courts, pony rides, a train for tots, and a merry-go-round. Not surprisingly, it was the first wild mountain lion ever photographed in Griffith Park.

Soon thereafter, biologists snared him, examined him—a male, roughly two years old, 125 pounds, in good health—and sent him away with a new satellite tracking collar and the name P-22. His blood profile traced P-22 to a tiny colony of some eight or nine lions stranded in the main body of the Santa Monica Mountains, twenty miles west. The Santa Monicas and their lions had been hemmed in on all sides by barriers once assumed impassable—westward by the industrial ag fields and urban sprawl of Oxnard, southward by the Pacific Ocean, and to the north and east by the eight-lane juggernauts of the Hollywood Freeway and Interstate 405, two of the most notoriously busy freeways in the country. P-22 became the first mountain lion ever known to cross them both, only to find himself trapped again, inside a playground of ten million people.

Which apparently came to suit him nicely. Freed from the daily threat of mortal combat with fellow lions, and lord of his own castle and hunting estate, P-22 settled in and went about minding his business. He tended toward the more rugged enclaves of Griffith Park, where he ambushed mule deer and the occasional coyote, and otherwise steered away from people. He remained elusive; almost nobody saw P-22.

But almost everybody was thinking of him. The Los Angeles Times featured profiles and periodic updates on their adopted lion, a sort of time-lapse reality show. Late in 2013, photographer Steve Winter and National Geographic magazine introduced P-22 to the world, with a miraculous flash portrait of him angling down a ridge, backlit by the iconic white letters HOLLYWOOD. In America's city of stars, P-22 shone the brightest.

His tracking collar not uncommonly betrayed him venturing into the surrounding city by night, and returning to his sanctuary by day, like a teenager toying with curfew. Seldom was anybody but his biologists aware he'd ever left. His rare public appearances made headlines. In March 2014, P-22 was famously photographed by a private security camera strolling past a Rolls-Royce in the Hollywood Hills. Thirteen months later, he was discovered holing up in an apartment crawl space in the middle of the day, in the toney neighborhood of Los Feliz. His Los Feliz drama went live. News helicopters hovered overhead while animal cops tried to shoo him with beanbags and tennis balls. P-22 politely declined to leave. America finally grew groggy and went to sleep. By the time they awoke, P-22 had helped himself back to Griffith Park.

P-22 was the most urban cougar in the state most crowded with urban cougars. He and the California lions had become daily confirmations of the Midwest fallacy—the antithesis to the beast of all blame, the indictment of the zero-tolerance culture. "They are certainly not too dangerous to dart, they are certainly not too dangerous to leave on their own," answered Seth Riley, the National Park Service's lead investigator of the Santa Monica Mountain lions. Riley and his cohorts had been tracking the Santa Monica lions for thirteen years without a single issue of safety. "There is no evidence of them becoming 'bold and habituated' and thereby becoming aggressive towards people. If people in Nebraska, or elsewhere, have some evidence for these claims, we would be interested to hear it."

Spatz couldn't have asked for a more accommodating ambassador than P-22. With his every new urban adventure splashed across the news scape came another opportunity to poke the lion's Midwestern bullies with a stick. P-22 had become his species' finest emissary since the Connecticut lion.

Yet, ultimately, P-22 was not the answer. California remained three thousand miles and a cultural world apart from the lands Spatz envisioned his lions once again roaming. Conspiracy theories notwithstanding, nobody was yet stepping forward with the political clout and nerve to suggest the unthinkable, of carting a starter colony of lions eastward. And as Spatz and company had pointed out so many times, the stepping-stone journey under the cats' own power was a far stretch to imagine in anyone's lifetime. For all the intoxicating potential on display in California, the fate of the eastern lion remained tenuously tethered to the hate-laden Black Hills, and the heroics of cats yet to come.

Oblivious to those towering mountains of doubt, the Connecticut lion had delivered one eternal promise of hope. That so long as there remained lions in the Hills, there would forever come another. There would arrive a night when, after weeks of pacing, a lone young lion would walk out of the forest and into the valley, down into the fields and the streamside groves at the prairie's edge. To the chorus of the crickets, he would draw near to the interstate running through the valley. And on that night, the trigger would finally trip, and he would dash for the far side of the highway. And one way or another, he would not be coming back.

ACKNOWLEDGMENTS

Thank you, Russell Galen and Kathy Belden, agent and editor, for believing in the lion from the beginning. Thank you, Kathy Stolzenburg, for enduring your mate's emotional absence till the end.

Thank you to Sara Kitchen, Rachel Mannheimer, Sara Mercurio, Anton Mueller, and others unknown to me at Bloomsbury, for pampering The Lion as if it were their own.

I gratefully badgered an awful lot of people to learn something of this lion and his world, some of them figuring in the story, some of them taking especial pains behind the scenes on my behalf. John Amos, president and remote-sensing guru of SkyTruth, instructed me in my baptismal flights over the lion's path as viewed on Google Earth, a lesson for which he is still owed a martini at the Press Room. Videographers Ben Thomas and Lawrence Cumbo both offered expert advice on their trade, regrettably little of which this reporter eventually conveyed to the field. And ethologist Marc Bekoff more than once steered me through the dreaded shoals of anthropomorphism.

My footwork on the lion's path was considerably lightened by various tour guides along the way. Dana Larsen-Ramsay escorted me on an anniversary's tour of the lion's visit to the Willow Lake Preserve in Vadnais Heights, Minnesota, where his presence two years gone was still palpable. In Wisconsin, Barry and Mary Anderson of Spring Valley invited me to their home overlooking the lion's first publicized stop in Dairyland, where Barry happily retraced his tractor-seat discovery. Jess Carstens and Jason Weber patiently waited forever for me to find my way to Jason's Downsville farm, and then went deep past the dinner hour sharing their experience and amazing video clips of the lion eating his dinner. The Runyons at Runyon's Country Lodging in Hayward invited me unannounced to dinner, and lent an extra hand at digging out from the blizzard. Adrian Wydeven and Sarah Boles generously provided me a warm place to stay in their snowy kingdom in the North Woods, and a step-by-step tour of the lion's traipse through Cable (as well as insider's tips on best spectating spots for the American Birkebeiner, the biggest ski party in the land). Larry Baldus and Bubba of Cable also opened their home on short notice to the stranger asking questions.

Carmel Severson, naturalist at the Sawgrass Recreation Area in southern Florida, introduced me to Orion and Mia, who allowed me the unforgettable privilege of touching a hand to the face of a purring Florida panther. Dave Onorato, biologist with the Florida Fish and Wildlife Conservation Commission, directed me toward prime panther habitat in the pine palmetto woodlands, as well as the female panthers' biggest barrier at the Caloosahatchee River.

John Kanta promptly handled many bothersome requests for numbers, dates, and sundry details on prairie lions shot in South Dakota. His retired predecessor, John Wrede, was especially frank and forthcoming with his views on the suspect science and politics governing the lions' fate in that state, as was the Lead veterinarian Tom Huhnerkoch. Dan Thompson and Brian Jansen—whose collared cats from the Black Hills blew the top off the preconceived limits of lion dispersal—offered the observations and speculations that most informed my take on the Connecticut lion's preflight behavior and first steps out of the Hills. Nancy Hilding, president of the Prairie Hills Audubon Society, compiled and shared map after map of the Black Hills' eastward casualties through the years, as did independent researcher Helen McGinnis. John Laundré patiently fielded far too many questions on the ecology and politics of fear, and on the featured cat's most likely paths between sightings on the prairie.

Jay Tischendorf was an invaluable resource on the early history of The Search, both in conversation and in loans of his library. Pat Rusz of the

Michigan Wildlife Conservancy generously shared reams of his intriguing articles in support of resident Michigan cougars. Stuart Kenn talked me through hundreds of miles of the lion's likely path through southern Ontario.

In Connecticut, Brendan Gilsenan of Greenwich graciously reenacted his unforgettable visit from the lion, as did Doug and Sarah Burdett. Joe Cassone showed me around greater Greenwich, and to every bush and bend where so many lions were said to lurk during the siege. Joanna Escandon and John Westerman of Airbnb in Milford, Connecticut, opened their lovely home as base camp for an exploratory stint of the lion's last steps. (And in the departed lion's absence, their convivial housecat, Noel, saw to it that I was never wanting for feline company.) Paul Rego and Jason Hawley, keepers of the lion's remains in Burlington, allowed me to touch, with no small sense of reverence, the pelt and paws of that most awe-inspiring adventurer.

And among all, Chris Spatz undoubtedly suffered most for this journalist's curiosities, stoically answering each of a thousand queries an average of three times over the long course of this investigation. Chris also led a private two-day tour of his idyllic home range in the haunted folds of the Shawangunks, where the lion, if Spatz has any say, will soon walk again.

NOTES

Full citations for all references noted here can be found in the complete bibliography, at [www.lionstrek.com], a tiny, merciful fraction of which appears in the book's selected bibliography that follows on page 225. In crude deference to brevity, all sources not dealing primarily with mountain lions have been assigned to the online listing. Newspaper articles were also, by and large, omitted from the selected bibliography. They were by far the most voluminous—and typically the most entertaining—source of public discourse on the lion and his journey, but their complete listing would threaten to dwarf the narrative. They, as well as many conference talks and presented papers, were thus arbitrarily omitted, except in instances where direct reference to the newspiece or presentation was made in the text.

Prologue
The lion's journey, from Black Hills to Connecticut coast, was reconstructed from accounts of those whose paths crossed his, the accounts' veracity weighted by the physical evidence of the lion himself: his hair, feces, urine, or flesh, and the matching genetic codes in each. As of this writing, a paper in preparation by Jason Hawley and several coauthors remains the only peer-reviewed analysis of the lion's journey, the frame of which this narrative attempts to follow. Though photos and sightings are notoriously prone to illusion and hoax, a few here were considered worthy of inclusion given their proximity in time and space with the lion's confirmed points of passage. Gaps in the particulars of his route remain open to speculation, and alternative routes are discussed in the notes for chapters 6 and 8.

Chapter 1: Black Hills
The natural history of the Black Hills is summarized by Edward Raventon's *Island in the Plains*; its geologic history, by Donald Trimble.

I roughly estimated the timing of the young lion's departure from his birthplace

215

based on several lines of corroborating evidence: patterns documented in the travels of his fellow Black Hills dispersers; his pace as later measured in his journey; and the date of his first confirmed public appearance in Champlin, Minnesota. South Dakota State University grad students Dan Thompson and Brian Jansen found the majority of young males dispersing from the Black Hills in late summer and early autumn. The lion's appearance in Champlin in early December, some six hundred miles east from the Black Hills, suggesting an average pace of four to seven miles a day—roughly his pace later measured across Wisconsin—would have had him leaving sometime between early July and mid-September.

The Pleistocene megafauna from which the lion's early ancestors emerged has been colorfully portrayed in books by paleontologist Björn Kurtén; the evolution of the great cats of North America in papers by Blaire Van Valkenburgh, Ross Barnett, and others. The megafauna's mysterious extinction is depicted by Paul S. Martin (2005)—with heavy leanings toward the aboriginal-overkill argument. A thorough overview of the science debating their disappearance is offered by Paul L. Koch and Anthony D. Barnosky (2010).

The mountain lion's Pleistocene retreat from North America and subsequent reinvasion has been informed by genetic work from M. Culver et al. (2000). The lion's survival during the hard times by way of its dietary flexibility is postulated by Larisa R. G. DeSantis and Ryan J. Haupt (2014).

The Europeans' meeting with America's mountain lion is reviewed by Chris Bolgiano and Jerry Roberts (2005) and by Stanley P. Young and Edward A. Goldman (1946). The oft-repeated story of Black Jack Schwartz's ring hunt was perhaps originally relayed by the historian Henry W. Shoemaker (1917). The lion's wholesale evaporation from the eastern United States is reviewed in separate analyses by Mark McCollough (2011) and Bruce S. Wright (1959, 1972). Its Midwest demise is summarized by John Laundré's "Phantoms of the Prairie" (2013).

The life and legend of lion slayer Ben Lilly was captured by the western historian and storyteller J. Frank Dobie (1997), and what was likely his last hunt, by Frank C. Hibben (1948). The western war against the lion and fellow predators was chronicled by Stanley P. Young and Edward A. Goldman (1946), among others.

Early reconnaissance of the Black Hills by white explorers is covered by James D. McLaird and Lesta V. Turchen (1974) and by Edward Raventon (1994). Custer's canvassing of the Black Hills and their subsequent plunder are variously discussed by Brian W. Dippie (2005), Richard Irving Dodge (1876, 1877), R. Bruce Gill (2010), Henry Inman (1897), Jeremy Johnston (2002), Richard Kime (1996), William Ludlow (1875), and Donald Worster (1994), in addition to the National Park Service's website for Wind Cave National Park (http://www.nps.gov/wica/learn/historyculture/history-of-the-black-hills.htm) and the PBS documentary Custer's Last Stand (http://www.pbs.org/wgbh/americanexperience/films/custer/). The annihilation of the bison is detailed by Dale F. Lott (2002) and Tom McHugh (1972).

The mountain lion's western expansion and subsequent hounding are detailed by Deanna Dawn (2002, 2007), Thomas Dunlap (1988), R. Bruce Gill (2010), and Ronald Nowak (1976), among others. The mismanagement of cougars via sport hunting is covered by Deanna Dawn (2002, 2007), the Cougar Management Guidelines Working Group (2005), and Christopher Papouchis (2006), among others. And the lion's return to the Black Hills and its subsequent study are chronicled in the dissertations and papers by Dorothy Fecske, Daniel J. Thompson, and Brian D. Jansen.

Information on the ensuing battle for the Black Hills, between lion defenders and detractors, was garnered largely via various dispatches from the *Rapid City Journal* and from conversations with game agency personnel and conservationists including John Kanta, John Wrede, Sharon Seneczko, and Tom Huhnerkoch, among others.

Chapter 2: Into the Void
The behaviors of young transients departing from the Black Hills were conveyed to me by Dan Thompson and Brian Jansen, two of the first students of mountain lions in the Hills. Their early life was described by Thompson, and that of their species more generally summarized in Kevin Hansen's book, *Cougar, the American Lion.* Observations on mountain lion dispersal in other regions were gathered from the works of various researchers across the field, chief among them Mat Alldredge, Charles R. Anderson Jr., Paul Beier, Mark L. Elbroch, Maurice G. Hornocker, John W. Laundré, Kenneth A. Logan, Becky M. Pierce, Toni K. Ruth, David C. Stoner, and Linda L. Sweanor.

Reviews of research on North American mountain lions are found in papers by Maurice Hornocker and in the book *Cougar Ecology and Conservation*, edited by Hornocker and Sharon Negri (2010). The cougar's reluctance to attack researchers is demonstrated anecdotally in any number of technical reports involving cougar capture and is directly addressed by Kenneth A. Logan and Linda L. Sweanor (2001, 2009), David J. Mattson et al. (2011), and Sweanor et al. (2005).

Confirmations of lions upon the Great Plains are summarized in papers by Michelle LaRue et al., and in various newsletters of the Cougar Rewilding Foundation. The speculated routes of and the barriers to eastward lions venturing over "the wall" are explored by John Laundré (2013). Data on individual lions killed on the South Dakota prairie were provided on request by John Kanta of the South Dakota Department of Game, Fish and Parks and summarized by Helen McGinnis (2012), formerly of the Cougar Rewilding Foundation.

Chapter 3: The Search

Accounts of the lion's emergence in Minnesota were shared by Champlin police officers Bob Penney and Jeff Martin, their video of the lion posted at several Internet sites, including http://minnesota.publicradio.org/collections/special/columns/news_cut/archive/2009/12/the_champlin_cougar_video.shtml. Chris Niskanen (2009) reported the Minnesota DNR's suggestions of killing the cat if it were cornered.

Chris Spatz provided much of his biographical information in conversation and personal essays, with contributions from Jay Tischendorf. Jeffrey Perls (2003) and Richard C. Williams (1980) added background and color on the climbing culture of the Shawangunks.

Information on the eastern cougar's early history and extirpation was gleaned from various sources, including Chris Bolgiano (1995), Bolgiano and Jerry Roberts (2005), Bob Butz (2005), Robert L. Downing (1984), Jay Kirk (2004), Mark McCollough (2011), Robert Tougias (2011), and Bruce S. Wright (1959). Biographical notes on Bruce Wright were provided by Jay W. Tischendorf ("Bruce Wright," 1996).

The lion's wanderings about the Willow Lake Nature Reserve in Vadnais Heights were reconstructed with considerable assistance from Dana Larsen-Ramsay and Dan Stark. The particulars of his scramble through Stillwater were shared by Minnesota Division of Natural Resources wildlife officer Alex Gutierrez.

Chapter 4: Crossroads

The chronicle of the lion's trek across Wisconsin was assembled from reports and internal correspondences shared by Adrian Wydeven and through conversations with Wydeven, Barry and Mary Anderson, Jason Weber, Jess Carstens, Harvey Halvorsen, Sarah Boles, and Larry Baldus.

The trek of the Milton cougar in 2008 was documented in news releases from the Wisconsin Department of Natural Resources. DNR conservation officers Doug Fendry and Boyd Richter contributed personal details on their chase of the cougar from the hayloft in the Milton barn. His eventual slaying in Chicago, and the public reaction to it, were covered far and wide by numerous sources, led by the *Chicago Tribune*.

Chapter 5: Attack

Details on the predatory relationship between big cats and early humans—and on Raymond Dart's and Bob Brain's contrasting views of it—came from writings by Travis Rayne Pickering, Hans Kruuk (2002), and Donna Hart and Robert Sussman (2005). My discussion of the hard-wiring of fear and the role of the amygdala was informed by Steven Johnson (2003) and Rob Dunn (2012). Evidence for meat's role in the ballooning of the human brain was presented by Manuel Domínguez-

Rodrigo et al. (2012), among others, and reported by Christopher Wanjek (2012) and Charles Q. Choi (2012). The leopard's role in human evolution was explored in papers by Robert J. Blumenshine and John A. Cavallo (1992) and by Klaus Zuberbühler and David Jenny (2002). George Schaller's experimental stint with Gordon Lowther as scavengers on the African plains is related in Schaller (1973) and Schaller and Lowther (1969). The relevance of saber-toothed cats to human evolution is explored in papers by Curtis Marean (1989) and by Marean and Celeste L. Ehrhardt (1995). The Tsavo lions' "reign of terror" was reexamined in blogs and papers by Kim Janssen (2009), Jennifer McNulty (2009), Bruce Patterson (2011), Justin D. Yeakel et al. (2010), and Ed Yong (2009). The Man-Eater of Mfuwe is reviewed by Darren Naish (2012). Modern instances of man-eating by leopards, lions, tigers, wolves, and mountain lions are variously considered in papers by P. S. Goyal (2001), Donna Hart and Robert Sussman (2005), David J. Mattson et al. (2011), Craig Packer et al. (2005), and Adrian Treves and L. Naughton-Treves (1999).

Attacks by mountain lions in North America have been examined in books and papers by David Baron (2004), Paul Beier (1991), Jo Deurbrouck and Dean Miller (2001), Kathy Etling (2004), E. Lee Fitzhugh (1988), Fitzhugh et al. (2003), Hans Kruuk (2002), David J. Mattson et al. (2011), Linda Sweanor et al. (2005), and Stanley P. Young and Edward A. Goldman (1946). Details of various attacks through history were provided by Linda Lewis and Tom Chester, whose online chronologies are apparently no longer updated. The attack on Anne Hjelle and Mark Reynolds was covered widely by various reporters, most intimately in an interview with Larry King (Hjelle 2004). The alternative hypothesis of Reynolds having died of a heart attack was presented by Tom Chester (2003).

The habituation hypothesis, with its popular implication that lions living near people are more apt to consider them prey, remains unsupported by science. For scientists' commentary on the subject, see Brian Handwerk (2005), Kenneth A. Logan (2004), and Linda L. Sweanor et al. (2005). A new paper by Rosatte and others (2015) reports six new pieces of evidence from Ontario between 2012 and 2014, including one set of tracks, a scat, three photographs, and the carcass of a cougar shot by police, several of them exhibiting signs of captivity, none of them genetically linked to cougars of wild populations.

Chapter 6: Northbound
The lion's hypothesized passage through the Upper Peninsula and across the province of Ontario remains the most conspicuous gap in his DNA chronicle. From the time he left his feces in Cable, Wisconsin, in February 2010, to the time he left his fur in a bed of snow at Lake George, New York, ten months later, no physical evidence of the lion was collected, so far as his leading researchers are aware. When queried, Ontario cougar seeker Rick Rosatte claimed he had received reports of "ten

credible sightings" roughly in line with what would have been a rather direct east-ward route across southern Ontario, though none would be verified by photo or DNA; nor would Rosatte reveal his sources.

At least two alternatives for how the lion proceeded eastward beyond Wisconsin have been suggested. The Cable cat, en route to New York, may instead have taken the long way around. He may instead have started back west, through Duluth into the boreal forest of northern Minnesota, before heading eastward again along the northern shore of Lake Superior into western Ontario and onward from there. The east-by-west jog would have meant traversing nearly the full length of the largest province in Canada, a province larger than the state of Texas. It would have added, at minimum, another six hundred miles to his trip.

Another suggestion imagines the Cable lion heading south, rounding the southern bend of Lake Michigan via Chicago, and traversing eastward through the agro-industrial landscapes of northern Indiana, Ohio, and Pennsylvania, through or around the cities of Gary, South Bend, Toledo, Cleveland, Akron, Youngstown, and Erie, before veering northeast into the Adirondacks of New York. Given the recep-tion of the Black Hills cougar who reached Chicago in 2008—and the Connecticut lion's propensity for leaving signs of himself—the prospect of the lion wandering unnoticed and unscathed through such a busy and unwelcoming corridor remains an outlying hypothesis.

The possibility of the lion's crossing of the St. Marys River is supported by aerial surveys of other wildlife species by Todd K. Fuller and William L. Robinson ("Some Effects," 1982 and "Winter Movements," 1982).

Chapter 7: The Deer Shepherd
The science measuring the ecological repercussions of big predators—and of primary concern lately, the consequences of their absence—has burgeoned over the past twenty years, much of it slotted under the technical term *trophic cascade*. The most popular dispatches have been springing from Yellowstone National Park. For starters, see the book by Douglas W. Smith and Gary Ferguson (2006), and various papers by William J. Ripple and Robert L. Beschta. For recent debates over the Yellowstone interpretations, see papers by Beschta et al. (2014), Scott Creel et al. (2013), L. David Mech (2012), and Arthur D. Middleton et al. (2013). Cougar-specific cascades are hypothesized by Ripple and Beschta (2006, 2007, 2008). For global reviews of trophic cascades, see James A. Estes et al. (2011), Cristina Eisenberg (2011), and William Stolzenburg (2008).

The concept of the ecology of fear, with particular focus on wolves in the Yellowstone ecosystem, is introduced by Joel S. Brown et al. (1999) and further explored in various works by John W. Laundré, and others. Fear-mediated cascades triggered by sharks are explored by Lawrence M. Dill et al. (2003), Michael R.

Heithaus and Dill (2006), and Aaron J. Wirsing and William J. Ripple (2011). The spider-fearing grasshoppers are featured in papers by Oswald J. Schmitz.

Aldo Leopold's story is gleaned from writings of Leopold himself and from biographies by Curt Meine (1988) and Susan L. Flader (1974). Leopold's essay on the Kaibab comes from *A Sand County Almanac, and Sketches Here and There* (1949). Theodore Roosevelt's hunt for cougars on the Kaibab with Uncle Jim Owens is recounted by Roosevelt himself (1913). And Christian C. Young (2002) delivered a more thorough reckoning of what actually happened there after the cats and wolves were killed off.

Deer and their recent history of runaway numbers and ecological damages are covered in various papers gathered in the book by William J. McShea et al. (1997) and in papers by Donald M. Waller, Thomas Rooney, and coauthors.

The worldwide rise of the mesopredator is summarized under a similar title by Laura R. Prugh et al. (2009). For the most recent systematic tally of damages by house cats in the United States, see the paper by Scott R. Loss et al. (2013).

The lion's speculated trip across Ontario was largely informed by interviews with cougar chroniclers Stuart Kenn and Helen McGinnis. The tale of Alice the moose was recounted by Ray Masters (2001). And the lion's appearance in the Egglestons' back-yard was first told by Phil Brown, "Wild Cougar Passed Through Adirondacks" (2011), and corroborated in conversation with New York conservation officer Louis Gerrain. The analysis of the Lake George lion's hair was conducted and reported by Kevin Hynes (2011), and the history of lion sightings in New York was summarized by Mark McCollough (2011) and Robert Tougias (2011). New York's deer-bitten forests are described by Rebecca Shirer and Chris Zimmerman (2010).

Chapter 8: The Gold Coast

The West's anti-cougar policies, as discussed at the Tenth Mountain Lion Workshop in Bozeman, Montana, were presented by Wendy Keefover (2011) and by Carl W. Lackey and Russell Woolstenhulme (2011).

Debate over the feasibility of cougars living in New York is found in Phil Brown ("Questions About Adirondack Cougars," 2011), Rainer Brocke (2011), and Christopher Spatz (2011).

The colorful histories of the Merritt and Wilbur Cross parkways are well docu-mented online by the website NYCRoads.com, by the Connecticut Department of Transportation's "Merritt Parkway Trail Study" (which can be accessed at http://www.ct.gov/dot/cwp/view.asp?a=4185&Q=491882&PM=1), and by a self-described highway historian and road geek named Scott Oglesby at his website kurumi.com. My description of the lion's King Street performance was largely informed by conversations with residents Brendan and Keegan Gilsenan and Doug and Sarah Burdett; Greenwich paramedic William Richards; Marcella Leone, director of the LEO Zoological Conservation Center in Greenwich; and wildlife officer Cynthia

Schneider of the Connecticut Department of Energy and Environmental Protection. The commotion over the lion's appearance was described by Joe Cassone of the Greenwich Conservation Commission and covered in online dispatches from reporter Barbara Heins, among others. The Sikorsky Memorial Bridge—beneath which the lion swam or upon which he crossed—is described by Michael Boyette (2006).

The lion's path between New York and Connecticut remains—like his jaunt across Ontario—another missing leg of the chronicle. Certain events suggest he may have toured a fair bit of New England en route. In April 2011, two months before and ninety miles east of where the lion met his end on the Wilbur Cross Parkway, the owner of a bed-and-breakfast in coastal Rhode Island awoke to a thumping on her porch and a growl of some sort. She waited until the morning light and went out to find hair on her porch and a deer partially buried near her driveway. Michael DiPietro, the conservation officer with the Rhode Island Department of Environmental Management who responded to the call, skinned the hide from the deer's neck and discovered two puncture holes spaced two and a half inches apart, each big enough to fit a pencil. Though colleagues in his department considered the deer roadkill, DiPietro believed he was examining the kill of a mountain lion. Two independent cougar authorities who later reviewed the report and photos of the suspected fang wounds agreed with DiPietro's assessment. DiPietro also talked with three people who each said they had seen, the day before, a big cat matching the description of a mountain lion. Adding intrigue to the mix, authorities a month earlier had received a set of photos of tracks in the snow beside Massachusetts's Quabbin Reservoir, tracks that some experts thought were of a big cat.

The timing and geography was right. Between the lion's unheralded appearance in the Adirondacks in December 2010 and his tornado touchdown in southern Connecticut in early June, he had travelled a straight line of only one hundred fifty miles in nearly six months, a rather pokey pace compared to his barnstorming of Wisconsin. He would have had plenty of time to explore as far east as Massachusetts and Rhode Island. He could have struck a fairly straight line through the Green Mountains of Vermont and the Berkshires of Massachusetts along the way. He could have hit the Atlantic somewhere below Cape Cod and followed the coast south and west en route to Greenwich. If the lion had proven anything, it was that anything was possible.

But there remain hitches in both the Rhode Island and Massachusetts accounts. Supposed eyewitnesses of the Rhode Island cat insisted they were still seeing cougars a year after the Milford lion was killed. Two big droppings collected near the deer carcass later turned out to be those of canid, perhaps a coyote or dog. Dogs were also suspected in the snow prints at Quabbin Reservoir. In neither case was a photograph or the DNA of a cougar recovered, hence the relegation of these hypotheses—as intriguing as they may be—to the back matter of this book.

Chapter 9: Resurrection

The lion's death on the Wilbur Cross Parkway was reconstructed from the accident report filed by state police officer Tamia Tucker and from conversations with the driver, Emarie Japitana; her sister, Sigred Lacson; and attending DEEP wildlife officer Todd Chemacki. Details on the lion's necropsy were provided by the veterinary pathologist, Tabitha Viner. The genetic analysis of his leavings and remain was explained by Michael Schwartz of the USDA's Wildlife Genetics lab in Missoula, Montana, and further reported by MariAn Gail Brown (2011).

Epilogue: Tolerance

Contrasting takes on the cougar's recolonization of the Midwest appear in reports by Michelle LaRue et al. (2012), Helen McGinnis (2012), and John W. Laundré, "Study: Cougars Again Spreading Across Midwest—Or Are They?" (2012). Christopher Spatz's views on the matter were gathered through interviews, a profile by Gary Sanderson (2015), and an essay by Spatz himself ("No Exit," 2013). Specifics on the Tulsa female were reported by Emilie Rusch (2012). Thoughts on the Connecticut lion's accomplishments were offered directly by various interviewees and in an essay by John W. Laundré (2011).

Nebraska's cougar hunt and Sen. Ernie Chambers's fight to stop it are reported in various dispatches by Joe Duggan and David Hendee and in the "No Exit" essay by Spatz (2013). Details on the controversial slaying of the injured Omaha cougar were provided by Emerson Clarridge (2015), David Earl (2015), Jordan Pascale (2015), and WOWT (2015).

The corncrib shooting of the Illinois cougar was reported and editorialized by the *Chicago Tribune* (2013), David Giuliani (2013), Ryan Gorman (2013), Peter Gray (2013), the *Quad-City Times* (2013), and Christopher Spatz ("Wild Cougars," 2013).

The shooting of the first Kentucky cougar seen in a century was reported by James Bruggers (2014), Sam Smith (2014), the Louisville *Courier-Journal* (2014), Keith Kappes (2014), and Christopher Spatz and Greg Costello (2014).

The smoke-bomb-and-backhoe-assisted killing of the Wall, South Dakota, cougar was reported by Daniel Simmons-Ritchie (2013) and later discussed by Christopher Spatz ("Smoke Bomb," 2014).

Details on Spatz's epiphany in the Santa Cruz Mountains of California can be found in Spatz ("California Dreamland," 2014). Science examining the Santa Cruz cougars' response to human development can be found in Christopher C. Wilmers et al. (2012). California's exceptional example of cougar conservation is outlined by Sharon Negri and Howard Quigley (2010).

Challenges for the urban lions of the Santa Monica Mountains appear in papers by Seth P. D. Riley et al. (2006, 2014). The tale of P-22, Los Angeles's Griffith Park cougar, are provided in numerous dispatches from *Los Angeles Times* reporter Martha Groves.

SELECTED BIBLIOGRAPHY

Altendorf, Kelly B., John W. Laundré, Carlos A. López González, and Joel S. Brown. "Assessing Effects of Predation Risk on Foraging Behavior of Mule Deer." *Journal of Mammalogy* 82, no. 2 (2001): 430–39.

Anderson, Charles R. Jr., Frederick G. Lindzey, and David B. McDonald. "Genetic Structure of Cougar Populations Across the Wyoming Basin: Metapopulation or Megapopulation." *Journal of Mammalogy* 85, no. 6 (2004): 1207–14.

Baron, David. *The Beast in the Garden*. New York: W. W. Norton and Company, 2004.

Beausoleil, Richard A., Gary M. Koehler, Benjamin T. Maletzke, Brian N. Kertson, and Robert B. Wielgus. "Research to Regulation: Cougar Social Behavior as a Guide for Management." *Wildlife Society Bulletin* 37, no. 3 (2013): 680–88.

Beier, Paul. "Cougar Attacks on Humans in the United States and Canada." *Wildlife Society Bulletin* 19 (1991): 403–12.

——. "Dispersal of Juvenile Cougars in Fragmented Habitat." *Journal of Mammalogy* 59, no. 2 (1995): 228–37.

Bekoff, Marc, and Cara Blessley Lowe, eds. *Listening to Cougar*. Boulder: University of Colorado Press, 2007.

Bolgiano, Chris. *Mountain Lion: An Unnatural History of Pumas and People*. Mechanicsburg, PA: Stackpole Books, 1995.

Bolgiano, Chris, and Jerry Roberts. *The Eastern Cougar: Historic Accounts, Scientific Investigations, New Evidence*. Mechanicsburg, PA: Stackpole Books, 2005.

Brown, Joel S., John W. Laundré, and Mahesh Gurung. "The Ecology of Fear: Optimal Foraging, Game Theory, and Trophic Interactions." *Journal of Mammalogy* 80, no. 2 (1999): 385–99.

Butz, Bob. *Beast of Never, Cat of God*. Guilford, CT: Lyons Press, 2005.

Cardoza, James E., and Susan A. Langlois. "The Eastern Cougar: A Management Failure?" *Wildlife Society Bulletin* 30, no. 1 (2002): 265–73.

Chadwick, Douglas. "Cougars: Ghost Cats." *National Geographic*, December 2013.

Cooley, Hilary S., Hugh S. Robinson, Robert B. Wielgus, and Catherine S. Lambert. "Cougar Prey Selection in a White-tailed Deer and Mule Deer Community." *Journal of Wildlife Management* 72, no. 1 (2008): 99–106.

Cooley, Hilary S., Robert B. Wielgus, Gary M. Koehler, and Benjamin T. Maletzke. "Source Populations in Carnivore Management: Cougar Demography and Emigration in a Lightly Hunted Population." *Animal Conservation* 12 (2009): 321–28.

Cooley, Hilary S., Robert B. Wielgus, Gary M. Koehler, Hugh S. Robinson, and Benjamin T. Maletzke. "Does Hunting Regulate Cougar Populations? A Test of the Compensatory Mortality Hypothesis." *Ecology* 90, no. 10 (2009): 2913–21.

Cougar Management Guidelines Working Group. *Cougar Management Guidelines, First Edition.* Salem, OR: Opal Creek Press, 2005.

Culver, M., W. E. Johnson, J. Pecon-Slattery, and S. J. O'Brien. "Genomic Ancestry of the American Puma (*Puma concolor*)." *Journal of Heredity* 91, no. 3 (2000): 186–97.

DeSantis, Larisa R. G., and Ryan J. Haupt. "Cougars' Key to Survival Through the Late Pleistocene Extinction: Insights from Dental Microwear Texture Analysis." *Biology Letters* 10 (2014): DOI: 10.1098/rsbl.2014.0203

Deurbrouck, Jo, and Dean Miller. *Cat Attacks: True Stories and Hard Lessons from Cougar Country.* Seattle: Sasquatch Books, 2001.

Dobie, J. Frank. *The Ben Lilly Legend.* Austin, TX: University of Texas Press, 1997.

Downing, Robert L. "Eastern Cougar Recovery Plan." U.S. Fish and Wildlife Service, Atlanta, Georgia, 17 pp.

———. "The Search for Cougars in the Eastern United States." *Cryptozoology* 3 (1984): 31–49.

Elbroch, L. Mark, Cristián Saucedo, and Heiko U. Wittmer. "Swimming by Pumas in Patagonia: Rethinking Barriers to Puma Movement." *Studies in Neotropical Fauna and Environment* 45, no. 3 (2010): 187–90.

Elbroch, Mark, Heiko U. Wittmer, Cristián Saucedo, and Paulo Corti. "Long-distance Dispersal of a Male Puma (*Puma concolor puma*) in Patagonia." *Revista Chilena de Historia Natural* 82 (2009): 459–61.

Etling, Kathy. *Cougar Attacks: Encounters of the Worst Kind.* Guilford, CT: Lyons Press, 2004.

Fecske, Dorothy M. "Distribution and Abundance of American Marten and Cougars in the Black Hills of South Dakota and Wyoming." Ph.D. diss., South Dakota State University, Brookings, 2003.

Fitzhugh, E. L., and David P. Fjelline. "Puma Behaviors During Encounters with Humans and Appropriate Human Responses." In *Proceedings of the Fifth Mountain Lion Workshop,* edited by W. D. Padley, 26–28. San Diego, CA, 1997.

Gugliotta, Guy. "A Glamorous Killer Returns." *New York Times,* June 10, 2013. http://www.nytimes.com/2013/06/11/science/cougars-glamorous-killers-expand-their-range.html?hp&_r=2&.

Halfpenny, James C., Michael R. Sanders, and Kristin A. McGrath. "Human-Lion Interactions in Boulder County, Colorado: Past, Present, and Future." In *Mountain Lion-Human Interaction Symposium and Workshop,* edited by C. S. Braun, 10–16. Denver, CO, 1991.

Hansen, Kevin. "*Cougar, the American Lion.*" Flagstaff, AZ: Northland Publishing, 1992.

Hibben, Frank C. *Hunting American Lions.* New York: Thomas Y. Crowell Company, 1948.

Holt, Ernest G. "Swimming Cats." *Journal of Mammalogy* 13, no. 1 (1932): 72–73.

Hornocker, Maurice G. "An Analysis of Mountain Lion Predation upon Mule Deer and Elk in the Idaho Primitive Area." *Wildlife Monographs* 21:3–39.

———. "Stalking the Mountain Lion—to Save Him." *National Geographic* (November 1969): 638–55.

———. "Learning to Live with Mountain Lions." *National Geographic* 182 (1992): 52–65.

Hornocker, Maurice, and Sharon Negri, eds. *Cougar Ecology and Conservation.* Chicago: University of Chicago Press, 2009.

Jansen, Brian D. "Anthropogenic Factors Affecting Mountain Lions in the Black Hills of South Dakota." Ph.D. diss., South Dakota State University, Brookings, 2011.

Keefover-Ring, Wendy. "Final Words About Beasts and Gardens." *Environmental Law* 35, no. 4 (2005): 1103–6.

———. "Mountain Lions, Myths, and Media: A Critical Reevaluation of *The Beast in the Garden.*" *Environmental Law* 35, no. 4 (2005): 1083–93.

Kemper, Steve. "Cougars on the Move." *Smithsonian Magazine*, September 2006. http://www .smithsonianmag.com/science-nature/cougars.html#ixzz1tekF643A.

Kertson, Brian N., Rocky D. Spencer, and Christian E Grue. "Demographic Influences on Cougar Residential Use and Interactions with People in Western Washington." *Journal of Mammalogy* 94, no. 2 (2013): 269–81.

Kirk, Jay. "Aslan Resurrected: Searching for Wild Panthers in a Domesticated World." *Harper's Magazine*, April 2004, 49–64.

Kurta, Allen, Michael K. Schwartz, and Charles R. Anderson Jr. "Does a Population of Cougars Exist in Michigan?" *American Midland Naturalist* 158, no. 2 (2007): 467–71.

Lackey, Carl W., and Russell Woolstenhulme. "Nevada Mountain Lion Status Report." In *Proceedings of the Tenth Mountain Lion Workshop*, edited by J. Williams, H. Robinson, and L. Sweanor, 17–29. Bozeman, MT, May 2–5, 2011.

Lambert, Catherine M. S., Robert B. Wielgus, Hugh S. Robinson, Donald D. Katnik, Hilary S. Cruickshank, Ross Clarke, and Jon Almack. "Cougar Population Dynamics and Viability in the Pacific Northwest." *Journal of Wildlife Management* 70, no. 1 (2006): 246–54.

LaRue, Michelle A., Clayton K. Nielsen, Mark Dowling, Ken Miller, Bob Wilson, Harley Shaw, and Charles R. Anderson Jr. "Cougars Are Recolonizing the Midwest: Analysis of Cougar Confirmations During 1990–2008." *Journal of Wildlife Management* 76, no. 7 (2012): 1364–69.

Laundré, John W. "Behavioral Response Races, Predator-Prey Shell Games, Ecology of Fear, and Patch Use of Pumas and Their Ungulate Prey." *Ecology* 91, no. 10 (2010): 2995–3007.

———. *Phantoms of the Prairie: The Return of Cougars to the Midwest.* Madison: University of Wisconsin Press, 2012.

———. "The Feasibility of the North-eastern USA Supporting the Return of the Cougar *Puma concolor*." *Oryx* 47, no. 1 (2013): 96–104.

Laundré, John W., and Tim W. Clark. "Managing Puma Hunting in the Western United States: Through a Metapopulation Approach." *Animal Conservation* 6 (2003): 159–70.

Logan, Kenneth A., and Linda L. Sweanor. *Desert Puma: Evolutionary Ecology and Conservation of an Enduring Carnivore*. Washington, D.C.: Island Press, 2001.

Maletzke, Benjamin T., Robert Wielgus, Gary M. Koehler, Mark Swanson, Hilary Cooley, and J. Richard Alldredge. "Effects of Hunting on Cougar Spatial Organization." *Ecology and Evolution* 4, no. 11 (2014): 2178–85.

Mallory, Frank F., Rebecca A. Carter, Jenny L. Fortier, I. Stuart Kenn, Linsay Weis, and B. N. White. "Cougars, *Puma concolor*, in Ontario: Additional Evidence." *Canadian Field-Naturalist* 126, no. 4 (2012): 320–23.

Mattson, David J., Kenneth Logan, and Linda Sweanor. "Factors Governing Risk of Cougar Attacks on Humans." *Human-Wildlife Interactions* 5, no. 1 (2011): 135–58.

McCollough, Mark. "Eastern Puma (=Cougar) (*Puma concolor couguar*) 5-Year Review: Summary and Evaluation." U.S. Fish and Wildlife Service, Orono, Maine, 2011.

Niskanen, Chris. "Cougar Faces a Deadly Fate If It Stays in Town: A Big Cat in a Populated Area is Viewed as Too Dangerous to Trap or Tranquilize." *St. Paul Pioneer Press*, December 8, 2009. http://www.twincities.com/localnews/ci_13952032.

Peebles, Kaylie A., Robert B. Wielgus, Benjamin T. Maletzke, and Mark E. Swanson. "Effects of Remedial Sport Hunting on Cougar Complaints and Livestock Depredations." *PLoS ONE* 8, no. 11 (2013): e79713. doi:10.1371/journal.pone.0079713

Pierce, Becky M., Vernon C. Bleich, John D. Wehausen, and R. Terry Bowyer. "Migratory Patterns of Mountain Lions: Implications for Social Regulation and Conservation." *Journal of Mammalogy* 80, no. 3 (1999): 986–92.

Ripple, William J., and Robert L. Beschta. "Hardwood Tree Decline Following Large Carnivore Loss on the Great Plains, USA." *Frontiers in Ecology and Environment* 5, no. 5 (2007): 241–46.

———. "Linking a Cougar Decline, Trophic Cascade, and Catastrophic Regime Shift in Zion National Park." *Biological Conservation* 133 (2006): 397–408.

———. "Trophic Cascades Involving Cougar, Mule Deer, and Black Oaks in Yosemite National Park." *Biological Conservation* 141 (2008): 1249–56.

Robinson, Hugh S., Richard Desimone, Cynthia Hartway, Justin A. Gude, Michael J. Thompson, Michael S. Mitchell, and Mark Hebblewhite. "A Test of the Compensatory Mortality Hypothesis in Mountain Lions: A Management Experiment in West-Central Montana." *Journal of Wildlife Management* 78, no. 5 (2012): 791–807.

Robinson, Hugh S., Robert B. Wielgus, Hilary S. Cooley, and Skye W. Cooley. "Sink Populations in Carnivore Management: Cougar Demography and Immigration in a Hunted Population." *Ecological Applications* 18, no. 4 (2008): 1028–37.

Robinson, Hugh S., Robert B. Wielgus, and John C. Gwilliam. "Cougar Predation and Population Growth of Sympatric Mule Deer and White-tailed Deer." *Canadian Journal of Zoology* 80 (2002): 556–68.

Roosevelt, Theodore. "A Cougar Hunt on the Rim of the Grand Canyon." *Outlook*, October 4, 1913: 259–66.

Rosatte, Rick. "Evidence Confirms the Presence of Cougars (*Puma concolor*) in Ontario, Canada." *Canadian Field-Naturalist* 125 (2011): 116–25.

Rosatte, Rick, Lil Anderson, Doug Campbell, Christine Ouellet, Brad White, Tasnova Khan, Paul Van Schyndel, Randy Pepper, Christy MacDonald, Wil Wegman, and Mike Allan. "Further Evidence of Cougars (*Puma concolor*) in Ontario, Canada." *Canadian Field-Naturalist* 129, no. 3 (2015): 277–81.

Ross, P. Ian, and Martin G. Jalkotzy. "Characteristics of a Hunted Population of Cougars in Southwestern Alberta." *Journal of Wildlife Management* 56, no. 3 (1992): 417–26.

Ruth, Toni K., Mark A. Haroldson, Kerry M. Murphy, Polly C. Buotte, Maurice G. Hornocker, and Howard B. Quigley. "Cougar Survival and Source-Sink Structure on Greater Yellowstone's Northern Range." *Journal of Wildlife Management* 75, no. 6 (2011): 1381–98.

Sanders, Michael R., and James C. Halfpenny. "Human-Lion Interactions in Boulder County, Colorado: Behavioral Patterns." In *Mountain Lion-Human Interaction Symposium and Workshop*, edited by C. S. Braun, 17. Denver: Colorado Division of Wildlife, 1991.

Seton, Ernest Thompson. *Lives of Game Animals, Vol. I*. New York: Doubleday, Doran, 1925.

Spatz, Christopher, and John Laundré. "National Cougar Recovery Plan, Part II: Federal Jurisdiction, Broad Public Support, and the Ecological Imperative for a National Cougar Recovery Plan." *Cougar Rewilding Foundation Newsletter*, November 2012.

Stoner, David C., Wendy R. Rieth, Michael L. Wolfe, McLain B. Mecham, and Ann Neville. "Long-distance Dispersal of a Female Cougar in a Basin and Range Landscape." *Journal of Wildlife Management* 72, no. 4 (2008): 933–39.

Stover, Dawn. "Troubled Teens." *Conservation Magazine*, November 18, 2009. http://conservation magazine.org/2009/11/troubled-teens/.

Swanson, Bradley J., and Patrick J. Rusz. "Detection and Classification of Cougars in Michigan Using Low Copy DNA Sources." *American Midland Naturalist* 155 (2006): 363–72.

Sweanor, Linda L., Kenneth A. Logan, and Maurice G. Hornocker. "Cougar Dispersal Patterns, Metapopulation Dynamics, and Conservation." *Conservation Biology* 14, no. 3 (2000): 798–808.

———. "Puma Responses to Close Approaches by Researchers." *Wildlife Society Bulletin* 33, no. 3 (2005): 905–13.

Thompson, Daniel J., Dorothy M. Fecske, Jonathan A. Jenks, and Angela R. Jarding. "Food Habits of Recolonizing Cougars in the Dakotas: Prey Obtained from Prairie and Agricultural Habitats." *American Midland Naturalist* 161 (2009): 69–75.

Thompson, Daniel J., and Jonathan A. Jenks. "Dispersal Movements of Subadult Cougars from the Black Hills: The Notions of Range Expansion and Recolonization." *Ecosphere* 1, no. 4 (2010): 1–11.

———. "Long-distance Dispersal by a Subadult Male Cougar from the Black Hills, South Dakota." *Journal of Wildlife Management* 69, no. 2 (2005): 818–20.

Tischendorf, Jay W., and Susan B. Morse. 1996. "The Puma in New Brunswick, Canada: A
    Preliminary Search." *Cryptozoology* 12 (1993–199): 66–71.
Tischendorf, Jay W., and Steven J. Ropski, eds. *Proceedings of the First Eastern Cougar Conference: 3–5
    June, 1994*. Fort Collins, CO: American Ecological Research Institute, 1996.
Tougias, Robert. *The Quest for the Eastern Cougar: Extinction or Survival?* Bloomington, IN: iUniverse, 2011.
Wielgus, Robert B., Dana Eleanor Morrison, Hilary S. Cooley, and Ben Maletzke. "Effects of
    Male Trophy Hunting on Female Carnivore Population Growth and Persistence."
    Biological Conservation 167 (2013): 69–75.
Wright, Bruce S. *The Eastern Panther: A Question of Survival*. Toronto: Clarke, Irwin, 1972.
——. *The Ghost of North America: The Story of the Eastern Panther*. New York: Vantage, 1959.
Young, Stanley P., and Edward A. Goldman. *The Puma, Mysterious American Cat*. Washington, D.C.:
    American Wildlife Institute, 1946.

INDEX

A NOTE ON THE AUTHOR

William Stolzenburg has written hundreds of magazine articles about the science and spirit of saving wild creatures. A 2010 Alicia Patterson Journalism Fellow, he is the author of the books *Where the Wild Things Were* and *Rat Island*. He is also the screenwriter for the documentaries *Lords of Nature: Life in a Land of Great Predators* and *Ocean Frontiers: The Dawn of a New Era in Ocean Stewardship*. He lives with his wife and dog and eight housecats in Reno, Nevada, where in the hills above home, lions still roam.

1. Black Hills, South Dakota: Birthplace of the Connecticut lion. Estimated departure: July–September, 2009.

2. Champlin, Minnesota, Dec. 5, 2009: The lion's first public appearance, approaching the Twin Cities of Minnesota nearly six hundred miles east of the Black Hills. Spotted crossing Highway 169 before dawn by Champlin police officers, he was videotaped scampering toward the banks of the Mississippi River.

3. Vadnais Heights, MN, Dec. 10, 2009: Five days after setting the Twin Cities on edge, the lion toured the Willow Lake Preserve, where he ate a deer and left his first DNA proof of identity in a patch of yellow snow.

4. Stillwater, MN, Dec. 12, 2009: His last appearance in Minnesota, the lion was seen and tracked meandering through a quiet neighborhood across from a shopping center before crossing the imposing St. Croix River—by water, ice, or railroad bridge—into Wisconsin.

5. Anderson's farm, Spring Valley, Wisconsin, Dec. 16, 2009: The lion's first appearance in Wisconsin, where Barry Anderson spotted the lion's tracks from the seat of his tractor. The ensuing investigation netted some hair, and thus the lion's second DNA identification.

6. Weber's farm, Downsville, WI, Dec. 19–21, 2009: The big cat's second capture on video, featuring a dinner of young deer under the stars. A sample of scat provides third DNA fingerprint.